Managing Your Move to Object Technology: Guidelines and Strategies for a Smooth Transition

Managing Object Technology Series

Charles F. Bowman
Series Editor

Editor
The X Journal
SIGS Publications, Inc.
New York, New York

and

President
SoftWright Solutions,
Suffern, New York

1. What Every Software Manager Must Know to Succeed with Object Technology, *John D. Williams*
2. Managing Your Move to Object Technology: Guidelines and Strategies for a Smooth Transition, *Barry McGibbon*

Additional Volumes in Preparation

Managing Your Move to Object Technology: Guidelines and Strategies for a Smooth Transition

Barry McGibbon
Independent Software Management Consultant

New York • London • Paris • Munich • Cologne

Library of Congress Cataloging-in-Publication Data

McGibbon, Barry, 1947–
    Managing your move to object technology: guidelines and strategies for a smooth transition / Barry McGibbon.
        p. cm. — (Managing object technology series ; 1)
    Includes bibliographical references and index.
    ISBN 1-884842-15-1 (pbk. : alk. paper)
    1. Object-oriented programming. I. Title. II. Series.
    QA76.64.M388 1995
    005.1—dc20   95-35609
                                                                CIP

PUBLISHED BY
SIGS Books
71 W. 23rd Street, Third Floor
New York, New York 10010

Design and composition by Kevin Callahan.
Cover design by Jean Cohn.
Printed on acid-free paper.

SIGS Books ISBN 1-884842-15-1
Prentice-Hall ISBN 0-13-242009-0

Printed in the United States of America
99 98 97 96 95   10 9 8 7 6 5 4 3 2 1
First Printing September 1995

DEDICATION

To Vicky, Craig, and Kirsty
for their love and support

ABOUT THE AUTHOR

BARRY MCGIBBON IS A SOFTWARE MANAGEMENT CONSULTANT SPECIALIZING in the management of object-oriented projects, software-improvement programs, and quality-management systems. Since he started building software systems in 1966, the author has been constantly involved in leading edge projects in the medical, publishing, manufacturing, and cartographic fields. He has used the object-oriented approach to system building since the early 1980s, when his research discovered the new user-interface concepts introduced by Smalltalk from Xerox PARC.

The author currently provides strategy directions for senior managers who are considering new development methods. Also, as an effective educator, the author has developed and presented a wide range of courses throughout the world on software management, software process reengineering, and object-oriented techniques. He has written many journal articles and technical reports and made presentations at international conferences associated with software development, and he takes part in major initiatives to improve development standards and management.

The author is a member of the British Computer Society. He has been married for 28 years, has two children, and lives in Herefordshire, England.

SERIES
INTRODUCTION

AS ITS NAME IMPLIES, THE MANAGING OBJECT TECHNOLOGY SERIES FOCUSES on the managerial aspects of object orientation. Specifically, this series provides readers with timely and accurate information dealing with a wide-range of issues related to managing object-oriented software projects. The books are written by, and for, the professional community and are aimed at individuals—mangers, consultants, developers, and educators—who are involved in managing systems developed using these new, emerging technologies.

It is my honor and pleasure to introduce *Managing Your Move to Object Technology: Guidelines and Strategies for a Smooth Transition,* by Barry McGibbon. This book addresses important business and technical issues involved in preparing your organization for object migration. More important, it provides a detailed description of the strategies, structures, systems, and skills your organization will need to acquire in order to effect a smooth transition to object-based development. I am sure you will find it a welcome addition to your technical library.

Charles F. Bowman
Series Editor

FOREWORD

THERE ARE PLENTY OF BOOKS THAT DISCUSS THE POTENTIAL BENEFITS OF using object technology or that discuss various aspects of the technology itself, such as programming languages or methodologies. In my experience, however, while mastering the concepts and techniques of object technology is vital, the real key to the successful adoption of object technology is an organization's ability to change its structure and culture to fit the new software development processes. I have had the misfortune to watch far too many organizations get sidetracked and bogged down in never-ending discussions and debates as to the "right" object-oriented programming language, or methodology, or CASE tool.

Using the McKinsey Seven Ss (strategy, structure, systems, staff, styles, skills, and shared values) as a framework, Barry McGibbon describes how an organization must change in fundamental ways to make the utilization of object technology successful. He challenges readers to assess whether their organization is ready, for example, to adopt an iterative development cycle, has the management skills to deal with the rapid development cycle of object systems, understands the need for multidisciplined, multidimensional project teams, or the need to treat software components as strategic assets to the enterprise that must be managed and capitalized upon.

Barry's book draws on his nearly 30 years' experience in managing and developing systems. The result is a very pragmatic presentation of strategies for ensuring a smooth transition to object technology. *Managing Your Move to Object Technology* should be read before, during, and after the introduction of object technology into any organization. It is a most welcome addition to the literature.

John Pugh
The Object People

PREFACE

OBJECT TECHNOLOGY, HEAVILY SUPPORTED BY MASSIVE MARKETING CAMpaigns, has been heralded as the "technology of the decade." Some rashly claim it is the "silver bullet" for all software development problems, but most managers are overwhelmed by conflicting statements by suppliers, pundits, journalists, and the leading lights of the IT industry. Suppliers state that their products are "object oriented," which might mean anything from using a graphical user interface to enclosing the old program in a single object wrapper. Pundits and journalists produce statistics, reports, and feature articles on how object technology has—or has not—improved some organizations' development. The leading lights of the IT industry say it will be the future and that the future is here now. Who is right? Who can you believe?

Well, in some way you can believe them all.

Object technology is a powerful new technique for building software systems:

- It *does* change the way we understand and express the problem, solution, and system domains.
- It *does* mean more flexible systems.
- It *does* give some much sought-after business benefits.

But it is only a technology. We need to move away from what object technology can do *for* you and focus on what will object technology do *to* you. As with any new technology, the challenge comes not from the methods, the toolsets, and so on, but from your organization's ability to change to embrace this new approach.

This book is about changes that your software development organization must undergo to make a success of object technology. It is aimed at IT development managers, project leaders, and team captains who want to improve the effectiveness of development staff using the object-oriented approach. It is also aimed at CEOs or managing directors of organizations who are considering using object technology for future product or systems development. It answers your questions about how your organization needs to change to make object technology successful. It is also frank about many of the difficulties that will be met in managing this new technology. By highlighting the management implications of object technology the book is also useful for organizations that may already have had problems introducing this technology.

As every organization is unique, every project is unique, and every individual is unique, this book can but raise the issues and outline possible solutions to be considered. It is up to you, the manager, to determine where you are now and where you want to be; every organization is different, and each will require a unique solution.

Successful adoption of object technology needs a mature development organization. The best known maturity model is probably the Capability Maturity Model (CMM) from the Software Engineering Institute (SEI) of Carnegie Mellon University as popularized by Watts Humphreys (1989). It identifies five levels of maturity ranging from "chaotic" at Level 1 to "optimizing" at Level 5. And one of the most effective methods of evaluating the maturity of any development organization is to use the McKinsey Seven Ss:

- **Strategy.** Plan or course of action leading to the allocation of a business's scarce resources
- **Structure.** Character of the organization chart
- **Systems.** Proceduralized reports and routinized processes
- **Staff.** Description of important personnel categories within the development group
- **Styles.** How key managers behave in achieving the business goals
- **Skills.** Distinctive capabilities of key personnel
- **Shared values.** Significant meanings or guiding concepts that an organization imbues in its members

This book examines each of the Seven Ss in the light of using object technology. It considers, for example, how the structure of your development staff needs to change to accommodate the new roles and skills necessary to gain full benefit from object technology. It also offers some radical suggestions, such as a payment scheme for authors of software components to encourage a culture of reuse within IT development. You will find many ideas you can introduce tomorrow as well as some that may take months to implement. All managers will be challenged to consider their present development activities and to develop a vision for the future using object technology. For managers unsure of their development group's current level of organizational maturity, Appendix A outlines the method of self-assessment.

The material for the book is drawn from nearly 30 years of experience in managing and developing software systems for many prestigious organizations in both the public and private sectors. As an experienced product developer, I have always sought new methods and tools to improve both the development process and the developed product. So it was in the early 1980s, while seeking answers to improving product flexibility and maintainability that I came across Smalltalk from Xerox PARC. This experience had a profound influence on all my future development activities, and I have used an object-oriented style of development since that time.

Now, as a software management consultant, I help organizations improve their development processes and introduce them to new development methods including object technology. Some will make a great success of it, but for others, it will be an uphill struggle. Those that fail will have underestimated the changes that must be made to their present development processes in order to meet the challenges of this powerful new technology.

Systems and product development using object technology needs to have aware and competent managers to lead its introduction. *Managing Your Move to Object Technology: Guidelines and Strategies for a Smooth Transition* is the software development manager's guide to reengineering software development processes to ensure success in adopting object technology.

References

Humphreys, W. (1989) *Managing the Software Process*. Reading MA: Addison-Wesley.

ACKNOWLEDGMENTS

MY FAVORITE PHRASE IS "THERE IS NO RIGHT WAY, ONLY THE ELIMINATION of wrong ways," so it's to all those past colleagues and students, former and current clients, and good friends who have contributed knowingly and unknowingly in helping me eliminate the wrong ways. In particular to colleagues Bob Bridges, John Lewis, and Howard Ricketts, as well as those students at QA Training with whom many a long hour has been spent understanding the complexities and frustrations of object-oriented development. To Martin Anderson and Oliver Sims at Integrated Objects, who have shown that cooperative business objects break down the barriers between applications and create a new world that can unlock the real business benefits of object orientation in commercial system development. To my old friends at Robinson Associates, who unknowingly took part in my experiments with people-oriented management and in the process built fabulous systems. My thanks to John Cato and Tina Monk who challenged me to start putting these ideas on paper and to the unknown reviewers who demanded clarity, consistency, and fuller explanations. Finally, my thanks to Charlie Bowman and Peter Arnold of SIGS Books Inc., who have guided and encouraged me in completing The Work.

CONTENTS

About the Author   *v*
Series Introduction   *vii*
Foreword (By John Pugh)   *ix*
Preface   *xi*
Acknowledgments   *xv*

1. INTRODUCTION   1

1.1. Don't Panic!   2
1.2. Chasing the Silver Bullet   9
1.3. Where Do Your Real Problems Lie?   11
1.4. The Managerial Challenge   14
1.5. The Software Development process   17
1.6. What Barriers Inhibit the Benefits of Object Technology?   20
References   22

2. STRATEGY   23

2.1. Strategy: The Vision Thing!   21
2.2. Levels of Strategy   25

2.3. Obstacles 30
2.4. Object-Oriented Development Strategies 32
2.5. Key Elements for Success 35
2.6. Some Final Words on Strategy 54
References 55

3. STRUCTURE 57

3.1. Types of Structures 58
3.2. Organizational Types 58
3.3. Structural Maturity 61
3.4. Structuring the Teams 65
3.5. The Software Component Factory 67
3.6. Providing Support 70
3.7. Conclusions 71
References 72

4. SYSTEMS 75

4.1. Layers of Systems 76
4.2. Object-Oriented Methods 79
4.3. Methods of Working 85
4.4. Process Maturity 96
4.5. Metrics 99
4.6. Quality Systems 101
4.7. Using and Choosing Tools 106
4.8. Summary 117
References 117

5. STAFF 119

5.1. Why Recruit? 120
5.2. Sources of Staff 123
5.3. Qualities to Look For 123
5.4. The Interviews 124
5.5. Using Agencies 127
5.6. Use Your Friends 127
5.7. Hiring Contractors 128

5.8. Roles and Responsibilities   130
5.9. The First 20 Days   135
5.10. The Next 30 Days   138
5.11. Summary   139
References   140

6. STYLE   **141**

6.1. Recognizing Our Differences   141
6.2. Creating Powerful Teams   145
6.3. Leadership   149
6.4. Maturity of Style   153
6.5. Managing with Style   155
6.6. Managing R&D   157
6.7. Do It with Style!   158
References   159

7. SKILLS   **161**

7.1. The Technologists   162
7.2. The Users   173
7.3. The Manager   175
7.4. Skills for Champions   179
7.5. Skill Profiling   181
7.6. Summary   182
References   183

8. SHARED VALUES   **185**

8.1. Corporate Goals and Objectives   186
8.2. Understanding Organizational Culture   187
8.3. Service to Customers   190
8.4. Building on Reuse   191
8.5. Empowerment   199
8.6. The Top Team's Values   204
8.7. People-Oriented Values   205
8.8. Embracing Change   206
8.9. Making a Culture of Quality   209

8.10. Encouraging Innovation   211

8.11. Summary   212

References   213

9. Growing in Maturity   215

9.1. Theme 1: Iterative and Incremental Development   215

9.2. Theme 2: Skilled Managers   217

9.3. Theme 3: Product Focus   219

9.4. Theme 4: Productive Teams   221

9.5. Theme 5: Class Organization   224

9.6. Theme 6: Reuse   225

9.7. Growth Towards Maturity   226

9.8. Setting Goals for Introducing Object Technology   229

9.9. Realizing the Vision   230

Appendix A

Self Assessment   233

Appendix B

The Concepts of Object Technology   249

Index   *259*

CHAPTER I

INTRODUCTION

THE COMPUTER INDUSTRY IS DOMINATED BY FADS. GENERALLY, THESE FACTS appear in times of difficulty and are hailed as powerful medicine that will cure all our problems. The latest fad fills our magazines and is on everyone's lips; and whether it is appropriate or not, we adopt it to show that we are part of the latest trend. After all, we don't want to be called old-fashioned!

Object technology is the most recent slogan. It is the final technical solution that will solve all your software development problems. Do you believe that? If you do, you may be in for a shock!

Object technology is a powerful new technique for building systems. It does change the way we understand and express the problem, solution, and system domains; it does mean more flexible systems; and it does deliver some much sought-after business benefits—but it is *only* a technology. And like any technology, the challenge comes not from the methods, the language, the toolsets, and so on but from an organization's ability to change to adopt this new approach.

After nearly 30 years of developing software systems, I take a pragmatic approach to object technology. It was in the early 1980s, while seeking answers to improving product flexibility and maintainability and searching for good user interfaces, that I encountered a description of the Xerox STAR user interface (Carfield Smith 1982).

This not only had a profound influence on my own user interface designs for clients' products, but as is now well known, it was both the precursor to the Apple MAC interface and the commercialization of the Smalltalk language. During 1982, I first used the object-oriented approach in analyzing and designing the control room systems for a U.K. motoring organization. I got further opportunities to use the object-oriented methods in analyzing, designing, and implementing a classified advertisement system for cable television. Although many cooperating processes made up the system, all the information (data and methods) was designed using the object paradigm. Later, these well-understood and practiced methods and techniques were used to develop a sophisticated building management system. Since then, I have been involved with hundreds of managers and software developers through consulting, writing, and teaching on object technology.

In the past 30 years, I have seen and tried most of the many ideas that have been thrust upon the development community. Some of those ideas have succeeded, but many more have failed. Often the reason for the failures is simple: lack of *commitment* to the new technology by the development organization.

It's a bit like dieting: The diet that works is the one you stick to. Despite this golden rule, the bookstores are full of ways to diet; every one of them will work, given the basic commitment by the dieter. It's the same with new technology solutions. Shelves are full of the newest products, advertising literature comes through the mail like confetti, and everyone tells you that *their* product will transform your development activities and make you sleep easier at night. You conclude that there is so much choice that it is better to wait to find the one that will work for you. The truth is that they will all work, but the organization must be committed to their success. Any failure of new technology—and object technology is the latest in a long line—lies in neither the concepts nor the difficulty in applying it to specific problems, but within the environment in which it will be used.

This book sets out to challenge you. It challenges you to change the way you develop systems or products as you move into object technology. It challenges you to investigate the reasons you want to use object technology. It challenges you to face up to the software crisis.

1.1 Don't Panic!

It does not seem fashionable to talk these days of the software crisis; perhaps we are behaving like children who are afraid to speak of something frightening in case it should happen. Yet, this crisis in delivering software products and services is all around us. How many of you can say that you have not been involved in some major development fiasco? If you have been blessed in that all your projects have been delivered on time and within budget—well done! However, software has a notorious reputation for poor deliveries.

Look in your weekly computer press to see the sad litany of disasters. Here are some from my own file of newspaper and magazine clippings*:

- $72 million system to support national training centers scrapped after 7,000 software bugs and change orders recorded over three years; major weaknesses in staffing, management and control, inadequate training and support, and poorly controlled use of consultants were identified (June 1993)

- Crime recording system five years behind schedule (August 1993)

- Insurance claims office support system running $10.5 million over budget on an original budget of $15 million; delay blamed on organizational changes caused by insurance losses and poor scoping and estimation (August 1993)

- Merchant bank scraps $15 million accounting and financial settlement system on a client/server architecture owing to change in business direction (January 1992)

- $60 million downsizing project for major insurance company abandoned primarily because of skill shortages in particular technology (April 1994)

- $4 billion lost each year by US industries through computer system crashes; each failure costs $330,000 on average, and there are usually nine failures a year for each of the 450 Fortune 1000 companies surveyed (August 1992)

- Paperless stock trading system abandoned at a total cost of $600 million (March 1993)

*Most of these examples come from news reports in *Computing*, published monthly by VNU Business Publications, London; dates of publication are given in parenthesis.

- $12 million spent on abandoned system to collect and distribute fees for performing rights (April 1993)

- A regional health authority's original cost estimate of $43 million for the development of a fully integrated computer system covering more than 270 hospitals has been revised to a final estimated completion cost of $90 million. (KPMG 1990)

- $1 billion was estimated as the cost of the UK government's ambitious set of projects to simplify the social securities benefit system. Early versions of the systems have caused staff to walk out in protest over the system's inefficiency. The revised cost estimate is $3 billion—nearly a 300% cost overrun. (KPMG 1990)

The list is endless. Each of the above examples, often known as *runaways*, shows the range of cost overruns that can occur in large projects, but such overruns are common to all software projects, large and small. Surveys* indicate

- sixty-two percent of all companies have experienced projects with severe cost overruns in the last 5 years,

- cost overruns in the range of 100 to 200% are common in every company,

- fifteen percent of all software developed for production use (i.e., excluding R&D) is never delivered,

- twenty-five percent of large projects (>25 staff years effort) are never completed.

In building construction, a cost overrun of more than 6% is viewed as a disaster, yet in software development, projects are rarely completed on time and within budget.

The examples so far, have mainly been about commercial applications whose failure would endanger the organization, but what about systems where lives are at risk?

---

* Survey carried out by the KPMG Peat Marwick Runaway Systems Management Practice in 1990 KPMG (1990). Further work by research group OTR in 1992 showed that 50 out of 400 top organizations lost a total of $1 million with 90% of big-budget projects overrunning in time and costs.

Safety-critical systems such as fly-by-wire aircraft control, railway signal monitoring, process plant control, and oil platform monitoring are now commonplace. Fortunately, there are only infrequent failures of such types of systems, but those failures that do occur have catastrophic results. The near meltdown of Three Mile Island nuclear plant caused by the display of an incorrect valve status is well known. So is the crash at the Paris airshow of the then new European Airbus aircraft when the pilot's commands for a steep climb were ignored by the onboard computer as "being out of normal flight profiles." The gentler climb angle did not miss the trees! Subsequent investigations cleared the Airbus computer systems, but another crash in January 1992 that killed 87 people reopened the fly-by-wire debate.*

Lets have a show of hands of all those who now hyperventilate when told your aircraft is flown by the latest computer technology.

Such safety-critical systems require a high level of discipline and well-defined software engineering methods. Good software development practices are rare, and poor development approaches are common. In the United Kingdom, the National Computing Centre (NCC 1991) produced a survey for the Department of Trade and Industry (DTI) in 1991 estimating that $1.5 million/hour is lost by the UK software industry through poor software development methods. Goodness knows how much is lost worldwide. Perhaps we don't want to find out.

1.1.1 Why Are These Projects Failing?

As a consultant, I tend to see only the disasters in software development. Rarely do I get invited to praise some major success story unless it was part of some major improvement program I helped implement. With this tendency to see only the darker side of projects, it does tend to color my perspective. It seems to me that most projects have a strong inclination to go wrong. Most of you will have your own horror story to tell; no company is immune from failures of software projects, so it's sobering to consider that "somewhere today, a project is failing" (DeMarco & Lister, 1987).

Why are these projects failing?

Blame is usually placed on technical problems, but there is much hard evidence that technical issues are rarely to blame.[†] For example, producing another

---

* July 1, 1994, another Airbus on a test flight in France crashed, killing all eight of the crew.

[†] UK Department of Employment abandoned a system after three years following over 7,000 software bugs and a catalogue of errors: weakness in staffing, management and control, inadequate training and support, and the poorly controlled use of consultants. *Computing*, VNU Business Publications, June 1993

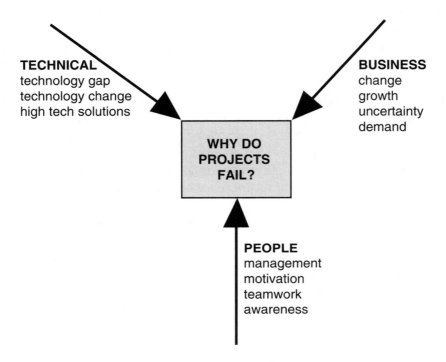

TECHNICAL
technology gap
technology change
high tech solutions

BUSINESS
change
growth
uncertainty
demand

WHY DO PROJECTS FAIL?

PEOPLE
management
motivation
teamwork
awareness

FIGURE 1.1. Why do projects fail?

accounts receivable program should be straightforward. It is a well-defined procedure that has been done thousands of times by thousands of programmers, yet it still causes problems. Why?

There are a number of reasons. Figure 1.1 shows that the main reasons why projects fail fall into three major areas: business, technical, and people.

Business issues are the following:

- Coping with change in the business processes and methods of working. The new emphasis on business process reengineering (BPR) throws a tremendous strain onto the existing IT systems, which generally cannot be changed in the timescales required.

- Demand for more products, more flexibility, faster development, higher quality, and lower costs is the perennial call of senior business managers.

- Demand for growth. All businesses now demand a year-to-year growth pattern that increases the pressure for the production of new systems to encompass new business areas or the modification of existing systems to meet increased levels of business.

- Increased uncertainty. The changing business and economic climate causes managers to focus on the short-term issues as the degree of uncertainty is greater.

This results in tremendous pressures to provide good (i.e., high-quality, robust, extensible) solutions on time and within budget. But when such pressure is applied, productivity usually falls, staff become disgruntled and key personnel leave, and delivered solutions are often of dubious quality. Software development management becomes crisis management as each new day brings another serious problem to be tackled.

Some relevant technical issues are the following:

- Hardware/software gap. Hardware has progressed significantly in its capability to provide raw processing power to the developer, but that power is unused or even not required for most product or application developments.

- High-tech solutions are rarely needed. Programmers apply the high-tech work done by researchers; very little, if any, research and development work is required for software development.

- New system architectures, building cooperatively processing application functions across client-server and distributed systems.

- Modern machine interfaces, enabling advanced object-based graphical user interfaces (GUIs) and inclusion of notes, multimedia, telephony, etc.

- Heterogeneous platforms, providing solutions for the wide variety of equipment and system environments found in major organizations.

- Constant product changes, with the inevitable problems of compatibility with existing and previous versions for the same vendor (i.e., upwards compatibility is no longer guaranteed).

- Plethora of products. Require understanding, deployment, and interfacing with existing system architectures.

These technical problems are significant and often critical. However, the main reason why technical issues are often cited as the cause of project failure is not because they are more crucial than other factors, but because they are easier to identify. It is easier to blame the failure on a technology issue such as inadequate disk space, lack of processor power, or inadequacies of the operating system than on such things as open-ended customer requirements, uncontrolled changes, arbitrary schedules, limited machine time, and the myriad details that slow or cripple any software project. These are all *management* problems. However, when new technology is introduced, the problems become unknowable, and the technical issues are no longer predictable.

Finally, issues concerned with people are

- Managing workers. The production-line approach of treating workers as interchangeable components is not applicable for software developers.

- Motivating workers. These highly skilled and intelligent workers are less motivated by money and prestige than by excitement, challenge, and pride in achievement. (This does not mean that money is not important as it is used as a measure among peers).

- Working in teams and groups. Programs are no longer the product of an individual effort but the results of cooperative working.

- Lack of awareness of process, methods, and best practices. The pressures to meet schedules generally forces out any efforts to define or improve the development activities.

All of these issues are sociological in nature. They constitute the project's sociology. Dealing with people issues can be a major concern and headache for development managers. Most managers are much more comfortable addressing technical problems and methods than coping with poor team cohesion or the reasons for antagonism between two groups. A typical manager's background also leads to the focus being on the tasks and how the job is done rather than on how the job is managed. Yet management is more about managing people than managing tasks.

1.2 Chasing the Silver Bullet

This crisis in delivering software projects was openly discussed in 1968, and it was about then that the first silver bullet was talked about: structured techniques. They would make the software crisis disappear. They didn't. Things did get better for a while, but once we felt confident, we started to tackle more complex problems. So along came computer-aided software engineering (CASE) tools; many will remember the excitement that they caused. Then a rash of power tools appeared, which would allow users to employ business modeling tools to provide the IT solutions that would meet their needs. The development department was to be a thing of the past. There were even serious articles in the magazines about how the days of the programmer were numbered; Ed Yourdon wrote of the demise of the programmer (Yourdon 1992). How many times have you heard that the days of programmers were over?

Nevertheless, programming has continued. There are strong demands for more staff to meet the increasing levels of software development. Structured techniques are widely adopted, CASE tools have moved beyond the initial level of office automation, and software developers have risen to the challenge by employing modern tools and skills to meet the needs of their organizations.

Software development has matured. Object technology is next in this line of progression toward mature development approaches; it's an evolution of programming techniques.

The core concept is decentralized control. Take for example, a simple program for a desk calculator. It selects the mathematical routine depending on the function key pressed; a central routine accepts input from the keypad and dispatches control to the appropriate routine. This central routine needed to know which routine to activate for each keypress. Conventional operating systems work in a similar manner; the routine to be activated is known to the central controller, which has interpreted the command. Think of traditional command-line operating systems such as DOS or Unix, where the command-line string is decoded, and the specified routine is activated, unless of course the command string is unrecognized.

With modern workstations' requirement to support multiple windows, this simple approach is no longer applicable. Here, the operations are requested through a mouse click, and the action to be taken depends on the position of the displayed cursor. This action is unknown to the operating system, and it

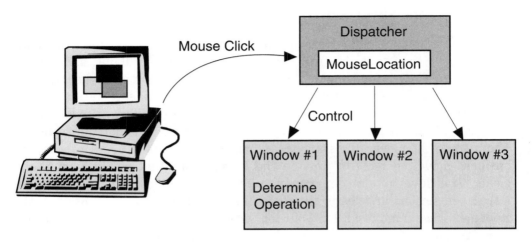

FIGURE 1.2. Control Decentralization in the Window "Objects"

depends on the type of window in which the cursor happens to be located when the mouse button is pressed. Each window then carries its own form of command interpretation. In short it is regarded as an object with its own behavior. When the mouse key is clicked, the dispatcher searches for the window descriptor identified by the current mouse location and transfers control to a routine assigned to that descriptor (see Figure 1.2). This routine is often called the *handler*.

Each different type of window will have a different type of handler for the command interpretation. Therefore, instead of control being centralized in a single program, which previously knew the identities of the destination of all commands, it is decentralized in the handlers whose identity and number are not known in the dispatcher's program text. It comes as no surprise to learn that much of the initial drive toward object technology was by the developers of these modern operating systems.

A fuller description of object orientation concepts is given in Appendix B. Object-oriented concepts—classes, inheritance, class relationships, and polymorphism—and the introduction of software components as frameworks and class libraries, perhaps provided by other suppliers, will lead to significant improvements in the productivity of software development. A real silver bullet. However, it might not solve your real problems!

1.3 Where Do Your Real Problems Lie?

Usually, the real problems lie in a number of major areas:

- The business environment
- The number of applications
- Decentralization
- Customer expectations
- Capturing user requirements
- Technical solutions
- Legacy systems

The business environment is constantly changing as attempts are made to meet the demands for competitive products, lower costs, and faster responses. These changes are being fuelled by the significant move toward business process reengineering being undertaken by many organizations. BPR focuses the mind of management to consider major reorganization of the way their businesses perform work (Hammer & Champy, 1993).

This drive has brought to light the problem of the explosion in the number of applications. Over time, separate business processes and functions have been supported by separate systems or, as they are more usually known, *applications*. Order processing has its own application, contracts another, and so on. Each department or function has its own developed application, which uses similar concepts of customers and orders, but which are implemented in different ways, often by different teams. This results in a "stable of applications." But in a newly engineered business environment where one person now provides most customer contacts, these applications form barriers to that process. For example, when a customer contact person wants to create an order and perhaps query the current level of the inventory and maybe check the contract details or change the telephone number, he will have to access all of these applications in turn (Figure 1.3). This, of course, may not be possible owing to hardware, access to information, incompatible information items, and so on. The business manager may wish to reengineer the business process, but the "walls" between the applications prevent this from happening. By creating cooperative

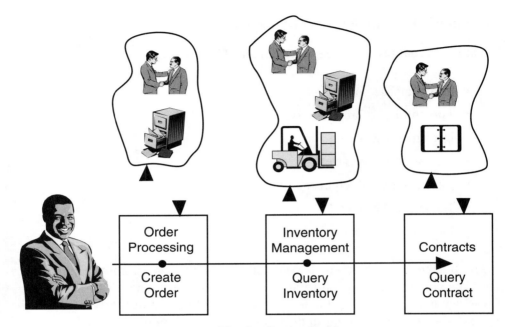

FIGURE 1.3. The Application Problem

business objects—customer, order, product item—these boundaries can be broken down (Sims, 1994).

BPR has also led to the decentralization of many organizations. This has meant a downsizing in the equipment (and often the staff) used to support the business. No longer is the mainframe the center of the IS universe, but its role has been changed to that of a "big server" in a new distributed client-server system architecture. Object technology is then used to not only encapsulate many of the existing application processes but to distribute objects around the network (e.g., to have multiple instances of customer or ZIP code information).

Encapsulation is also used to overcome the problems with complex data structures—voice, pictures, mixed information, and so on (i.e., no one other than the object itself needs to know the complexity of the stored information). This means that a `Display` message can be sent to a customer, a picture, or a map object, and each will be able to deal with its own internal information.

Customer/user expectations about the look and feel of the screen has changed dramatically. Despite there being far more character-based user interfaces in businesses, the demand is for graphical user interfaces on all machines. When the computer you have at home has a more sophisticated user interface than the one at work, it not only frustrates but highlights how old your business systems may be. Introducing modern graphical user interfaces (GUI) with direct manipulation (drag and drop) is one of the driving forces for the adoption of object technology. Most modern GUIs come with extensive libraries of components to allow the developer access to the rich functionality of the user interaction. New developments that do not have the magic foursome—windows, icons, menus, and pointer—will be considered old-fashioned and no longer able to meet today's requirements.

If you have problems capturing the customer/user requirements, prototyping may help. Previous attempts at using prototypes relied on special languages, so the effort spent in building the prototype was lost (i.e., you understood the user requirements, but the software was discarded). Object technology allows components of the prototype to be used in the final delivered system, thereby making effective use of the resources spent capturing the customer/user requirements.

The final and major real problem is your present, or legacy, systems. Throwing new technologies at old systems usually results in some hybrid, misdesigned fragile system that crashes at regular intervals instead of the more efficient, better defined, and more reliable system you hoped for. Yet these legacy systems cannot be abandoned. They need to be carried forward not only to support the business but to move toward the newer platforms of tomorrow.

This is a big step for most organizations—the costs and risks are formidable. In fact, some organizations shrink from the task and, as a result find themselves getting further and further behind in the technology. One UK bank has yet to move from assembler language programs that provide the applications that support their large customer databases.

Object technology can help with this transition, but only with a well-defined conversion strategy such as

- defining a mechanism and infrastructure to support communications between existing components (e.g., dealing with global data),

- modifying the present physical architectures of the legacy systems to fit the newer object-oriented architecture (e.g., client-server structures),

- incorporating the logical components of the present legacy systems into the newer object-oriented logical architecture (e.g., matching to problem domain classes).

- supporting the legacy systems within the newer object-oriented infrastructure

1.4 The Managerial Challenge

A number of challenges face developers and customers and users today (Figure 1.4). These result from the differing perspectives on the work of IT development. We have always succeeded in overcoming most technical challenges and are confident of coping with new technology. We learn the techniques and, with time and practice, we become proficient. But this is not sufficient. The management challenges are always greater.

1.4.1 Critical Misconceptions

Like all industries, a number of misconceptions are repeated about software development. We have already discussed the misconception that technical problems are the main reason for software failure. Others are the following:

- Software management is different

- Quality can't be measured

The Developer
• Application integration
• New architectures
• Client/server connections
• Advanced GUIs
• Multiple platforms
• etc.

The User
• Short time to market
• Usable systems
• Flexible systems
• IT **off** the critical path

FIGURE 1.4. Different Challenges

- Better people are needed

- Requirements must be fixed

- Testing removes all the errors

Software management is different from other engineering disciplines in that it is a relatively new field and it produces an intangible product (the program itself), which is an artifact of the mind, yet the main elements of the program, the functions, are visible to the user and so are the focus of most complaints. Everyone expects equipment to fail, but they do not expect the program to fail or even behave unpredictably. This is unlike other engineering disciplines, where physical objects, which can be viewed, handled, and appreciated both for their usefulness and their physical properties (i.e., their style, ingenuity, etc.) are produced.

Software is considered a black art despite the widespread use of the term *software engineering.* It therefore is considered difficult to manage. As software has many unique characteristics, these require more management discipline, not less. It is ironic that the same managers who insist on detailed designs, tracking systems, and technical reviews for hardware let their software teams get by without them.

A further difficulty of software management is that associated with managing any group of highly skilled knowledge workers. Such staff are usually relied upon to be self-motivated and often self-managed (i.e., the work task is defined, a schedule is given, and the worker is left alone to produce a result). In theory, this is a classic example of management by objectives (MBO), but in practice it often fails because the task is ill-defined, the schedule is unreasonable, or the delivered item does not meet hidden expectations.

Measuring software quality is difficult but not impossible. The industry's present focus on quality improvements implies that quality can be measured and improved, but the messages from the exponents of quality improvement are general motherhood statements such as "do it right the first time" or "if it's not broke, don't fix it." The call is to define some grand benchmark against which all software can be measured. But this is not feasible. What is feasible, however, is the identification of the key areas where factors that determine quality can be measured and expressed in numerical form. Using this approach, action plans to improve the quality of the software can then be defined and monitored.

The call for better people for software development usually comes from senior business managers. The premise is that if staff make constant errors, they should be replaced by better people. This is the approach to other functions within a business, so why not software development? The fault, of course, does not lie in the people but in the process. Poor requirements definition is not the fault of the programmer who caused the error, but of inadequate mechanisms to capture the requirements. Similarly, a lack of test equipment may have curtailed the test and verification phase causing the delivery of a less-than-perfect solution. Who's at fault—the tester, the programmer, or the manager?

Another major fallacy is that the requirements must be fixed before the development is started. While every attempt must be made to define the customer requirements, it has to be recognized that these will change as the project progresses. Gone are the days when specifications were sketched on the back of a cigarette packet, but now the swing toward requirements definitions that are totally complete, comprehensible, and unchangeable has gone too far. Defense procurement now involves such long schedules in the requirements phase that the reason for the system may disappear before the project starts! The more insistence that the requirements are fixed and signed-off, then the far greater risk of delivering a system that, while it may meet the defined (fixed) requirements, no longer meets the customer's needs. Subsequent wrangles over the contractual responsibilities for the changes often sour business relations for a very long time.

Finally, there is the misconception that testing removes all the errors. Every programmer knows that testing exposes the presence of bugs, not their absence. As we build larger and more complex systems, testing becomes a less reliable indicator of program quality. In a common multi-programming environment, the sheer number of logic combinations and instruction selections make comprehensive testing near impossible. Instead, the approach has to be to develop small, well-understood program components—clusters of classes—that can be fully tested so that there is a degree of confidence in the resulting system. Also, as these components are reused in different contexts and under differing conditions, our confidence in their quality will increase. This development must be based on the establishment of a high quality software development process. We cannot just rely on testing alone to improve the quality of a product.

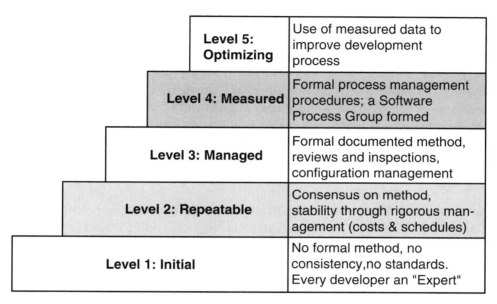

FIGURE 1.5. The SEI Model of Software Maturity

1.5 The Software Development Process

Processes and business process reengineering have come of age. After years in the shadow of quick fixes, silver bullets, and other sure-fire ways to build a better organization, the focus once more returns to the root cause of failures: the process. The way of working. The everyday "doing the work" that makes all organizations function and allows the creation of new products and services.

BPR challenges organizations and businesses; object technology challenges software development. It poses the question: is your software development process sufficiently mature to successfully exploit object technology?

Whenever there is talk of the maturity of a software development organization, the Capability Maturity Model developed by the Software Engineering Institute (SEI) of Carnegie Mellon University led by Watts Humphreys is normally used (Humphreys, 1989). Figure 1.5 illustrates this model, which is now widely accepted and is being developed further by various groups, including the International Standards Organization (ISO) through their working group on software process improvement.* Briefly, each level can be described as follows.

---

* ISO/IEC JTC1/SC7 formed a working group on Software Process Assessment in June 1993. Working Group 10 is creating a standard through a project called SPICE—Software Process Improvement and Capability Determination.

Level 1: Initial
At level 1, the work process is ad hoc and often chaotic. There are no formalized working procedures, cost estimates, or project plans. Any tools that are used are not integrated into the tasks, and different types are used throughout the organization. Changes are not controlled with the result that the delivered product does not meet the customers requirements, if it works at all! Software maintenance and support is a serious problem in this level of organization. Project planning is done, but there is often poor management control in meeting these plans. When crises occur, this level of organization reverts to coding and testing.

Level 2: Repeatable
Level 2 organizations provide stability through rigorous management of costs and schedules. The work is under control as long as it relies upon the previous experiences of the professional involved.

Level 3: Managed
At level 3, the organization has formal documented methods, undertakes reviews and inspections, and ensures proper configuration management. These give a strong foundation for major and continuing progress. Such organizations often deliver high-quality products on time and within budget.

Level 4: Measured
Level 4 organizations have instigated formal process measurement procedures and formed a software process group. This group defines useful process information to be collected and uses the results of the analysis to define further process improvements. The group also ensures the propagation of good working practices throughout the organization.

Level 5: Optimizing
The most mature development organization is at level 5. It uses all forms of automatically collected measured data to improve development process on an ongoing basis.

While recent quality initiatives such as ISO 9000 and TickIT have placed more organizations at level 3, most are still at levels 1 and 2; that is, they are usually in a state of permanent crisis. Unfortunately, it is these organizations that believe adopting object technology will solve their current problems. What do you think? Do you think that it will help or will it create such chaos that not only will expectations not be met, but object technology will be proclaimed a failure?

1.5.1 McKinsey's Seven Ss

The Capability Maturity Model, while helpful as a scoring system, does not help greatly to identify the particular areas within the organization that need attention. So another critical set of organizational attributes is needed, and the one most commonly is the McKinsey Seven Ss (Pascale & Athos, 1981):

Strategy.	Plan or course of action leading to the allocation of a business's scarce resources over time to reach identified goals
Structure.	Character of the organization chart (i.e., functional, decentralized, etc.)
Systems.	Proceduralized reports and routinized processes, such as meeting formats
Staff.	Demographic description of important personnel categories within the development group (i.e., designers, coders, analysts, etc.)
Style.	Characterization of how key managers behave in achieving the business goals; also, the cultural style of the organization
Skills.	Distinctive capabilities of key personnel
Shared values.	The significant meanings or guiding concepts an organization imbues in its members; can also be described as superordinate goals or culture of the organization

These are such powerful and useful indicators of capability that they have been chosen as the framework for this book. Each of the following chapters explores one of the Seven Ss and details the changes you will need to make to ensure success with object technology. There will be as many questions posed as answers given as each of you will need to consider your own unique situation.

1.6 What Barriers Inhibit the Benefits of Object Technology?

Most of all the writing about object technology focuses on the benefits it will bring. Typically, these are

- Reusability. Construction from proven components
- Flexibility. Responsiveness to changes in the current problem domain
- Extensibility. Ability to add new functionality without changing existing solutions
- Maintainability. Ease of repair through smaller components

Object technology also offers numerous benefits to management:

- It gives increased control of projects through shorter delivery cycles.

- It makes progress more visible with working prototypes.

- It gives the opportunity to enter new business or technology domains through the use of supplied components (e.g., graphical user interfaces).

- It installs a unified development approach based on a well-defined methodology, toolset, and language.

- It increases the consistency of the development approach through the phases from conception to completion.

These focus on what object technology will do *for* you, but what will object technology do *to* you? What are the barriers and issues that will need to be tackled?

First, there are the conflicting expectations of those involved with product and system development. Programmers see it as the "hot" new way to develop software, to be at the front of the technology wave, and to make themselves more marketable in the future. Customers and users really don't care about the technology, but if you have spent some time in convincing them of the benefits (see above), they will look for shorter delivery times, improved quality, and flexible solutions. If these things are not delivered, your customers and users will once again think that pouring money into software development is a waste of resources and will buy off-the-shelf packages or out-source their IT services. Senior managers have also bought the benefits, but with a different emphasis than customers and users. Managers want improved productivity—lower costs—and they want to remove IT from the critical path of major organizational changes.

These expectations need to be reconciled. One of the first things all development managers considering adopting object technology must do is reduce expectations. Don't oversell the benefits of object technology. If you have created such a climate of high expectation—wittingly or unwittingly—any failure to meet those expectations will be laid at the door of the development group and the move toward objects. Considerable benefits are there to be gained, but they do not come immediately, nor are they achieved without strong resistance.

Resistance comes from the people and the culture of the organization. Any change is resisted; companies seek the steady state. Unfortunately, the business and commercial world does not stand still. It's messy out there and this messiness always ends up inside the software system. For example, if a new business product is provided—whether insurance, banking, or some other service product—the ability to change the way the system can support that product needs to be changed. With the trend to product variations announced almost on a daily basis, rapid changes are constantly required to these systems. But people in the development organization have just learned how to do it the old way. They have become competent and confident in the approach to their way of working. Now, that is once again under threat, so resistance grows. New skills are expected, new tools have to be used, a different way of working is required, and new deliverables are expected. These changes mean that what worked before may not work with object technology.

Moving to a new technology also insists that choices are made. What methodology will be used? Are toolsets going to be provided and, if so, which ones from which suppliers? Is the programming language going to be changed? What about the old systems—the legacy—how will they be supported? Making these choices can be very difficult for many organizations.

Finally, the concept of failure needs to be accepted. Introducing object technology may fail. You might have chosen the wrong tools, provided insufficient training, underestimated the learning curve, or made the pilot project too ambitious. While there is only one way for a project to succeed, there are a thousand ways for it to fail. Moving to object technology confronts you with the possibility of failure.

Hopefully, by carefully considering many of the concepts and ideas in the rest of the chapters, you will not fall into the many tar pits that await the unaware manager. The ideas and concepts presented here are based on the practical experiences of successful developers as well as from on those not-so-successful development projects.

This book is about the changes in each of the critical areas of strategy, structure, systems, skills, staff, style, and shared values that any development organization must undergo to make a success of object technology.

Let's explore the key question: How do you manage your move to object technology?

References

DeMarco, T., and T. Lister. (1987). *Peopleware.* London: Dorset House Publishing Co.

Canfield Smith, Dr. D. et al. (1982, April). Designing the Star user interface. *BYTE.* pp. 242–282.

Hammer, M., and J. Champy. (1993). *Reengineering the Corporation—A Manifesto for Business Revolution,* New York: Harper-Collins.

Humphreys, W. (1989). *Managing the Software Process.* Reading, MA: Addison-Wesley.

KPMG Peat Marwick. (1990). *Runaway Computer Systems.* New York.

National Computer Centre. (1991, December). Metrics Club Report to the Department of Trade and Industry.

Pascale, R.T., and A.G. Athos. (1981). *The Art of Japanese Management.* New York: Penguin.

Sims, O. (1994) *Business Objects—Delivering Cooperative Objects for Client-Server.* New York: McGraw-Hill.

Yourdon, E. (1992). *The Decline and Fall of the American Programmer.* New York: Simon & Schuster.

CHAPTER 2

STRATEGY

W HY DO STRATEGIES FAIL? WHAT'S THE REASON THAT THE MOST THOROUGH strategies created with the best of intentions and expertly communicated seem rarely to make a difference? You need to know, as this sets the tone for considering your own approach to object technology. Object technology is less a strategy in itself; rather, it supports the execution of the strategy at different levels: the business, the organization, and the information technology (IT). I look at the benefits and the support, and highlight the conflicts between them. Business strategies, which any IT development needs to support, begin with consideration of five crucial questions. Organizational strategies that support the innovation necessary for successful object development, involve broad job assignments, decentralization, and an openness with information. For the IT strategy, the benefits of the object approach are considered and the different levels of maturity are outlined.

The object-oriented development strategy has a number of key elements:

- A focus on the products—business products, lines, or services—produced by development activities ensures that the expectations of the customer/users are identified early in the project. It also involves resolving the differing needs of the customer, the technologist, the business manager, the project manager, and possibly the sales staff.

- A new development life cycle based on an iterative and incremental approach and its impact on the customer/user and scheduling. Prototyping can be a boon or a curse. I outline the three different types of prototype and examine their usefulness in a variety of situations.

- Classes are the building blocks of object systems and these classes need to be organized for reuse perhaps in a multicultural environment (i.e., multiple hardware platforms, operating systems, languages, etc.).

- Multiple dimensions are also associated with the teams and staff involved in object-oriented projects. I look at these multidimensional teams.

Object technology can face a number of obstacles: the existing systems and databases that may preclude some types of development, the culture of the present development organization and the significant learning curve with its paradigm shift. Each is covered in detail to help you avoid some of the pitfalls.

2.1 Strategy: The Vision Thing!

Oh no, I hear you groan, not another mission statement. In the beginning, we had aims, then objectives and now the mission statement. These days, almost everybody is talking about their vision for the future. Most of their utterances are banal and not worthy of the term *vision*. They are muddled, they are confused, and we are expected to agree with them, but more often than not, they outline a straightforward short-term objective—reduce costs, improve productivity, raise quality, etc.—dressed up in some visionary verbiage.

This camouflage results in our tendency to mock mission statements as the product of some advertising or public relations agency. They're motherhood style statements, they're hard to write yourself, they're ignored by even the most senior managers, and so on. Most of us have experienced situations in which the exhortations for superb quality ("quality products from a quality company") are quickly replaced by "ship it *now*" when patience with the delays in testing finally runs out. Even Tom Peters says of mission statements, "They can hinder and make a mockery of the process if the vision and values are merely proclaimed, but not lived convincingly" (Peters, 1987).

Why is this?

One of the prime reasons is that any mission statement not produced by yourself does not generate the kind of commitment that will make it work in the long term. For brief periods, most people will suppress their own hopes and aspirations to support some corporate goal given form in a mission statement, but they will not support it forever. There need to be objectives, but these objectives must be in line with the personal objectives of the individuals. While the corporate objectives may be permanent and stable, individual objectives are constantly changing. For example, there will always be a small number of technical people who are driven by the challenge of new technology and want to use the latest techniques and tools. Sadly, when the next silver bullet appears, then they will cast off the old and put on the new. Does this sound familiar to you? Does this apply to the discussions you are having at the moment with developers about object technology? If so, then beware that you may not be making a strategic decision, you may be simply responding to a technical solution that excites some developers.

If your group already has a mission-style statement, do a reality test. Ask your developers to state the mission of the group. Don't be too disappointed with the replies or shocked at the reaction. Some will look at you as if you had asked for their innermost secret, others will waffle, and few will have any concept of the mission or the strategy. Are you surprised? How often do you state the strategy? How often in meetings is it used as a touchstone for a decision? In fact, do you clearly understand your own set of objectives, your own strategy?

As an example, there's the classic story of three stone masons. When asked what they were doing, one replied, "I'm earning $15 per hour." Another replied, "I'm cutting this rough stone into a block measuring three foot by two foot by two foot." The last mason replied, "I'm building a cathedral." Which one do you think knows the overarching objective and the strategy? How many of the other type of masons work for you?

If you are a bit cynical about mission statements, call them "sets of objectives."

2.2 Levels of Strategy

Sets of objectives and their strategic implications are very important. They provide the foundation for the future direction of the organization, they identify the goals and targets to be achieved, and they provide a touchstone when considering new ideas, new technology, and more important, a framework when things go wrong.

These strategic objectives operate at a number of levels: business, organizational, and IT development. Whenever an objective at one level conflicts with one at another level, we can be sure there will be trouble. Unfortunately, this is usually the result of a lack of communication following the change to a previous objective. This is obvious and most of you will have experienced it ("Well, I didn't know *that* had changed!") but for object-oriented development these objectives need to be communicated clearly and often. Most changes happen inside the development group—component libraries, building frameworks, etc.—but there will be significant impact on the customers. For example, the incremental delivery approach requires very close cooperation with the customer/users for the numerous releases of versions of the product or system. Can the customer/users accept this shorter development cycle? It may be that speed is of the essence—business strategy objective—in which case, the customer/users will welcome each new version. But if exceptional quality is a requirement, thorough and exhaustive testing will mean more time between version deliveries.

To develop your own strategies there needs to be a clarity of vision, which can only occur when all the critical driving forces have been identified and their potential impact embraced by analysis. Those responsible for developing sets of objectives for the future must take the time to identify, immerse themselves in, and learn about the complex of interacting variables they are seeking to control. It is only when the underlying concepts of their business are fully understood that the objectives for bringing them about can be defined, together with a knowledge of the skills required to achieve them.

2.2.1 Business Level Strategies

From the business perspective, objectives usually answer five critical questions:

1. What is the focus for future business development?
2. What is the scope in both product and market?
3. How do we prioritize our scarce resources?
4. Do we have the capabilities to achieve these objectives?
5. Will they meet our growth and return expectations?

The answers to these questions developed by the top team are crucial to the IT development manager as there must be an alignment between the business and IT goals. This may seem obvious, but all too often this occurs by accident rather than design. The acid test is if the processes change within the business, how long will it take to change the supporting IT? Or, can the use of IT provide some strategic advantage that will benefit the organization? As an example, a Japanese bank spent $15 million in IT development to shave three seconds off a particular trading process; the increased revenue paid for that development in the first quarter (Leigh, 1994).

This is what is happening with the business process reengineering revolution. Old ideas are being thrown away, and managers are considering reinventing the corporations. There are some obstacles to this process as we shall see later.

2.2.2 Organizational Strategies

Object technology means becoming a highly innovative organization. This attitude toward innovation—a shared value—becomes widespread throughout the entire organization. There is a willingness of the top team to consider new ideas and fresh approaches to problems. Change is seen as a positive force, and there is a constant search for improvements to the processes and the business.

This innovative attitude is reflected in a number of key areas:

- Broad job assignments

- Decentralizing

- Establishing a culture of pride

- Open information

Setting broad job assignments is often expressed by mottoes such as: "do the right thing," "solve the problem," "make it happen." People's jobs are broad rather than narrow, and they are encouraged to seek opportunities, to share in the success and the failures of the work undertaken, and to be involved in the wider issues. If you ever hear, "It's not my job," consider yourself or, more properly, the organization, a failure in this area. Such a cry is commonly heard in organizations that have undertaken large-scale decentralization. To manage the impact of the shift of power, tighter controls in the form of restricted job descriptions are put in place. This is often experienced as responsibility without authority.

Yet the aim of decentralization is to ensure that power is placed close to the front line of the organization; that is, the customer or end-user. Successful organizations are adopting the "small is beautiful" approach to create many smaller "businesses" consisting of those groups or departments needed to make and execute a decision (Schumacher, 1973). These are called "case teams" by Mike Hammer in his book on reengineering the corporation (Hammer & Champy, 1993). In smaller organizations, people are more likely to suggest ideas and be enterprising about innovation and change. This is often for the following reasons:

- Fewer levels of management structure (usually three)

- Increased awareness of the activities of others

- Informal groupings and communication pathways

- A sense of belonging and of importance to the organization (one is not just a cog in the wheel)

A culture of pride respects people, recognizes their achievements, and expects outstanding work from them. Constant recognition is a reminder that people are the greatest asset to an organization. This environment makes it possible for change to be embraced and for it to be seen as an opportunity, not a threat.

The final characteristic, access to information, is crucial to encourage innovation, and to develop coalitions of groups to produce new products or systems. Obtaining information in most organizations is difficult at best and nonexistent in most. For example, can you as a product development manager or team member access the sales figures and customer information to identify possible partners in the next product development? Yes? Well done, you have broken down the walls surrounding most departments. No? Join the club of the excluded and the uninformed.

If these characteristics reflect your organization, adopting object technology will be another step in creating successful products or systems. If not, then you may need to address some of these areas before changing the way people will need to work.

2.2.3 IT Strategies

There a number of benefits to be gained from setting IT strategies. It

- encourages management of software as an asset, which like other assets, has a business life and will need replacing as it ages;

- reduces number of system variations, which leads to a faster response to customer/user requirements because developers have the skills and knowledge to focus on business applications rather than software needed to connect incompatible applications;

- permits interworking of the various applications supporting the business functions through compatible products and system purchases;

- provides flexible choices on hardware platforms, which will support the various applications.

However, even IT strategies have a number of levels of maturity with a progression—smooth or otherwise—from one to the next. IT strategies usually begin with policy decisions about the acquisition of hardware and software products (e.g., whether to use open systems architecture, to use Microsoft products, to buy only XYZ equipment from a local supplier). Little attention is paid to the selection and skill development of the IT staff by management. Simple applications, usually covering the financial aspects of the business, are installed. These are most often adaptations of standard packages, which may have been modified by outside contractors or suppliers. This approach works for a while, but when the group expands and a permanent IT staff exists, an IS audit is undertaken.

The IS audit is the first attempt to determine the customer/user requirements. A move is made to explore other areas of the business and to provide automation for many of the operational processes. These systems reflect what is being done at the current time with little thought or effort in looking into the future changes. Usually there is an increasing backlog of systems to be built and an increasing demand for more money to be spent. Identification and attack on this lack of overall planning leads to the next level of maturity.

To overcome this ad hoc approach to systems and the lack of control over the myriad development efforts, there is a move to form the centralized IT group.

This centralized view means that top-down planning is now undertaken. This is linked to the attempt to have IT support the business and, therefore, the IT strategy needs to support the business plans. Any developments are now planned in the longer term and gauged against the overall plans for the business. The IT department often becomes remote from the customer/users and is seen as a centralized dictatorship.

Because of the conflicting requirements of the many plans, the first steps in breaking down the barriers between IT and the customer/users begins. Arguments and debates begin to resolve the differing priorities of the customer/users for the scarce resources of the IT development group. Customer/users become involved in the systems and as long as the IT group responds to the changing business requirements, all will be well. However, should delays and restrictions be placed on the customer/users, there will be attempts by the more confident customer/users to create their own systems separate from all other systems.

A mature IT strategy uses technology as a provider of strategic benefit to the business. Opportunities in changing technology, such as geographic information systems (GIS), are explored and used to create a competitive advantage or provide support for the decision making processes of an effective organization. This involves a constant reassessment of all uses of IT and the introduction of corporate strategic alliances with many third-party suppliers. A forward-looking view dominates all consideration of IT policy and strategy.

2.3 Obstacles

Before detailing an object technology strategy three main obstacles must be considered: the existing IT systems, the current development culture, and the learning curve.

Obviously, not all systems can be changed overnight, nor should they be. Many systems perform well and would not benefit from the new technology. But they are often information sources for newer systems. You know you can't replace your accounts' database, but the new system needs the client names and addresses and sales order values. So a strategy to build wrappers that encapsulate the existing systems is required. If access to existing relational databases is required, numerous products provide class libraries to support interfaces between the old and new systems.

The problems are not, however, at the physical level; they are usually at the logical level. For example, a customer object may contain information on name, address, zip code, telephone number, account number, personal identification, etc., which consists of a number of discrete tables of a relational database schema. Imagine the scenario of a car when it goes onto a ferry: in the object world, the car is stored on a particular deck, but on a relational database, the tools come out and the wheels are removed and put on the wheel shelf, the doors go onto the door shelves, the engine onto. . . . And to leave the ferry, it has all got to be put back together again!

Packing and unpacking the information for the customer object may be complex, and it will definitely be slow, but performance is one of the key areas in evaluating the success of pilot object-oriented projects. Interfaces between the old and the new are prone to failure and require much effort. Don't underestimate this task.

The other major obstacle is the culture of the development organization. If you have tried it, you know that changing a culture is one of the most difficult things to do. This is why many large organizations set up separate teams staffed by outsiders recruited for their skills and, indirectly, for their culture. There is little point in hiring a developer from a traditional engineering background to provide investment analysis tools in the fast-changing world of trading floors.

There may be such a strong culture in place that it exerts a firm control on the way we think, feel, and act that nothing new is possible until we rid ourselves of it. It is the sum total of the intellectual and creative values of the people as well as the skills, knowledge, behavior, customs, and judgments, which, in organizational relationships, define the work of the staff at a particular time. When that culture is no longer relevant to present circumstances, a powerful negative influence is felt. But to throw such a culture out in a wholesale manner may mean losing the baby with the bath water. A thorough evaluation of the changes required and the ability of the organizational culture to assimilate these changes is an important method of overcoming this particular obstacle.

One of more significant obstacles is the learning curve associated with the move to object technology. Many, including myself, say that it's a more natural and intuitive way of expressing system solutions. However, to express these solutions much has to be learned: from the analysis and design perspective, the object models, the design of classes and the interaction between objects. From a programming perspective, the language, the operating system features, the existing class library components, etc. The shift in thought models and patterns can be daunting to many development staff who may have written solutions in a very narrow development environment (e.g., COBOL).

2.4 Object-Oriented Development Strategies

Object orientation is an approach and a technique for developing software systems. As such, it is more associated with the *execution* of a strategy rather than the strategy itself. The software development strategy could simply state that all systems development is undertaken in an object-oriented approach, but that would be missing the point.

The point of a strategy is that it is a course to steer by; it is a set of objectives that consider the long term and are bolder than usual. Strategies come from the top—from the top team and from the manager of software development. Attempts at bottom-up strategies are usually unsuccessful mainly because the resources and the commitment need to be there to carry the strategy forward through the many difficulties in its execution. However, input for the strategy must come from all levels of the development organization.

As strategies are guides to the general direction to steer, then they need themselves to be general in nature. So what could the software development managers' set of objectives be? After what I have said about writing your own objectives, you might find this suggested mission statement a bit strange, but take it as starting point for developing your own mission statement.

All managers should have this sign in two-inch high letters above their desks:

> To deliver quickly, cheaply, and with greater control, the high-quality systems of today and tomorrow that meet our customers' expectations

Please pause and reread it again as it's a significant challenge to most software development organizations. Notice it does not mention object technology; this is to reinforce the point that object technology is an approach and a technique to achieving this objective for the development of software.

Let's use Occam's Razor and look at the keywords in detail:

- *Deliver* shows that it's about producing an outcome, not simply performing some series of tasks in developing the software; these tasks underlie the working but the focus is on deliverables. Object development that stresses the evolution of the components means that working portions are delivered.

- *Quickly* indicates avoiding developing everything from scratch, using powerful tools, buying in software components from other suppliers, and reusing existing components or systems so that there is a shorter time to market for your products.

- *Cheaply* means less expensively as most systems cannot be said to be cheap. It implies reusing existing components as well as effective use of the resources and skills of the team members in order to contain costs.

- *Greater control* lets you monitor the project progress through the deliverables, manage change, and estimate the impact of such changes. With object orientation, the concept of the object as a deliverable item means that objects can be readily identified: hence they can be tracked and controlled explicitly.

- *High quality* is always assumed with every new technology. No one willingly adopts a new technology that will lead to lower quality of their products, yet this is often the result of inappropriate solutions. By reusing an object that has been proven in another system context, then not only is a higher level of confidence in that object assumed but the quality requirements are transferred to the provider of the object.

- *Systems* indicates the relationship of the components as a whole rather than as individual building blocks of applications. Object systems tend to become sets of applications that can communicate, usually via the operating system facilities such as Microsoft's object linking and embedding (OLE). It is better that they become sets of cooperating objects that can communicate directly with each other (i.e., remove the application barriers).

- *Today* recognizes that you need to produce practical solutions with the present resources and current systems and equipment. It also means meeting the business requirements for systems to save or make money, and the lower the cost the better. So the new object-oriented approach must result in savings of time, money, or effort or it must contribute to the business' bottom line in some way.

- *Tomorrow* means flexibility, dealing with changing requirements, looking to the longer term, and dealing with the unknown and the unforeseen. Object technology will encourage the building of components (objects) that can be modified and extended to meet these changes. Such modifications can be controlled and contained without unforeseen side effects on the remaining objects.

- *Meet* matching the requirements whether in time, cost, scope, facilities, etc.

- *Customer's expectations* shows the focus is always on the needs and expectations of the customer/user rather than the whims of the developers or the politics of the organization. By building objects that reflect the business operations of the customer/user, there is a much closer understanding of their needs, requirements and expectations. The language is not of database tables, schemas, and tuples, but of order form, credit checking, and delivery address.

Put this mission statement above your desk in a prominent position so you can see it every day. It will then sink into your subconscious. It will become your touchstone. Whenever a suggestion is made or a decision required, you will think "will this lead to greater flexibility?" or "how could this be done less expensively?" This is where the power of objectives comes from. It becomes the set of values that guides every business decision. We need those guides, we need this powerful mission statement.

So we have the vision: to deliver quickly, cheaply, and with greater control, the high-quality systems of today and tomorrow that meet our customer's expectations. Now we need to convert that into tangible elements for object technology development.

2.5 Key Elements for Success

The key elements of a successful object technology strategy are product focus, incremental delivery, class organization with component reuse, and development by multi-dimensional teams.

2.5.1 Product Focus

The first, product focus, is probably the most important. Products—the term *products* is used to indicate business products, product lines, or services—drive the software development activities. If the product is a banking service, software development will be involved in the delivery of fast, accurate, and secure customer-based services over a wide geographical area as well as corporate systems that support these services. If the product is an intelligent machine tool, the system is concerned with repeatability, safety, and flexibility that may be tailored to individual customer/user needs. These two examples require different emphasis in the development of the software system or set of components.

A product focus means always having a view of the results of the development activities. By results, I mean those that are meaningful to the customer/user, or as they are sometimes called, "user discernible deliverables." It may be interesting to know that the analysis phase is completed, but the customer/user does not care. I would also suggest that you don't know that the analysis was actually completed until the project is finished. Despite all the reviews, walkthroughs, and inspections, you cannot be certain sufficient information has been collected. Furthermore, you will find that as more details are produced, the risk of change to this volume of information is correspondingly greater.

2.5.1.1 Differing Wants

This aspect of the differing perspectives of the people involved in delivering the product is important. The customer/user is unconcerned at the various tasks undertaken by the developers, the techniques used, or the particular programming language. They want it to work. That seems simple enough, but the software industry has an appalling record of delivering working systems. They also want it on time—no comment needed on that! They want to change it—we are

TABLE 2.1. Differing Perspectives of Those Involved
in the Product Development

Customer/user	wants it to work
	wants it on time
	wants it to meet the needs of their job
Business Manager	wants it quickly
	wants it cheaply
	wants it flexible
Project Manager	wants control of the deliverables
	wants it produced within budget
	wants it delivered on time
	wants no surprises
Technologist	wants a technical challenge
	wants to use latest innovation
	wants new system development
Sales Staff	wants it to sell itself
	wants it yesterday
	wants infinite variations

slow to respond. Table 2.1 gives some idea of the differing perspectives that need to be reconciled.

These differing views are a prime source of misunderstanding and conflict between business managers. For example, in one organization the different viewpoints were the following:

- Marketing/Sales saw the product as a set of standard components with alterations to meet specific client requirements—a combination of proven technology and customized system.

- Management/Financial saw it as a combined set of low-cost existing components and high-cost alterations funded by the client in a once-off payment.

- Development/Manufacturing saw it as a specific variation of a previously proven and delivered system within market sectors that would be fully supported indefinitely.

These views obviously conflict. While the basic internal view outside development was of a core product that was adapted for individual customer needs, within development the product was built from previously delivered systems within each discrete market sector. Attempts to form a core or baseline product for use by other development groups had only partially been successful. The reason for this failure, or more accurately, the expenditure of excessive development time in relation to the supposed benefit, was that the underlying product architecture did not meet the special needs of the separate development groups—there was no set of common objects. Furthermore, the continual support offered to customers by development had a significant impact on development schedules and costs as no separate support group existed at that time.

2.5.1.2 Involving the Customer/User

Changing to a product focus involves the customer/user. As soon as the customer/user becomes involved in the project—as they should be—the risk of change increases. Customers work with a constantly changing environment: commercial, business, legislative, etc. So instead of ignoring the changes needed by a customer as soon as the requirement specification is signed off, as has often been the case, the development teams must recognize that the changes in the customer/user environment mean changes to the system. Continually involving customer/users often leads to improved understanding of how their business changes and leads to awareness of how the applications affect the present business processes; (i.e., how business process may be altered by new software systems).

Involving the customer/user also means including them in any evaluation or selection process for third-party products or components that will be used to support their work. It also means their involvement in prioritizing the various projects.

2.5.1.3 Meeting Expectations

"Meeting customer expectations" seems a simple enough phrase, but it does suggest that you know who your customers are and what their expectations are. Who are your customers? Are they the end-users of the system or product? What roles do the various end-users need: operator, maintainer, tester, supplier, etc.? Could the customers also be next in line in the development process (e.g., the QA test department)?

Gauging expectations is another mine field. What do they really need rather than want? Do they have long-term visions for the future that they would like to do, but are unable to express them or are unaware that the technology could take them towards it? Can we use a language to capture the expectations? One less publicized benefit of object technology is that it does provide a common language. If the customer/user deals with payslips, then a payslip object will be present in the final system. No longer will the talk be of database tables, unique keys, tuples, etc. Instead, the language will be that of the customer/user: information and behaviors. Many developers find this hard. They have preferred to communicate with machines rather than with other people. So you may also have to look at the interpersonal skills of your staff. Who will relate well with the customers, and who should stay in the back room?

If your customers are identified as the business managers who commission the product, a further important expectation to meet is that of the projected *benefits* to the business. If the cost of the project is estimated to be more than $500,000 then it should be a matter of policy that relevant business benefits— such as financial, performance, or effectiveness—are identified at the start, tracked after delivery, and compared with the earlier projected benefits. Hopefully, you will be able to show significant return from the new system.

The customer/user wants to see results and wants to see them soon. Much of the impetus toward object-oriented development has been to provide early results to show to the client. I will admit that graphical user interfaces (GUI) had a major impact on the move toward object thinking. It was through these components which could be modified and adapted, that partial systems could be shown to clients early on in the development process. But GUI technology is at the widget level of components. GUIs provide the elementary components needed to present the result to the customer/users and permit interaction with the system. This presentation and interaction accounts for only 40% of the usability of the system; the other 60% is the user's conceptual model of the underlying business objects, properties, and behaviors and the common metaphors that reflect the business tasks (Figure 2.1). It is often this 60% that makes the difference between a usable system and one that confuses and confounds.

You must be clear what is the product and what the customer/user wants to see.

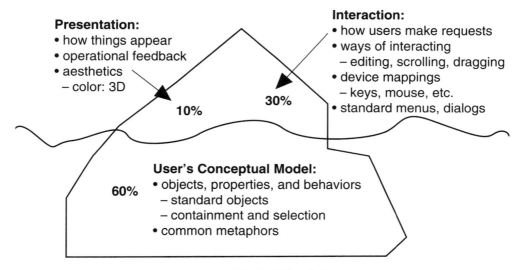

Presentation:
- how things appear
- operational feedback
- aesthetics
  - color: 3D

Interaction:
- how users make requests
- ways of interacting
  - editing, scrolling, dragging
- device mappings
  - keys, mouse, etc.
- standard menus, dialogs

10%

30%

User's Conceptual Model:
- objects, properties, and behaviors
  - standard objects
  - containment and selection
- common metaphors

60%

FIGURE 2.1. The Usability Iceberg

2.5.1.4 Outcomes not Tasks

Focusing on the product is a restatement of Michael Hammer's first principle: organize around outcomes, not tasks (Hammer & Champy, 1993). So what are the outcomes from the development activities?

The most important is obviously a valid and verified system. However, "valid and verified" means checks and tests, perhaps using live or contrived data to ensure and prove to the customer/user that the present delivered system meets their expectations. Often this test and verify phase is a major part of the project and requires a significant amount of effort in generating test data or building test harnesses. These things do not disappear with the use of object technology. In fact, they can get worse. Testing individual components is straightforward. Many toolsets support test generation and validation on static pieces of code. Even clusters of classes can be validated using such tools. But object systems are fundamentally *dynamic* systems. Objects are created and destroyed, they communicate using messages; there is a flurry of messages on every action and this is the glue that holds the system together. Who tests this glue? How can we be sure that all possible messages and links have been explored? Some approaches to testing are outlined in Chapter 4.

A further set of outcomes are internal to the development process: the object models. The final result is the delivered system, but to move from conception to completion, three distinct models are produced (Figure 2.2) All of the object-oriented development methodologies give these models different names or use different notations and diagrams to express their contents; the attempt here is to give a generic view of the deliverables from the various phases of development.

The problem domain model focuses solely on the scenarios—sometimes called use cases—within the scope of business or problem being considered (Jacobson, 1993). This model is a product of the definition phase when an understanding of the work is made. The next model, which encloses the problem domain, is the solution domain. This model is the product of the design phase when various solutions that take account of the numerous constraints are explored. Finally, the system domain, a product of the build phase, is the realization of the chosen solution. Classes in the problem domain should still be discernible in the system domain, just as solution classes will appear in the system domain, which will have further classes unique to itself (Figure 2.3) These relationships are important as any ill-conceived change to a problem domain class

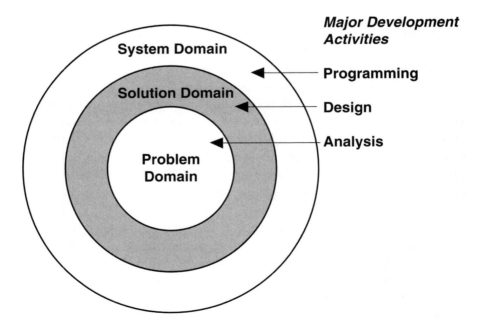

FIGURE 2.2. The Three Model Domains

made by an inexperienced programmer has a direct impact on the behavior of the problem scenarios. But it is also true that in poorly designed object systems, classes can disappear between each of the domains (e.g., a customer class in the problem domain ends up as a series of fragmented classes in the system domain; see Figure 2.4)

Documenting these domains is another major outcome of the development activity. While analysis and design documentation is accepted as necessary, most developers are reluctant to complete the documentation of a delivered system (i.e., describe what was built). Yet as soon as a maintenance programmer gets close to the system, the first thing sought is information on how the system goes together. Don't be mislead by the fact that object systems tend to have smaller components that are easier to understand. Sales literature will tell you that object systems are easier to maintain, but they are only easier to maintain because of the encapsulation of information and behavior in objects defined as classes.

Furthermore, while overall maintenance costs are unlikely to be reduced, the cost to maintain an individual system will be lower. With the faster application

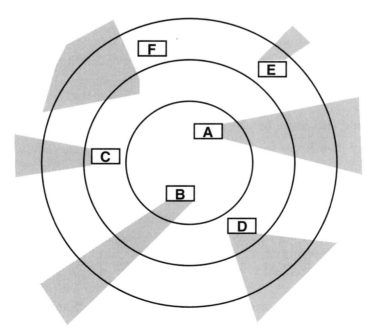

FIGURE 2.3. The Span of Classes across Domain Models

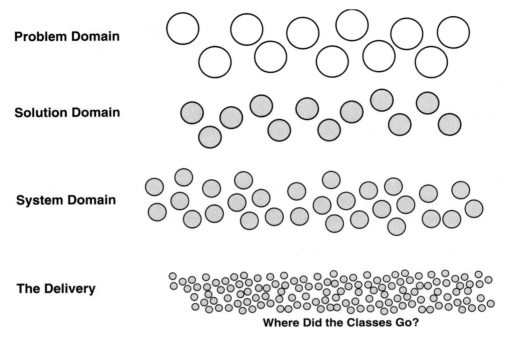

Problem Domain

Solution Domain

System Domain

The Delivery

Where Did the Classes Go?

FIGURE 2.4. The Disappearing Classes

development process, there will be more systems to maintain at the same cost, a significant gain in maintenance productivity.

2.5.2 Iterative and Incremental Delivery

The next key element is to change the work processes. The traditional waterfall development process is not appropriate for object-oriented projects. Much more emphasis is required in the analysis and design tasks with significantly more communication taking place between analysts, designers and programmers. Traditional process models inhibit this feedback. There are numerous hand-offs from one group of developers to the next. Each hand-off results in a delay and a requirement that sufficient level of detail be provided to make the information understandable, comprehensive, and unambiguous. Remember, someone either has to ask for clarification or guess at uncertain requirements. Also, as the product evolved through each stage any form of traceabilty of requirements got lost. A functional requirement may be uniquely tagged for identification purposes, but as this requirement was developed in the solution

FIGURE 2.5. Example of a One in Four Chance of Getting it Right!

and then the program code, it got diffused and fragmented. Experience of the pain and effort required in resolving these problems can inhibit any move to a newer development cycle that encourages multiple deliveries.

Even with high-quality objectives the risk of the delivered system being unacceptable was one in four (Figure 2.5). Is it any wonder that systems delivered using traditional development process models often failed to meet customer/user expectations?

An object-oriented approach can be undertaken using the waterfall process model, but this is effectively saying "we will use object technology as a technique for building, but we will ignore the opportunity to reduce the time to delivery." Another approach is needed to gain the benefits of early visibility, flexibility, and extendibility of object systems.

Barry Boehm introduced the spiral approach to software construction and enhancement (Boehm, 1988). In this model, shown in Figure 2.6, each turn around the spiral is determined by the need to reduce the risks of the next increment of the new development. Clear objectives and alternative solution models are used to plan each delivery cycle. The build phase may use different techniques and methods, and after evaluation of the delivered version and future capabilities a decision is made to commit to the next turn or stop development at that point. As each turn around the spiral increases the costs, these increments of small fixed-budget contracts can also be used to control the costs.

One thing the spiral model does not stress is that each delivery should be a functional version of the final system. A functional version is a properly engineered, fully working portion of the final system—100% of 35%, 100% of 56%, etc. This is not the same as the misunderstood and misused word often associated with object orientation: *prototype*.

2.5.2.1 Different Prototypes

There are three types of prototypes (Graham, 1991):

1. Evolutionary prototyping is used when the target system is constructed in the original prototyping language (i.e., each new prototype is a functional part of the final delivered system). Components of an evolutionary prototype would be included in the functional version described above.

2. Revolutionary prototyping is when the prototyping language is not used in the final delivered system. This is the term used when a 4GL or similar rapid application development environment is used to obtain, for example, customer/user requirements prior to development

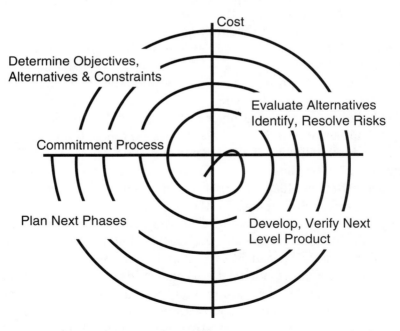

FIGURE 2.6. The Spiral Model of Development

in a standard language. This is often called the *rapid prototype* in object literature.

3. Revelationary prototyping is the exploration of ideas or concepts in a research environment using unusual or specialist tools. It is this type of prototype when subsequently delivered as the final system that has given prototyping a bad name.

Revolutionary and revelationary prototypes are portions of the system that are built to reduce risk. For example, if the system requires high-speed communications with another system, the communication components need to be built early on in the project. If the prototype shows that the speed cannot be obtained, more innovative approaches need to be sought or the project abandoned. Such prototypes are used to reduce risk by experimentation and exploration, and components are generally not reused in the final system. If they are to be used, proper design and engineering is required.

Instead of throwing away the components, the evolutionary approach to prototyping is used instead. Such prototypes are often used to capture the customer/user requirements. Then the components, which are in the language of the target system, are incorporated into the delivered versions. Any effort expended in developing these prototypes can be applied to the final system.

There is a downside to this evolutionary development approach: it can lead to problems of inappropriate system architecture and complex class structures, which can ruin the final larger systems. It's like building a skyscraper with the foundations of a bungalow; it looks OK for a while, then it falls over! In an object-oriented system, the system architecture is in effect the class hierarchy—the inheritance trees and the class relationships. Whenever inheritance is used it fixes the architecture, which is why many experienced object developers recommend wide and flat hierarchy trees over deep and narrow trees; see Figure 2.7.

2.5.2.2 Iterative and Incremental Delivery Cycle
Once these risks have been explored and removed through prototypes, the driving force is the iterative and incremental (I&I) delivery cycle. Complete versions of portions—the increments—of the final system are developed and delivered to the customer/user. I want to stress again that each version is a fully working set of scenarios or use cases within the scope of the new develop-

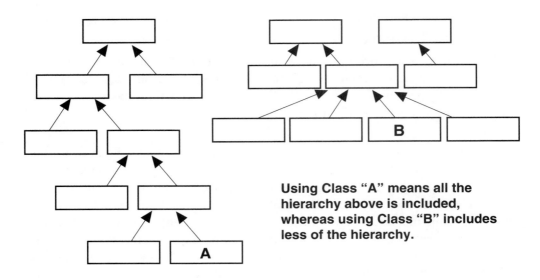

Using Class "A" means all the hierarchy above is included, whereas using Class "B" includes less of the hierarchy.

FIGURE 2.7. Inappropriate Class Architecture

ment (Figure 2.8) When all the scenarios and use cases have been delivered, we have the completed system. However, if for economic reasons, the project is curtailed, even 100% of 85% of the full system may still be useful and effective in supporting the customer/users—85% of 100% of the software components is not useful; it does not work!

One thing to ensure in this I&I approach is to deliver a number of scenarios or use cases, say between 5 and 15 cases. Why? If a smaller number of scenarios are delivered (i.e., narrow segments of the domains), there is an increasing risk that when they interact with other scenarios, major changes may be needed to the previous delivered version. It has been found that significant rewriting or even total replacement of previous delivered classes has a detrimental effect on team motivation and morale. It also may indicate insufficient understanding of the user requirements. If this is the case, call it rapid prototyping, use a high-level language such as Visual Basic, determine the requirements, and then undertake I&I delivery for the final system.

Also, during the I&I delivery cycle portions of the system may need to be reworked or modified. These are the iterations of the I&I approach. The benefit of both iterations and increments is that there is a convergence toward the final solution that meets the customer/user's needs.

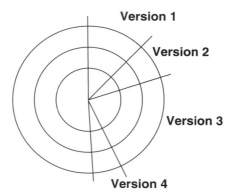

FIGURE 2.8. Versions Delivered in an Incremental Way

Care is needed after every delivery. During the build process, classes are extended and modified to meet the current delivery requirements, but the resultant architecture may be inappropriate for the next build cycle. After a delivery, time needs to be taken to review the class hierarchies, reconsider the abstractions, identify more appropriate generalizations and specializations, and then rework the present version of the system to provide a baseline for the next increment. You must allow such time in the schedules.

Figure 2.9 shows that the iterative and incremental development project cycle is based on a product view of the delivery in terms of user features and a process view that identifies the analysis, design, and build tasks required to deliver the next functional version. So the project is planned with the deliveries of major user features, represented as use cases, at sensible intervals and the development activities are planned within those major milestones. Within each major milestone, user discernible deliverables, the minor milestones for monitoring technical progress are defined (e.g., completion of the analysis models).

When planning the project, the milestones, which tie together the technical and managerial aspects of the project, are laid down as time boxes and the development processes and matching resources are planned only for the short term. Major milestones and resources loading and costs are planned for the whole project but for the detailed allocation of individuals or teams to specific tasks, only the next two major deliveries need to be considered. Any plans that show allocation of people to tasks on days more than three months ahead should be treated with extreme caution as the uncertainty factor is so high as to make such plans meaningless.

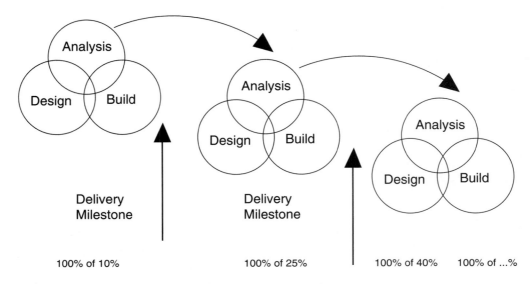

FIGURE 2.9. The Iterative and Incremental (I&I) Development Approach

2.5.2.3 Can Your Customer/Users Handle I&I Development?

Customer/users have become used to a long wait for new systems. They expect teething problems during the early days and have a cut-over point to the new system. Now you come to them and announce that the first delivery will be in three months and that further deliveries will take place at six-week intervals. Imagine the consternation. They will think that each delivery will give as much heartache as in the past and will not want to be put through that experience every month. You need to convince them and demonstrate that

- the delivered version will be of high quality,

- it will be useful,

- support will be given,

- it can be changed if it does not meet the requirements.

If the deliveries will cause a major disruption to the present operation of the customer/users, it is wise to set up a beta test group who can assess the delivered versions. These testers will be part of the team as discussed in Chapter 3. What will fail will be internal deliveries within the development group; the customer/users must be heavily involved from the outset.

All this means more work for the manager of object-oriented projects. Can your teams handle the testing, the disciplines of customer delivery and support, the inevitable changes? Is there a well-established change control mechanism? There must be; object technology promotes flexibility, and that flexibility must be controlled.

This change to an I&I delivery cycle combined with the product focus has the added benefit of making the progress of the project visible to both the project manager and the customer/user. No longer can developers pull the wool over your eyes. When each delivery means a demonstrable version of a portion of the system, its behavior and its information, it either is complete or not; it becomes a boolean-style decision: true or false. Now, not all deliveries will be successful, but a release note accompanying the version clearly indicates what it contains and what it does not.

This leads to one of the problems with the I&I approach. Deferring requirements to later deliveries of the product can lead to the "snow plough" effect where as the original completion date nears, the amount of work to be achieved is considerably more than first planned.

However, an iterative and incremental delivery cycle can become a uniform project management, control, and reporting method.

2.5.3 Class Organization with Component Reuse

The next component of a successful object technology strategy is class organization with component reuse. Classes need to be organized at the group level. The term *group* is used to indicate a business or infrastructure domain.

Business groups imply functions such as accounts, engineering, manufacturing, sales, etc. These business groups will have libraries that contain classes that reflect their business operations: account number, drawing number, job number, and so on will all be different. There will also be common classes that can be used across many of the business groups—these are often called *enterprise classes*. Grouping the classes into business and enterprise domains, rather than a single library of vast number of components, encourages version control of the contents of the libraries and ensures that these classes will always be considered for further new developments in that domain.

Infrastructure groups develop special classes that support the computing environment of an organization, such as real-time, networking, user interfaces, etc. There are four main components of the software infrastructure:

1. User interface
2. Data management
3. Communications
4. Operating environment

The user-interface component is more than the class libraries provided by a supplier. It is also the standards and guidelines that provide a uniform look and feel to all the organization's products and systems. Many class libraries are available from third-party suppliers in a variety of languages. These class libraries provide the basic building blocks for the user interface (e.g., windows, buttons, scroll bars, etc.). Such components, now called "widgets," may be used directly or can be constructed into *frameworks* that supply a higher-level abstraction for the developer. For example, in the ABC Company, instead of collecting the individual classes for each new development, a previously developed set of GUI infrastructure classes could be formed into a framework such as ABC_Window, which would give the standard window, buttons, logo, etc. as used in all ABC user interfaces. Visual C++ and Visual Basic products provide a similar style of framework; from a series of straightforward selections, fully operational windows (without content functionality) can be created in a few minutes. Such work traditionally took weeks of effort.

Data management components provide the information and data access to the variety of storage techniques used by the organizations. It would be simple to say that object systems use object-oriented database management systems (OODBMS), but the vast legacy of existing information sources precludes that statement. Adapter objects to access the various types of database management systems (relational, hierarchical, flat-file, etc.) with the appropriate access language (usually SQL), have to be provided (Figure 2.10). As movement toward object databases gain momentum, these adaptor objects will be replaced with persistent object storage mechanisms. However, legacy databases will exist for many years to come, and tools to aid their interface with object-oriented systems will appear.

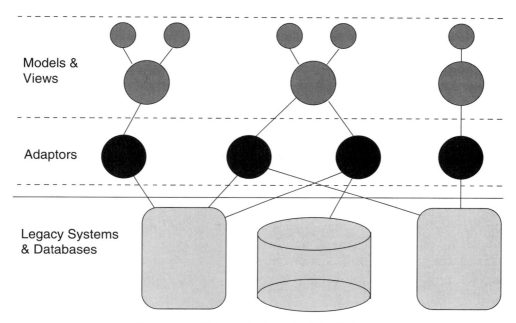

Models &
Views

Adaptors

Legacy Systems
& Databases

FIGURE 2.10. Using Adaptors for Interfacing to
Legacy Systems and Databases

There is similar requirement for communications components. Adapter
objects for APPC, TCP/IP, NetBIOS, and the many other internal and external
communication protocols have to be supplied.

Finally, the components supplied with the operating and development environment have an impact on the system infrastructure. Choosing the right products for this part of the infrastructure is possibly the most difficult decision the
software or systems manager has to make.

The aim of these infrastructure components is

- to provide a common set of standard components,

- to provide a uniform processing environment,

- to ensure major systems/applications are not developed from scratch,

- to guide and support changes to future procurement policy.

Procurement of these components to support the business and infrastructure domains is dependent on your organizational style. If you are fully decentralized, the decisions will be devolved to the development groups. If, however, you are in the early days of object technology, it is wiser to adopt a coordinating style where you decide on the standards, and infrastructure and buy the components, and the development groups develop the classes for their business domains. Use of these standards, infrastructures, components, etc. by the development groups will give prompt feedback on their ability to meet the needs of the development organization. If they don't work, change them. Avoid persevering with things that do not fit your development activities—it's not a mistake if you change it, it's a mistake if you don't!

In developing or procuring these components, a strategy also needs to be considered for what can be called *multiculturism,* or the various decisions on supporting multiple languages, multiple operating systems, and multiple hardware platforms. Most organizations already have some form of multiculturism in place.

2.5.3.1 Component Reuse

The major claim of productivity increases with object technology is based on a high reuse of existing components, but this can only occur when the classes exist, developers know of their existence, and managers are encouraged to exploit these assets. Useful classes cost money as they need to be bought or especially developed. However, a cost saving of 75% can be made in a development project within the same business domain by reusing existing business domain classes (customer, order, product), and a cost saving of 25% can be achieved between different business domains by using the infrastructure domain classes (GUIs, communications, etc.)

To exploit the concept of component reuse, a new structure needs to be put in place. This has been called the software factory or the software foundry; see Chapter 3 for fuller details. However, moving to such a structure is not without problems. In a normal factory environment when widgets are checked those with faults are added to the reject pile. When the stack gets to a noticeable or significant level, some action is taken to improve the process that created the widget. No such thing happens with software components. They are invisible, and as they are soft, they can be changed easily and frequently. Poor components become visible only when they fail for the customer/user. At that point, the managers consider the pile of rejects and may take corrective action to improve the development process. Unfortunately, there is a tendency to fix only the broken component and continue to work in the same way with the same tendency to produce poor components.

This makes a mockery of one of the most publicized benefits from object technology, that of improved quality. While it is true that quality improvements can be made by using pre-tested and proven components, detecting defects is still left to the developers and all to often left to the customer/user. Even with object technology, programmers still have to design and write code segments, and the process can be as error-prone as any other. Only professional software engineers will apply high-quality standards to the components created by their teams.

In time, the main role of object technologists will be to provide components for the business and infrastructure domains, which will then be used by the customer/user to build their own applications. If software developers resist this trend, it will only encourage user departments to "do their own thing." It's already happening with the advent of languages such as Visual Basic with its in-built database, which are clearly being marketed at these power users. Such user-built applications will never be a match for fully engineered *core applications*. They can fill a need for short-lived "fancy queries" often required by business functions, but if reliance is placed on such small-scale applications for day-to-day operational activities without adequate professional advice, standards, and controls, this proliferation could slowly sink your organization.

Recognize this trend and provide well-engineered components for your customer/users. Get them to buy only your components because, after all, you know your own organization better than anyone.

2.5.4 Multidimensional Teams

No longer are significant developments undertaken by individuals; the tasks are too complex and the timeframes too short. The boundaries between the problem, solution, and systems domains are more blurred with object technology. More effort is needed in the analysis and design stages to ensure the problem domain and possible solutions will meet the user's expectations. As stated before, changes in any of the layers has an effect on the other layers, so informed decisions are required. This means that the roles of analyst, designer, programmer, business expert, tool maker, etc. are all required for object-oriented developments. No longer can teams remain in their functional groups, all the skill and knowledge is needed on a daily basis. The team needs to be multidisciplined; it needs to be multidimensional. This multidimensional team provides the powerhouse for successful object-oriented software development.

2.6 Some Final Words on Strategy

It's here at the strategy level, that the seeds of success or failure in adopting object technology are sown. In writing this chapter I was continually struck how everything that follows has its roots in strategy. Miss one of the key elements, and the whole may fail; embrace them all, and radically change your way of working and success is assured. You will be able to add other strategic elements to suit your organization, but you should start out with this overarching mission statement:

> To deliver quickly, cheaply, and with greater control, the high-quality systems of today and tomorrow that meet our customer's expectations

Then put in place your own version of the key elements for a successful object technology strategy:

- A product and customer/user focus ensures that the expectations of the customer/users are identified early in the project and the differing needs of the customer, the technologist, the business manager, the project manager, and possibly the sales group are resolved.

- Changes in the development processes to support iterative and incremental development also mean an impact on the customer/user and on scheduling. The three different types of prototype are useful in a variety of situations.

- Organization of the classes into domains with the right framework for component reuse in a multicultural environment—multiple hardware platforms, operating systems, languages, etc.

- Build high-performance teams with a wide range of skills and knowledge.

References

Boehm, B. (1988, May). A spiral model of software development and enhancement, *IEEE Computer.*

Graham, I. (1991). *Object-Oriented Methods.* Reading, MA: Addison-Wesley.

Hammer, M., and J. Champy. (1993). *Reengineering the Corporation—A Manifesto for Business Revolution,* New York: Harper-Collins.

Jacobson, I. (1993). *Object-Oriented Software Engineering—A Use Case Driven Approach.* Reading, MA: Addison-Wesley.

Leigh, A. (1994, May). How to reengineer hears and minds, *Management Consultancy.*

Peters, T. (1987). *Thriving on Chaos.* New York: Knopf.

Schumacher, E.F. (1973). *Small Is Beautiful—A Study of Economics as if People Mattered.* London: Blond & Briggs.

CHAPTER 3

STRUCTURE

T HIS CHAPTER EXPLORES THE CHARACTERIZATION OF THE OBJECT-ORIENTED development organization (e.g., functional, decentralized, etc.). It's important that the size and shape of the structures enhance the development activities rather than inhibit the creative and thoughtful work necessary for object development. Most organizations are a mixture of two types of structures that are under threat by the move toward decentralization of the business. What's happening is that the traditional organizational pyramid is being turned upside-down, and this has an impact on what and how you manage.

Structures have a number of levels of maturity ranging from the IT developers being part of business functions (e.g., finance), to the the fully mature organization with coalitions between IT specialists and the business groups. These levels help you to plan the next stages of maturity for your organization.

Teams play a significant part of the success of any development project, but what's their shape, how are they organized, and what roles need to be filled? I look at the Shamrock concept for team structures to provide a new shape made up of the core team, the services, and the contractors. In each of these teams, the roles and skills are outlined. This leads to the concept of the software factory vaunted by many. The implications of such a structure and the types of components that may be usefully produced from such a factory are explored. Also, a radical approach to work allocation developed by HP is discussed and shown to be possible in the context of the team when it might not be acceptable to the organization.

Finally, support for these new structures is considered: overcoming the "developers curse" caused by the accommodation and the range of services needed to support the team activities and communications.

3.1 Types of Structures

Since the early 1970s it has been noted that the structure of a system tends to reflect the structure of the enterprise that built it. This means that a highly structured hierarchical organization tends to produce strongly structured systems, even when developed by a single individual within that organization. Similarly, a less-structured enterprise produces a less-structured system. This indicates that our mindset is influenced by the external environment in which we work.

It may also explain the eagerness with which certain organizations select different object-oriented methodologies. For example, a strongly structured group would have a tendency to choose Booch or Rumbaughs' Object Modeling Technique (OMT) as it reflects their strong structural view of the world, whereas a loosely structured group may prefer the looser style of Wirfs-Brock or Object Behavior Analysis (OBA) developed by Adele Goldberg of ParcPlace Systems.

Why are these findings on system structure important?

Well, successful object systems tend to be loosely coupled and decentralized. This implies that the organization that constructs them needs to be decentralized and loosely coupled. This is then reflected in the structure: the shape and size of the development group that needs to tackle object-oriented projects. Like most things, it is not as easy as it appears. You can simply say to your current project teams, "I've read of the benefits of object technology, so I want you to now develop in an object-oriented way." It may work, but do you honestly think it will succeed in the longer term? No, it needs a more considered approach, so let's start with some principles.

3.2 Organizational Types

Most organizational structures fall into two categories: hierarchical and free-form—although a mixture of both is usually evident. Hierarchical structures are more common in well-established enterprises in which layers of managers control and direct the activities of the subordinates. Such a structure implies regimentation, although this may not be the case. It does clearly provide a structure for authority and a strong mechanism for dealing with crisis. Control comes from the top. Authority usually lies near the top, but responsibility can be quite low down in the organization. This often results in a lose-lose situation: you are responsible when something goes wrong, but have no authority to avoid the error. In such hierarchical organizations, there are usually numerous layers of management, although the recent trend in downsizing or restructuring has led to significant reductions in these layers.

The new movement toward a customer focused organization introduced by Tom Peters (1987), Mike Hammer (Hammer & Champy, 1993), and others (Kanter, 1989) has led to the traditional organizational pyramid being overturned (Figure 3.1.) Instead of working for your boss, you are now thought to be working for your staff, and the real heroes and heroines are the customer contact people (Peters, 1987). I'm not naive enough to think that you ignore your own boss, but if the pyramid is fully turned over, then of course the boss should also be seeking ways for you to improve your effectiveness. This attractive model is still some way off for most organizations, whose senior managers profess customer service but still hold the reigns tightly from the top; the pyramid is on its side!

When hierarchies get in the way of innovative work—adopting object technology is innovative—the skunkworks first appear.* Skunkworks break the rules, crack the structures, jump the boundaries, ignore the conventions. They are necessary to create the highly motivated teams for creative and inventive tasks. They are the ultimate free-form type of organization.

Free-form organizations imply many relationships between individuals and groups. In these types of organizations the project team is the normal center of activity. Unfortunately, in the past these teams were formed along functional lines, whereas the real power comes from a common objective and multidisciplined team members. Leadership and authority lie within the team, but unless this is clearly stated or when relationships become confused then troubles

---

* *Skunkworks* is the term brought to light by Tom Peters and Nancy Austin in their book *A Passion for Excellence* (1985). The term was first used by Kelly Johnson of the Lockheed California Company, who created powerful teams for designing and building many of today's aircraft: skunkworks. A short history of Kelly Johnson's approach is on page xxiv of the introduction to Peters and Austin's book.

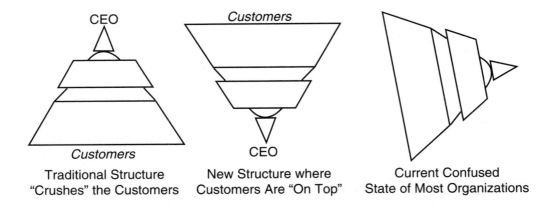

FIGURE 3.1. Overturning the Traditional Structural Pyramids

occur: "it's not my responsibility. . . ." You have all heard that type of reply when your system has crashed, even in the most structured enterprise!

Despite the differences, both hierarchical and free-form structures require individuals to be strongly self-disciplined. This means individuals must have a clear understanding of their roles and responsibilities; more of this in Chapter 5.

The new style of organization means breaking down the barriers of the traditional functional-style structure. No longer are the developers grouped into functional teams: analyst team, design team, etc. Instead, these barriers, which often led to "over-the-wall" development—the specification is thrown over the wall to the analysts who after some work through it over the wall to the designers who may throw it back over the wall to the analysts, and so on—are disappearing. As mentioned in Chapter 2, Michael Hammers' first principle of business process reengineering is to organize around outcomes. This inevitably leads to a process-oriented organizational structure where the structure reflects the business products or services. So instead of a separate development group, multidisciplined development teams are part of the business groups (i.e., coordinated but decentralized).

You may think that this is too radical, but look outside your window. Look at what is happening in the business community: megacorporations are decentralizing (Peters, 1987). For example:

- Asea Brown Boveri redeployed its central accountancy staff to their business units. Now the accountants work in the front lines in the business division or company.

- Mars. Inc. have only thirty staff guiding a $7 billion company. Where are the rest? In the field!

- Intel Corp. have decentralized approval and eliminated middle-management layers to remain agile within the structure of a big organization.

So why shouldn't developers of business systems work in the front line. A major Irish enterprise has recently dispersed all its developers to its divisions and group companies to make them more responsive to their clients' needs. Before this change, requests for new applications or updates were formally submitted by the various business groups. Unfortunately, it became difficult to assess the priorities of the numerous demands for resources; every group's request was of the highest priority to that group but not necessarily to the whole organization. Needless to say, if a request got deferred, the users were extremely unhappy, complained bitterly to the IT group, and to everyone else in general. (Anyone out there recognize this scenario?) Also, what tended to happen was that the more forceful managers from the various groups got the lion's share of the new work. More complaints and more recriminations would inevitably follow.

Now the development staff can set local priorities and meet local demands. A small central staff of three set corporate guidelines, monitor technology advances, and provide training. They do however, recognize that one of the potential dangers of this change is the isolation of the developers. It's understandable that members of a small team of developers in a remote location will feel isolated.

The key to this redeployment is identifying what parts of the organization should join together and what parts should be kept apart—doesn't this sound a bit like the principles of object-oriented design? But beware, Peter Drucker in his classic work on management advised against putting the wrong things together (Drucker, 1991). For example, treasurers deal with money and accountants deal with figures, so there's no need for them to be in the same structure.

3.3 Structural Maturity*

At the initial level, the IS or IT group is part of one of the normal business groups, usually finance or accounting. A small staff provides a limited service supplemented by the use of outside contractors. When it gets larger, it becomes

---

* There have been many studies into process and growth models (Galliers & Sutherland, 1991; Bailey & Basili, 1981; Gibson & Nolan, 1974)

a centralized entity and the DP manager, who usually has a technical background and controls the power, appears. Customer/users feel poorly supported, there is some rebellion, and they start running free with their own systems. At the next level, the focus changes to information and the name is usually changed to "information services" or "information center" and the manager is now renamed the "IS Manager." This is also when the QA department is formed as part of the group, and libraries of components start to appear. However, this stage usually creates a "them and us" situation between the developers and the customers. There is a backlog of systems and a defensive attitude to the users' problems.

At the next level of maturity the strong infrastructure is extended into coalitions between the business and IT units, but the control is still from the IT or IS centre. These coalitions are formed only to satisfy the current development need. The final stage of maturity is solid coalitions with the guiding hand of central coordination.

How are these levels reached?

Larger organizations are breaking down the functional divisions and creating focus groups, listening teams, quality circles, and the like. All are multidisciplined teams organized for application-oriented tasks. Such team structures are necessary for truly innovative work, and in developing object-oriented software, innovation and abstraction are key elements to success.

These multidisciplined project teams are usually small, but how small is small? Ideally, these teams have 7 to 15 members; this is the ideal number as shown by most sports teams, the primitive hunting bands and the 12 disciples. This is not to suggest that we become primitive hunting bands of developers or don sackcloth and ashes, but that history has shown the powerful effectiveness of small, highly focussed groups. Some even consider that 15 is too large a number and point to the fact that such a team is normally broken down into subteams; rugby football has forwards and backs, and in American football there are offense and defense teams with linebackers, running backs, etc.

Development teams are then made up of developers, clients, agents, and the different types of customers (e.g., end-users, testers, installers, maintainers, documentation writers, etc.). The team is fully empowered—even as far as being given its own budget—is self managed, and tends to have a flat structure. Team leaders are responsible for the technical content and quality of the delivered software, and project managers ensure the activities are within budget and time constraints.

There is still the need for leaders. There will need to be a permanent head of the team, who is the point of contact and the seat of authority and responsibility. One useful title is chairman or chairperson, as it more properly suggests the role of this leader. Leadership during the project lifespan may be adopted by other individuals for the duration of a particular activity. For example, during analysis and design, the leaders are the architects, and during construction, the leaders are the builders. This free-form structure does not mean a loss of authority or control, nor does it imply a move toward a democratic style of management, which frightens many senior managers who are used to powerplays.

The team needs to maintain focus on the outcomes, and there always needs to be a single point of authority for when things go wrong and when major decisions, usually of a commercial nature, need to be made. This focus and direction can be achieved in a democratic way without entering the tar pits of committee decision making. Remember, the requirement is to achieve a creative and innovative environment and at the same time ensure proper discipline in the development of the outcome. This is why *software engineering* is the correct phrase for the work. Whether the technique is object oriented or traditional, developers must balance creativity with discipline; they are required to engineer the software.

3.3.1 The Shamrock Organization

For smaller enterprises, the shamrock organization introduced by Charles Handy (1991) is the most appropriate. For nongardeners, a shamrock is a small, three-leafed clover seen as the Irish national symbol (Figure 3.2) One leaf of the shamrock is the core of professionals who are permanently assigned to the

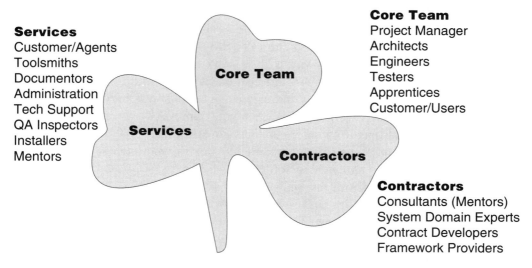

Services
Customer/Agents
Toolsmiths
Documentors
Administration
Tech Support
QA Inspectors
Installers
Mentors

Core Team
Project Manager
Architects
Engineers
Testers
Apprentices
Customer/Users

Contractors
Consultants (Mentors)
System Domain Experts
Contract Developers
Framework Providers

FIGURE 3.2. The Shamrock Organization

team. These professionals are usually the most skilled and highly trained of the team. They provide the strong architectural framework, maintain continuity for the duration of the product, and ensure the quality of the delivered system components. They are highly influential in the design and building of the delivered system. As a manager, your task is to assemble and maintain this team of core professionals.

This core team forms the development organization. It is their skill and expertise that differentiates your organization from any other. These are the essential staff, those that the business cannot do without. Often they are very well paid—with such golden handcuffs as fringe benefits, low interest rates, company cars, etc.—in return for this expensive package, results are expected and demanded. Long hours and hard work are normal. Many companies have used this approach and found that even with a significantly reduced workforce, their turnover has gone up! These staff may be very highly effective, but their quality of life can be questionable: do you miss your child's ballgame for another meeting on class library components?

One of the other leaves of the shamrock is the services provided by others within the organization (e.g., publications, contracts, networking services). These professionals are part-time members of the team seconded for the necessary periods when their skills and expertise are required; they are the specialists in testing, documentation, infrastructure components, etc. These team members should not be core members of other teams, as this would lead to a conflict of priorities.

Services may also be supplied by outside agencies such as external suppliers of class libraries and toolsets. You can take the attitude of simply buying their products and throwing them away if they don't meet your needs. It would be better if you formed a stronger relationship with certain suppliers. Microsoft may appear to be interested only in large corporations, but they do rely heavily on smaller innovative enterprises that use their products in new and less well-known areas. Smaller suppliers of class libraries, especially CASE toolsets, are only too willing to become partners in your developments; they want a strong customer focus as much as you do.

The final leaf—and there are only three leaves unlike the lucky four leafed clover sought by many—are contractors and other professionals hired to satisfy a shortfall in skill or experience. These outside contractors will need to be closely managed. It is unfortunate that the software industry, which relies so much on these freelance professionals, has an appalling record on the use of contractors.

Many managers lay the blame on the contractor, when the responsibility usually lies squarely with the managers. A typical scenario goes like this:

> "Here's the specification, it's not complete yet but tell me how long you will take."

> "That's too long, see if you can cut some out and Jane will finish it for you."

> "What do you mean it will take longer, you saw the spec."

> "Never mind those new requests, I want it finished by Friday."

> "Where's the documentation? You must provide documentation."

> "That's the trouble with contractors, they don't finish the job, never provide documentation; still I'll not pay that final invoice until I see it fully documented."

Have you been there?

So the shamrock organization has highly skilled and committed professionals as its core team supported by services from within or outside the organization and contracts with other highly skilled professionals to meet shortfalls.

It's not a perfect solution. There are three different workforces to manage: core, services, and contractors, each with different levels of commitment and priorities. But by careful management, this will be the future structure of most organizations whose work is based on knowledge.

3.4 Structuring the Teams

The shamrock concept is equally applicable for the structure of the team to build and support object-oriented systems. Traditionally, the focus has been on the builders of the new applications: let's call them the *applications team*. This team focused on meeting the requirements of the users, usually by building applications, but in some organizations they are, of course, building operating systems, real-time controllers, etc. Members of this team usually consist of the sponsor of the project, the lead customer/user for at least half of his or her time, as well as the developers.

This then is your core team supported by services and contractors—the other shamrock leaves—as appropriate.

One such support team is the *class team*. This team looks after the library components, but they are much more than simple librarians. Members of the class team need to be of the highest technical level. Their skills in modifying submitted classes for generic use and ensuring high-quality improvements are obvious. These members also need to be good communicators, who meet regularly with the development teams to discuss appropriate classes and guide reuse solutions. Large organizations even publish newsletters—new classes added to the library—and hold awareness seminars. This awareness of the contents of the class and domain libraries is crucial as the most common excuse for poor component reuse (i.e., "I didn't know it was there.").

What if your organization is not large enough to warrant a separate team or it's early days for your object-oriented development? Then you need to allocate these roles to members of your core team. For a period every week, a small group get together and review the past work to identify generalizations and specializations—the key concepts of abstraction—for further refinement. This process is always done after a version release of the system and prior to further new work.

Evidence suggests that one-third of your development staff need to be concerned with the class libraries (Henderson-Sellers, 1993). This may be separate staff or an allocation of time to present team members to undertake these important activities.

One radical approach to teams has I believe, been tried by Hewlett-Packard (HP)*. This is their concept of project bidding. On a special notice board, details of forthcoming projects are posted. Members of staff seek out others to join them in submitting proposals for the project indicating their capabilities, their team structure, and their management organization. A committee then sits and selects the most appropriate team given their project proposal and their availability—it could not be used as a mechanism to get off a current project. Surprisingly, even the most mundane and boring projects had teams bidding for the work. This seems to indicate that *who* we work with—we choose the members of our team—is more important than *what* we work on. Managers, take note.

---

* I remember reading of this some years ago, but can no longer find the reference. I would appreciate any readers who know of this experiment and could provide further details to contact me.

This approach turned out to be very successful in trials and has spread to other HP plants. Maybe it could only work in a highly innovative organization like HP. When I conducted a straw poll on this idea with groups of developers, they all indicated they would love to work this way, but they all say that their own organization would throw a fit if it was ever suggested! However, while you may not be able to change the organization as a whole, it is certainly within your power to change it within your project; pin the next set of project activities on a board and select individuals and teams from the resulting bids.

There is a downside, of course. What happens to people whom no-one picks for a team? (This is similar to school days when football teams were chosen in the playground.) Does that indicate something about that staff member? Is communication training required? Is career guidance needed?

3.5 The Software Component Factory

An extreme form of class team is the software component factory. In the factory concept, the focus is on the prime goal of the object-oriented approach: the construction of the system from existing components. This goal statement does raise some questions:

- Do the components exists?

- Are they reliable?

- Who built them?

- How much would they save?

- Can I change them?

To deal with these questions, the concept of the software component factory has been introduced. The factory produces high-quality components for use by application development teams within the organization. The factory concept has been around for a long time in certain organizations. It has not always been successful as the languages used tended to inhibit effective reuse, and the library needed more work than the given return. Now, thanks to object-oriented languages, with their encapsulation and extension, the idea once more has merit.

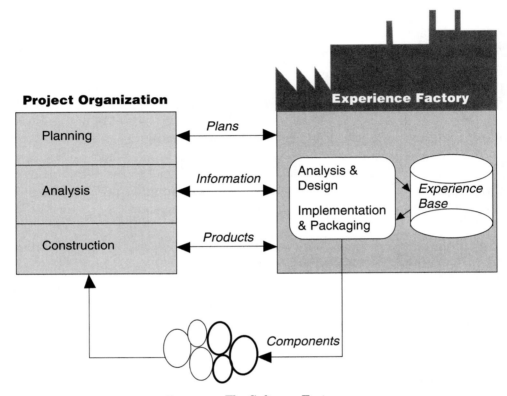

FIGURE 3.3. The Software Factory

Project teams provide production managers with information on future business directions and current plans for new applications (see Figure 3.3). The factory team review these plans, and based on their experience, produce components that can be assembled to provide the relevant solutions. These components are available for other project teams. Over time, the library components will meet most, if not all, of the business domain and infrastructure requirements.

It's an attractive idea, but it has some assumptions. What does it do to you?

When full component production is envisaged, proper production management is required. Firstly, strong paths of communication need to be established between the project groups and the factory: user groups, strategy teams, business developers, marketers, etc. Then, design activities need to look to the future business directions, design for genericity and to ensure that performance targets can be met. Construction must focus on quality with all the necessary and costly reviews and inspections. Software components have become more like widgets, so production planning, scheduling, design, and construction are required. If the production line is producing a significant number of broken widgets, the production process is failing. Unfortunately, with software it can be difficult to identify the number of rejects in the production line.

Once the components are available, sales literature needs to be produced. This brochure details functionality, performance, reliability, size, documentation and perhaps even price of the components. Sales can be made internally but there will be a growing market for the sale of good components to others. Substantial income could be made from the components (Love, 1993).

Attractive though the software factory may seem it does have some flaws. Experience shows that the best software components come from application developments. It is by scanning these developed systems that candidate classes can be identified and reworked to form the more generic components for the future. This approach ensures that the components meet the needs of the business. A factory would always have to predict the future—our past record shows that we are hopeless at that. The future is constantly changing and unless these components were restricted to stable concepts such as windows, buttons, sliders, etc., they would need constant revision. Who pays for this revision?

Microsoft and the other component builders can successfully supply you with classes as long as they stay within a well-defined scope. As soon as they attempt to supply business components, they will be subject to the constantly changing business environment. Current classes available from suppliers reflect this narrow scope:

- Foundation classes—strings, collections, etc.

- Graphical user interfaces

- 2D and 3D drawing

- Charting and plotting

- Databases

- Financial—money, rates, formula, etc.

- Mathematical—general, DSP/time series, statistics, etc.

- Modeling and simulation

The software component factory is a powerful concept, but you must realize that managing the production of invisible components is not straightforward and not inexpensive.

3.6 Providing Support

To support these new structures, changes may need to be made to the accommodation and to the services. Teams members need to be near each other. Object orientation means they need to spend much more time talking with each other and to be aware of what's happening to the system. All changes can have serious impact on the final system. For example, a builder changing a class hierarchy tree may reduce the ability for that class to be reused in the future as planned by the designers.

I know of one object-oriented development group that is split between Scotland, England, and the US. The manager spends all her time commuting between the three sites trying valiantly to create a common purpose and to handle the stretched communications. You and I know that should it ever succeed, it will be a testimony to the architects who designed the components and the interfaces as well as to the manager who maintained the organizational glue. However, I doubt if she will ever again have the energy to manage even a small project—burnout also happens to managers as well as to high-flying technicians.

Communication means talking, talking means noise, and noise disturbs other developers. Creativity—yes, we come back to that again—needs peace and quiet, time without interruptions, time to reflect and build those models of the mind. Most developers will tell you that they hate open-plan style offices; see Figure 3.4. You can test this yourself. Conduct a survey of your developers' working hours and you will find many come in early or stay late in order to get some work done. Maybe you don't need to do this. Maybe you come in early or take work home for exactly the same reason. What does this say about the quality of your working environment?

Often, open plan is an economic choice over the structure of the building, although some open-plan offices may have more to do with managers requiring supervision over the bowed heads of their workers. Economically, it is not cost effective; the lost productivity far outweighs any cost savings on buildings. You pay for it now or you pay later—either way you pay. For those skeptics, read *Peopleware* by Tom DeMarco and Tim Lister (1987) to find out how much it really costs.

If your organization insists it cannot change the floor space, at least insist on having many small meeting rooms to keep the work area as quiet as possible. Or, as introduced by one major organization that required large experimental

FIGURE 3.4. The Developer's Curse

areas for their large systems, set up quiet rooms where people can go to hide; no phones, no talking, no terminals, only silence in which to tap the creative part of their powerful minds. It may come as a surprise, but they have been hired for their brains not their bodies!

New tools and services may also be needed by the object-oriented teams. Some form of groupware is required to support the development teams. This may be supplied by the CASE toolset you are using to develop the object-oriented system or it may be extra support in the form of repositories or configuration management tools (see Chapter 4). No matter what form of structure you adopt, you must put the infrastructure in place; if you don't control the flexibility inherent in object-oriented systems, you will disappear under a mountain of partially completed systems.

3.7 Conclusions

I've shown how the new driving forces in business will mean changing the structures of the development organization. It will mean multidimensional teams, ideally of no more than 7 to 15 members, as the leaves of the shamrock. One leaf of the shamrock is the core of professionals permanently assigned to the team. These professionals are usually the most skilled and highly trained of the team. Another leaf of the shamrock is the services provided by others within the organization (e.g., publications, contracts, networking services). These professionals are part-time members of the team seconded for the necessary periods when their skills and expertise are required. The final leaf is the contractors and other professionals hired to satisfy shortfalls in skill or experience.

The impact of the concept of a software factory means highly skilled staff, more communication, more care in the design of components, and more management of production, which is neither straightforward nor inexpensive.

Finally, I've tried to highlight the problem of noise as the main curse of developers, which is most often caused by open-plan accommodation. Such a curse inhibits the concentration and creativity of many developers, which results not only in reduced productivity but in poor system designs.

I am often challenged by these ideas for structural changes. Often, the main reason is the inflexibility of the organization. That's entirely my point. If the organization is that inflexible, it will be very difficult to gain the benefits for this powerful technology. If it's that bad, set up a skunkwork; break the rules, jump the boundaries, form unusual alliances. Do something to release the creative spirit.

References

Bailey, J.W., and V.R. Basili. (1981). A meta-model for software development and resource expenditure. In *Proceedings of the 5th International conference on Software Engineering*. Parsippany, NJ: IEEE.

DeMarco, T., and T. Lister. (1987). *Peopleware*. London: Dorset House Publishing Co.

Drucker, P. (1991). *Management*. Oxford: Butterworth-Heinemann.

Galliers, R.D., A.R. Sutherland. (1991). The "Stages of Growth Model" Revisited. *Journal of Information Systems*, 1(1).

Gibson, C., and R.L. Nolan. (1974). Managing the four stages of EDP growth. *Harvard Business Review*, 52(1).

Hammer, M., and J. Champy. (1993). *Reengineering the Corporation—A Manifesto for Business Revolution*, New York: Harper-Collins.

Handy, C. (1991). *Age of Unreason*. London: Business Books.

Henderson-Sellers, B. (1993). The economics of reusing class libraries. *Journal of Object-Oriented Programming*, 6(4), 43–50.

Kanter, R.M. (1989). *When Giants Learn to Dance.* New York: Simon & Schuster.

Love, T. (1993). *Object Lessons.* New York: SIGS Books.

Peters, T. (1987). *Thriving on Chaos.* New York: Knopf.

Peters, T., and N. Austin. (1985). *A Passion for Excellence.* New York: Random House.

CHAPTER 4

SYSTEMS

"IT AIN'T WHAT YOU DO, IT'S THE WAY THAT YOU DO IT" IS AN APT INTRODUCTION
to systems, the third of the McKinsey Seven Ss we are exploring. By *systems*, I don't mean the fruits of our development processes, but the processes of working and the procedures used in the development activity. This definition then includes the systematic flow and relationships of tasks and information needed to produce the product and methodologies employed to accomplish the task, the metrics used to measure the success of the tasks, the tools used to support the activities, etc. Figure 4.1 illustrates the different type of systems in most organizations.

This chapter explores each of the different types of systems and, given their variety and complexity, it must cover a lot of detail. It begins with an examination of the different levels of systems that are usually in place in the organization and how they may need to be modified to fit the object-oriented approach. Then there is a look at some of the major contenders for object oriented methods such as Rumbaugh's OMT and Booch. Note that they are called *methods*, not *methodologies*, which really means a "study of methods." This leads to an examination of the basic working patterns for software development and the

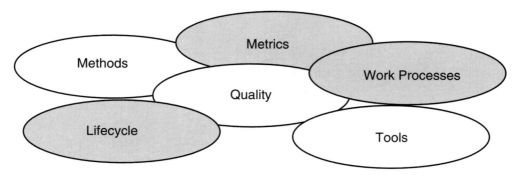

FIGURE 4.1. The Different Types of Systems

impact of object orientation on these techniques of working. Choosing and using methods means an understanding of the process models and process architectures within development. A generic model is shown to help you to map your own organization's working processes and thereby gain knowledge of potential process problems.

Systems also have levels of maturity, which were first outlined by Watts Humphreys of the Software Engineering Institute. While these maturity models focused on organizations, Watts Humphreys is now considering how such concepts can be applied to teams and to individuals; these new ideas are covered.

Metrics for the measurement of object systems development are also detailed. This is followed by the types of quality systems that are needed, including what to look for in class design and what to consider in the development processes. The final section covers using and choosing tools to support all object-oriented development work. This includes CASE toolsets, configuration management, verification and validation using testing tools, and all the support tools that will be needed for group working (i.e., groupware).

It's a lot a detail, so let's start by looking at the different levels of systems in an organization.

4.1 Layers of Systems

In any organization there are different layers of systems. They can be thought of as three concentric circles (Figure 4.2), where the outer ring is the organizational systems (i.e., the accounting, budget reporting, etc.). In the next ring are the specific tasks and their relationships with each other that make up the

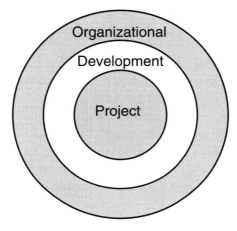

FIGURE 4.2. The Three Layers of Systems

development department or group (i.e., define, plan, build, deliver and support stages). In the center are the procedures and techniques required to accomplish a single task (i.e., production of the object model and class relationship diagrams).

In a similar way to changes in the object domain models having significant impact on the problem domain model, it holds true that the components of the organizational systems have an effect on each of the other circles. A change in the organizational reporting of resource expenditure, for example, may mean new data capture methods for an employee and changes to the sequence of development activities. Similarly, new work patterns required by object-oriented development may not fit into the present organizational system procedures.

A typical example of this misfit is the outdated use of timesheets. There will be howls of derision from our financial friends [sic]. "We must know where the money is going." "We must know how to charge a customer for their desired widgets." And so on, and so on. This is not a suggestion that there should be little financial control of projects but a query on the usefulness of the common procedure of timesheet reporting.

On the whole, timesheets are a waste of time; time in filling them in, time in entering the data into the database—there is always a financial database—time in calculating the charges, and time in reading the monthly reports. Little is achieved by this obsession. The accountants believe the figures, the managers distrust the figures as they all know the number of developers who call them "lie-sheets," and the cost of collecting this misinformation rises all the time. I recently heard of an outrageous situation in which timesheets had to be completed two weeks *before* the actual dates to give the accountants time to calculate the invoices to the clients. Utter madness.

If you question this assertion, ask yourself, "Are the weekly reports really telling me who worked on what activity, how long it took and whether it is different from that planned?" In most organizations, you might see the summary report, but it will only tell you some financial budget figures. If you want to keep track of the projects, then you usually must collect your own information, and timesheets are not often appropriate.

For example, hands up those of you who have received little if any feedback from this timesheet system on your performance in achieving the goals of the company

Why this tirade against timesheets?

The focus of timesheets is on the *money* and not on the real, crucial goal of the development organization: to deliver quickly, cheaply and with greater control, the high quality systems of today and tomorrow that meet our customer's expectations.

This is not to say that money is unimportant or to encourage a free-for-all with the budgets. They are important to the organization, but timesheets for the reasons of money are not good predictors of the future. The focus needs to be on the management of object technology projects. It's a bit like playing tennis, but watching the scoreboard rather than the ball. Unfortunately, the scoreboard is for another game—the accountants' game—so it bears little resemblance to your own activities and performance.

What are the "balls" we should be watching?

Given the interrelatedness of the procedures and techniques—the systems—it becomes very important that the systems reflect the goals of the organization. If, for example, a company goal is service to customer or customer care, then the systems under which all development is done must reflect that focus. Customer care implies

- ensuring the delivered system works,

- delivering on time,

- responding quickly to new demands,

- providing customization facilities for their own use,

- involving the customers in the development process,

- actively seeking their ideas and identifying their concerns.

The list goes on and on, but you get the point. Similarly, if quality is the focus, what mechanisms and checks need to be in place to ensure the highest possible quality of your delivered product? Do the schedules permit enough time for thorough acceptance tests? Are tools available to automate the tests? Will sufficient resources be available? Are you able to delay delivery to ensure the quality is up to standard or will you be "shot"?

If technical innovation is important—it is often called leading edge in mission statements—are lots of small starts encouraged? Are genuine failures permitted? Are libraries of components honed for ease of reuse to speed new products?

Consider now your own organization's goals. What is its mission statement? Do your systems support this mission statement? There is often a glaring misfit between many a mission statement on the walls of numerous organizations and the systems and work patterns of the development group. A large organization— nameless for obvious reasons—prides itself on the highest quality of its safety-critical systems, yet it permits unsupervised, inexperienced programmers to patch the code of existing live products. Talk about disasters waiting to happen.

4.2 Object-Oriented Methods

Before outlining some of the issues on choosing a method some words of caution are needed: Master the method, don't let the method master you.

If your team follows the method slavishly, there is a chance that you will have a successful development, but there is an equal chance that you will have a disaster! Methods can hinder as well as help to establish new ways of working.

All object-oriented methods have to be considered as formalized statements about patterns of work and working procedures. They provide an aggregated approach based on the concept of best practice. When a project is completed successfully, the work processes are analyzed and used to provide a template for the next project. Normally, further successful projects usually occur through the continuance of the previous successful team and little or no attempt is made to document the best practice.

Others have done this work for us. They have formalized their view of successful working practices. But they are only that; they are methods of working, not to be confused with magic sequences or tasks that will always guarantee success. In fact, many of the so-called methods are simply a set of diagrams that provide views of the object model with various notations. Such methods do not explicitly discuss the working technique or the processes, only the outcome as diagrams and code.

A development method therefore requires that the working technique be formalized and documented and that a set of notations are defined. However, this is not enough. There has to be an established set of users of the method. We all have a method of working but cannot call our personal approach a method, unless others use it.

4.2.1 Review of Some Popular Methods

At the time of writing there are something like 47 different object-oriented methods! Fortunately, we can ignore many of them as they are either still in early stages of development (and unlikely to oust the leading contenders) or are used exclusively by a single organization. This is similar to the earlier days of structured methods when there were also very many so-called methods but only a handful in wide use within the software development industry. For object technology the leading contenders at present are

- Booch
- Coad/Yourdon
- Jacobson (Objectory)
- Rumbaugh (OMT)
- Shlaer/Mellor
- Wirfs-Brock
- Fusion

No matter which methods are in the list, some readers will think it an insult that their particular favorite has been ignored. If you want to learn more about all the methods, other books provide fuller details (e.g., Carmichael, 1994). I also have no intention of recommending any particular method over another. In my experience, every organization has a unique set of requirements, so help can only be given by suggesting ways to go about choosing a method and a toolset.

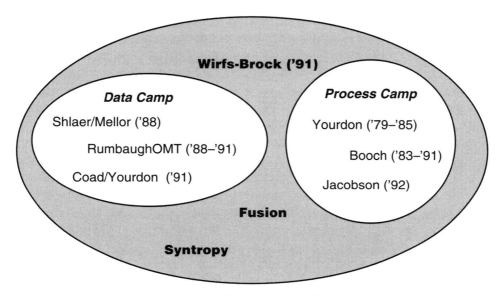

FIGURE 4.3. Different Method Camps

For the purposes of our review, Figure 4.3 shows the methods as belonging to various "camps"—I call them camps as there are regular skirmishes between the various factions. While there are real differences in the approaches, usually such warfare* is about the syntax of the diagrams, rather than the process models and the architectural issues, which are far more important.

Most of the methods in the Data Camp have their background in entity relational modeling and structured design approaches, which have been modified to accommodate the new object-oriented paradigm. Most systems in this camp handle large amounts of information and therefore tend to create entity-like objects.

On the other hand, the Process Camp has its roots in real-time programming applications and encapsulation. Grady Booch published a seminal paper on object-oriented programming using ADA in 1986. Since then, he has developed his model into a full development method, which has recently been updated.

---

* Ivar Jacobson wrote a plea for such a cease-fire in "Time for a cease-fire in the methods war" in the July/August 1993 issue of *Journal of Object Oriented Programming*. The same issue had an open letter from all the major methods developers (Booch, Shlaer, et al.) titled "Premature methods standardization considered harmful"

Ivar Jacobson with his object-oriented software engineering approach supported by the tool Objectory has now become well known throughout the industry
(Jacobson, 1992).

In 1991, Wirfs-Brock used the work done at Xerox PARC, to produce the
first object-oriented method that has come wholly from that background
although it draws heavily on psychology and cognitive science.

One of the interesting features is the increasing overlap between all the modern methods. Scenarios first introduced by Adele Goldberg of Smalltalk-80 fame
(she also has her own object method called OBA), appear as use cases in Jacobson and responsibilities in Wirfs-Brock. Booch and Rumbaugh now have similar
elements in their methods. Fusion, the method developed by the Hewlett-
Packard team led by Derek Coleman (Coleman et al., 1989) set out to select the
key elements from the other major methods, such as object model and processes from OMT, visibility from Booch, and object interaction from Wirfs-Brock.

While there is a form of convergence, perhaps speeded by the present collaboration of Rumbaugh and Booch, it will not generally lead to a single object-
oriented method. Differing requirements by object developers and their
organizations will preclude such a product.

4.2.2 Fundamental Models

Two fundamental models must be described in any object-oriented method: the
physical model (the architecture of the system components) and the logical
model of classes and objects. The logical model needs to be able to not only
describe the contents of a component but be capable of describing complete systems. This latter point is crucial, as many methods are good in a particular area
(e.g., describing objects), but they are poor when it comes to describing the
other models.

Earlier I wrote about structures affecting the delivered systems and mentioned that I also thought that the structure also suggested which appropriate
method would be chosen. I do think that this has an impact on which method is
appropriate for an organization.

If past projects used structured methods in designing systems to process
large volumes of information, one of the methods from the Data Camp may be
more appropriate. If, on the other hand, your work involves more process-oriented systems for machines, one from the Process Camp may be better. Each
has roots and focus in that particular application development environment.

Table 4.1 Differences between Structured and Object-Oriented Approaches	
Structured Analysis and Design	**Object-Oriented Analysis and Design**
Functional view	Object view
Process focus/data focus	Encapsulation of process and data
Separation of process and data	Process and data equal
Top-down or bottom-up approach	Known/unknown approach

For those who are used to structured methods the essential differences are shown in Table 4.1.

In the UK, banks and financial institutions are generally choosing Rumbaugh's OMT whereas telephone and communications organizations are using Booch. You must decide for yourself which method fits your applications environment, your staff, and your methods of working. Each organization's business domain is unique, and each will have special requirements.

4.2.3 Basic Object-Oriented Work

Object-oriented analysis and design provides all the information necessary for the construction of the system in a form that can be understood by others. The latter point is important, as some of the notations for object models do not lead to a clear understanding. Overall analysis and design are necessary to clarify the requirements, to discover and resolve omissions, and to build a visible model of the structure, relations constraints and boundaries of the problem, solution and system domain models.

The basic purpose of object-oriented analysis is to

- assess what is needed,
- identify the right problem and establish the vocabulary,
- produce a definition of the needs to be met by the new system,
- provide a visible representation of the problem,
- provide a basis for other specifications: user manual, build plans,
- meet cost and time constraints.

The purpose of design on the other hand, is to

- find the appropriate system architecture,
- discover and/or create classes that can be implemented,
- ensure the solution is complete, correct, and viable,
- apply known techniques using well-established principles,
- meet cost and time constraints.

There are differences in the emphasis and focus of each of these stages. Analysis focuses on the problem and finds as much information as practical, design is focused on providing a practical solution. For example, during analysis, a class is identified and defined in terms of its behavior, public information, relationships, and possible operations (services); in design, this definition is transformed into a full specification detailing the attributes, states, methods, and message contracts.

The solution model is independent of the system domain model with good reason. A detailed solution domain model should be capable of being realized on multiple platforms, with different languages and perhaps with different operating environments. Modern systems of today need to be portable.

The product of the analysis and design stages are

- scenarios and scripts,
- object models,
- class models,
- class definitions and specifications,
- message definitions and specifications,
- user interaction model.

These models are then refined and implemented during the build—program coding, test, and validation—stage. With the object-oriented approach, the build stage is much more straightforward as full component specifications are available. This is not to underestimate the work involved in the programming as great care is needed to use the appropriate system model, but the object models and specifications provide much more information.

4.2.4 Further Challenges

Most organizations report that they currently use some particular method, object oriented or otherwise, but how mature is your use of your chosen method? There are five levels of maturity:

1. *Not aware of the state of the art.* No interest nor concern at this lack of interest

2. *Aware but no use.* Knows about some methods, but no intention to use one

3. *Aware but casual use.* Experiments and pilot projects, but not in any mainstream development; little or no training

4. *More use than not.* Indicates use in the mainstream development, but often abandoned for smaller projects; some trained and skilled staff

5. *Fully exploits the state of the art.* Full compliance, all staff trained and skilled

Where is your organization on this scale? If you are currently at level 2 in your development method, there is considerable work ahead to introduce an object-oriented method. If, on the other hand, you consistently use a method (levels 4 or 5), with training and with commitment, you will be able to introduce the object paradigm.

4.3 Methods of Working

Methods cover the development process, although some are mainly concerned with the syntax of the diagrams. You do need to understand the software development process itself and you need to establish task descriptions and procedures of working for your own developers. These may be based on either a well-known method or adaptations, sometimes extreme adaptations, of other existing practices. But all methods need to be adjusted and tailored to fit your own organizational requirements. These are usually turned into standards documents.

Most established organizations have standards documents that formalize the task descriptions and procedures for working. In fact, the recent drive toward certification for ISO 9000, TickIT, or BS 5750 makes this formalization compulsory. Many hours were spent in identifying these work procedures, much discussion ensued, many changes made and announced with great fanfare to the staff. They then sat on a shelf, were pointed at occasionally when asked what procedures are followed and rapidly became out of date. How many of you have coding standards, when were they last updated and when were they last looked at? Are they "shelfware"? Most are. The only one who read them last was the newest recruit, who then looked at the delivered code and found little or no conformance. You probably get by now my lack of excitement over standards, especially as applied to working methods.

Methods as a way of working, as patterns of techniques are valuable.

Methods form the essential elements of every developer's toolbag, but ones that are codified and prescribed are detrimental to the creative activity of software development. It's like painting by numbers. Here's the "work of art" with the blocks in numbered outlines, all you have to do is find the right color and apply where marked. But what happens if some colors are missing, or the paint pots have the wrong numbers? We blithely go on painting unaware of the error until the result once again becomes so much scrap. When challenged, we report that "we followed instructions—we could see it did not look right, but that's what the numbers said".

I do not decry attempts to formalize the way of working, but you must accept that they may be ignored, that they are very expensive to implement—to create, to gain certification, to maintain, and possibly to police—and that they really document the past. Unless these standards are enforceable, they are useless. One manager ran a tool on the software code and found that the programming standard had been broken every 168 lines. But how is it possible to enforce programming standards?

When setting up your standards on methods of working, ensure that you are developing the *skillbase* by adding to the toolbag of the developers and not forcing some form of cookbook approach that makes you feel that everything is fine because the blocks have been colored in.

Some will challenge this lack of de-emphasis on standards saying that they need to ensure new recruits get guidance on how to work in their organizations. Fine, I can understand that. But are standards the way to do it? Could a form of user guide with samples such as a specification or code segments be sufficient? Could the master-apprentice approach not yield better instruction? Does giving a pile of standards manuals to read really replace a short induction course by a range of personnel: developers, customers, service engineers, etc.? Look at your new recruits; what are they doing? Reading standards manuals? Are they learning? Does Figure 4.4 reflect what really happens?

FIGURE 4.4. Typical Situation for New Recruits?

Object technology means faster delivery of flexible systems. Keep that sense of urgency. Don't let a weight of development standards and procedures slow you down. They were built for a different age—one of waterfalls.

4.3.1 Development Process Models

To understand development process models, the work activities are partitioned into tasks and grouped into stages as shown in Table 4.2. Every organization will have similar names for the different stages and variations will exist from the version shown in the table. For example, only one test task may be used rather than two. Nonetheless, the essential activities within the two tasks would be performed under the definition of the single task. The work specifics are not different, only the segmentation and the stage names.

The segmentation is mainly meant to show how partitioning of the development process is accomplished and not to force exactly five stages upon an operation. They provide a framework or checklist to use when developing the process architecture models.

Although the process has been segmented into stages, which are described and shown serially, the actual work occurs in parallel to various degrees across the product lifecycle. This overlap of activities from different stages is both natural and necessary.

You will notice that terminology associated with object technology appears in the task lists only in the consolidation stage. That is because the tasks are generic for all software methods; it is the *deliverables* that are different for the object-oriented development models. The object-oriented model may alter the product components from subsystems and modules to processes and objects but

Table 4.2 Process Stages and Tasks

Stage	Task
Define	Requirements Definition Requirement Analysis
Plan	Project Planning System Level Design
Build	Detailed Design Code and Unit Test Functional Verification Test
Deliver	System Verification Test Package and Release
Support	Early Support Program General Availability
Consolidate	Component Evaluation Component Construction

the development stages remain the same. The point is that the programming pieces may be different, but the development process stages remain the same. This is the power of the process stages.

In fact, the iterative and incremental development cycle clearly shows that each version is a minidevelopment in its own right, each of which still requires all the stages (i.e., define, plan, build, deliver, and support). You cannot simply deliver a new version of the system and not expect to support it.

4.3.1.1 Stage 1: Define

Requirements definition is the capturing and documenting of the requirements for the new system or extension to existing systems. It is a major activity sometimes carried out by a separate group and may use rapid prototyping techniques or joint application development methods to capture the functional requirements.

Requirements analysis is the thorough examination of the defined requirements to ensure that the right problem or business scenarios are solved and that these are fully understood. The product of this task is the problem domain model, which aims to give a robust and flexible object structure that will meet the requirements. This model often provides the basis for the other documents, such as the user manual.

4.3.1.2 Stage 2: **Plan**

Project planning involves not only the completion of the business proposals but defines the management system under which the project will be controlled. For large projects, this may involve considerable effort in establishing tracking and reporting mechanisms, whereas for smaller projects, a simplified form of reporting mechanisms may suffice. Notice that the detailed planning comes after a full understanding of the problem domain. If planning is done earlier, accept that your project is controlled by the budget and consider it a constraint: "What can I build in this timeframe for this amount of money?"

System level design is the definition of the solution domain that will meet the requirements. This includes both the highest level design statements and the major quality objectives (e.g., efficiency, reliability, understandability, etc.). Functions are partitioned into subsystems or components and the hierarchical relationship between them are defined. The principal classes and their relationships are also defined; domain libraries may be explored.

4.3.1.3 Stage 3: Build

Detailed level design is the detailed design of each section of the system domain for the specific solution. Full class and message details are defined; classes from the domain libraries are used.

Code and unit test is the transformation of the detailed level design into a language suitable to produce object code for the target computer. Test plans and test cases are also produced that are used for the individual testing of the logic and test cases for each cluster or ensemble of classes. Groups of classes are combined together to perform the scenario or use case tests.

Functional verification test is the execution of all product function tests in the test environment. These tests are carried out from a development viewpoint and are to prove the correct functionality of the product.

4.3.1.4 Stage 4: Deliver

System verification test is the execution of all product function tests in the target environment. These tests are performed from a customer/user's viewpoint and are to prove not only that the functional requirements have been met but that the quality objectives have been met. At the end of this stage, the product is normally announced to the market or released to the customer/users. Also part of this task is the testing under different stress load conditions: performance, reliability, availability, and usability. At the end of this stage, the product should meet all the customer requirements.

Package and release is the bringing together of all the product components: master program disks or tapes, publications, and installation guides as the user will see them. The result of any test will ensure that the customer can install the product and operate it successfully.

4.3.1.5 Stage 5: Support

Early support program is the provision of field and customer support to selected or early customers. It also ensures that the delivered product still meets the requirements and expectations.

General availability is the delivery of the product to the marketplace. All manuals, price lists, field service, and marketing materials must be completed before this stage can be completed.

4.3.1.6 Stage 6: Consolidate

Component evaluation is when the delivered system is examined to identify classes that are candidates for inclusion in the enterprise or domain class libraries for wider reuse throughout the organization. Also, application classes may be reconsidered as useful abstraction for the next cycle of development. This work may be done by a separate group, the class team, or undertaken by the project team itself.

Component construction is when the candidate classes are reworked, checked for quality, documented, and added to the domain libraries.

4.3.2 Process Architecture

The process architecture is a formalized description, usually in graphical form, of the work activities and stages—processes—involved or undertaken by the software development group. It begins at the highest level with the development context model as shown in Figure 4.5. This enable-deliver-monitor architecture is universal to all organizations and depicts the external interfaces that the development group must meet. At the next level in deliver development

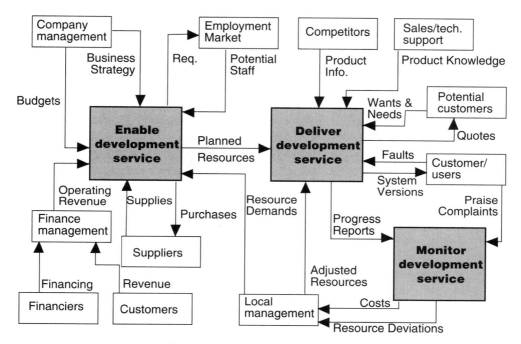

FIGURE 4.5. Universal Process Model Product Development

service, the unique work processes and the flow of information is shown; an example is shown in Figure 4.6.

These models are developed to a sufficient level of detail to fully investigate and validate the present working activities and information flows. As every organization is different, so is every model unique. What makes these differences?

They come in many guises. First are the process stages themselves; they may all be under the responsibility of the development group or some stages may be external. For example, who produces the requirement specification? In some organizations this is done by the sales team with technical support provided by senior developers i.e. technical sales support. Or who supports and maintains the software? Sometimes it is development, sometimes it is a separate organization and sometimes it may be done by hardware service engineers.

The next set of differences apply to the process model that reflects the product production method. This model should indicate unique product production or flexible mass production as necessary. I say *should* because often the production

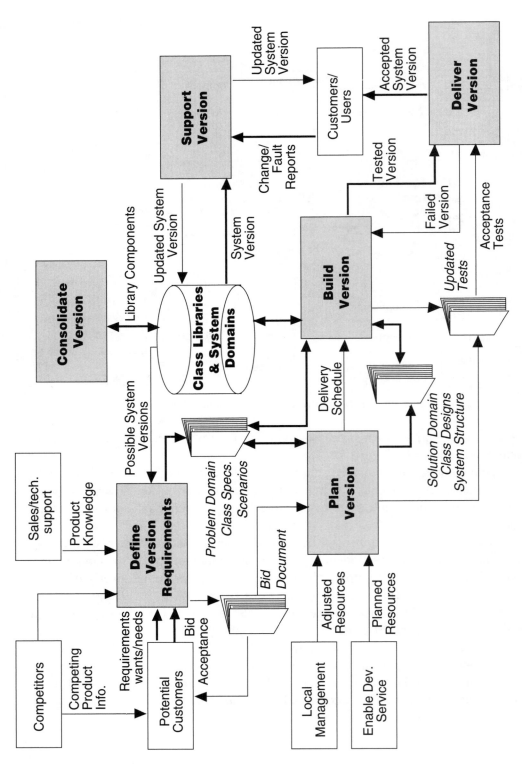

FIGURE 4.6. Universal Model of Deliver Development Service

model does not match the process model and this is the major reason for poor development productivity. For a product that is tailored for each individual customer, e.g. a process control system, then the process stages reflect a build procedure based on standard components. Whereas a unique product such as a satellite communications system has the form of a research project when much experimentation (i.e. prototypes) is undertaken.

The final set of differences is in the information that flows between the process stages. Again this is unique to every organization.

So to stress again: the process stages are common, the types of documents are common, but every process architecture model will be different for each organization.

4.3.3 What These Process Models Can Tell Us

One of the most powerful features of a model is simply the act of describing in a formal manner and showing the work processes and the information that flows between them. The models promote understanding of all the processes as a complete entity, rather than the usual focus on an individual work stage.

Discussion, controversy, and disagreements arise from the first showing of the process model. Information items and flows between activities are the most common sort of errors and omissions. It becomes clear that the documents that support the projects—the information—are crucial to the ordered development of any product. Specifications need to be produced at the appropriate stage in the development process, test plans require development, and supporting documentation, such as user manuals, need to be drafted. It also shows when documents are not used properly (e.g., client fault reports not being monitored by management).

It also becomes clear that some functions may be missing—these are process discontinuities. Complete stages are often not formally recognized in the organization. For example, a client company in the process control field, has a good reputation for the support and maintenance of its existing customers. Yet there was no support group! All support was done by the development staff who had previously worked on the project thereby causing enormous disruption of new work. It took $750,000 to equip and staff the support function, but the immediate benefit was felt in timely delivery to new customers and less harassed staff.

Not only do models show process discontinuities and guide us in fitting the production method to the product as described above, they are a useful and powerful management tool in planning for the future. They help discussions and form estimates of the impact of changes to the organization. For example, what happens when an existing group is split into two new groups to handle different development stages? What information then needs to be produced, what procedures will need to be established, and what reporting mechanisms must be put in place?

A sample of questions that can be answered by models are the following:

- Who needs to be involved in producing the specification guideline?
- Where can formal review mechanisms take place and what will they check?
- What existing information that is currently not collected, would be useful as a control metric?
- What new information could prove useful to monitoring the performance of the stage?
- If we had to give this work to an outside agency, what would we need to provide, and what would we expect in the way of deliverables and as management information?
- How much would we save if we bought-in this facility?

These and many more questions can be answered when there is a commonly agreed and understood model of the development process—the process architecture. Like all models, it must be kept up-to-date to reflect the current situation to remain useful.

4.3.4 Product Lifespan

The viewpoint discussed so far has been of the development activities rather than of the product. Unfortunately, the same term, lifecycle, is also used with the product, but it is more accurate to describe it as the product life span, which better indicates the stages of growth and decay of a product. The typical stages illustrated in Figure 4.7 are shown in Table 4.3.

These stages are of prime importance to the business as a whole—spending large amounts of development resources to support a senile product does not make business sense, but many development organizations are doing just that.

Table 4.3. Stages of the Product Life Span

Infancy	The main stage during the development of a new product; high development resources are needed
Youth	When the product enters the market place, early and usually heavy support is needed by development
Maturity	The product has become well established and development involved mainly in enhancements and extensions
Senility	A tired product that needs a major overhaul to rejuvenate, fast approaching "death"

It can be seen that each product needs a different development process model depending on its position in the product life span. Those in their infancy and youthful products are best supported by an iterative and incremental development cycle: developing on the existing product to produce new versions quickly. A mature product requires a more ordered approach as the changes will have a significant impact upon the present system. Senile products should be left to "die," but if you must support them, it is best to do it with the minimum effort and the easiest solutions.

FIGURE 4.7. How mature is your product?

Table 4.4. Process Maturity Levels

Level 1	Initial	No formal method, no consistency, no standards; every developer an "expert"
Level 2	Repeatable	Consensus on method, stability through rigorous management (cost and schedules)
Level 3	Managed	Formal documented method, reviews and inspections, configuration management
Level 4	Measured	Formal process measurement procedures; a software process group formed
Level 5	Optimizing	Use of measured data to improve development process

4.4 Process Maturity

One of the main strides in the last few years has been the concept of a process maturity model. Probably the best known is the Software Capability Maturity Model (CMM) from the Software Engineering Institute (SEI) of Carnegie Mellon University and popularized by Watts Humphreys (Humphreys, 1989). Other models are used throughout the world and an initiative has been launched by the International Standards Organization (ISO) to develop a universal standard.*

The basic model of CMM has five layers shown in Table 4.4.

Ivar Jacobson, creator of the Objectory technique and CASE tool†, suggests that Industrial Systems Development can begin at level 3 and set the foundations for levels 4 and 5. Adopting the object-oriented approach means that some basic maturity needs to be in-place before launching into major mission-critical developments.

As much has already been written about this subject, it's not my intention to add much more except to say that the CMM model is aimed at organizations rather than the individual developers.

---

* ISO/IEC JTC1/SC7 formed a working group on Software Process Assessment in June 1993. Working Group 10 is creating a standard through a project called SPICE—Software Process Improvement and Capability Determination.

† *Objectory* from Objective Systems SF AB, Box 1128, S-164 22 KISTA, Sweden, telephone +46 8 703 45 30

This is changing. One of the newer developments in this field is the concept of Personal Software Process (PSP) from Watts Humphreys*. One of the problems of many maturity improvements was that it was focused on larger teams; small projects—the one-person variety in particular—were not well covered. PSP changes the focus of concern to every software individual regardless of the size of the project.

PSP is a metric-driven change, as well as an empowerment-driven thrust. In a nutshell, PSP is a closed-loop professional process. The PSP practitioners establish personal goals for their processes, define the method they will use, measure their work, analyze the results, and based on those analyzes, they adjust their methods to better meet their personal goals. The process is an iterative learning process from one's own work and the work of peers. Data is gathered and analyzed, so that individuals could decide what works best, and adjust accordingly. The process could be applied to any domain of intellectual activity.

The purpose of PSP is to make individuals aware of their own performance and of their improvements with use of measurements. All processes, including the improvement, requires personal commitment and self-discipline. The rationale for PSP is that when engineers understand what happens, they plan for improving. The assumption to implement PSP, is that the individual should work in a stable organization environment, above level 1 (i.e., "out of chaos"). The approach for PSP has been to derive the improvement framework from large-scale intellectual work (CMM) by identifying the large-scale practices, which could be adapted to a small-scale environment.

There is no such thing as a single process with a fixed set of details that could fit all sizes of environment. Every layer—organizational, group, team, and individual—of the multi-layer model shown in Figure 4.8 has some degree of freedom. For example, every project has its own process, providing it fits in the general guidelines and standards of the organization process. The personnel process is ultimately different between individuals. A minimum set of critical concepts are shared between those processes, and this is what Watts Humphrey is addressing. Also these PSP are not independent, because they have to be designed to be compatible with the higher level processes they have to interface with. Another critical aspect of this multi-layer framework is that it involves a

---

* Much of the material on PSP was provided by Gerard Chabert (ger@msg.ti.com) of Texas Instruments. A new book by Watts Humphreys giving full details of the approach will be published during 1995

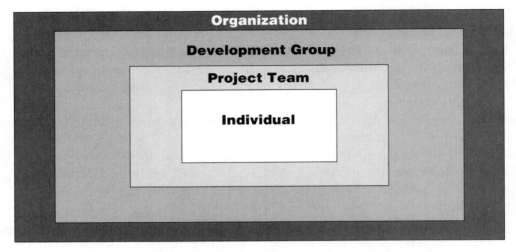

FIGURE 4.8. The Multiple Layers Process Models

top-down approach from the organization and the projects to the individual (individuals have to accept an organization and project discipline), as well as a bottom-up approach from the individual to the teams and the organization (the organization has to benefit and respect self-discipline).

The critical subprocesses of the global process are the following:

- The collection of personal measurements—time to delivery and defects
- The planning of the personal activity—size and resources expended
- The management of quality—defects
- The integration of elementary PSPs into a development process

PSP is not the new answer to the software crisis, it is one component of the answer, which reinforces other professional approaches. Some of the potential benefits of the PSP are the following:

- PSP should accelerate the organizational process improvement.
- It will enable software professionals to learn to define their own process and give a good understanding of how to improve it.
- It helps the organization meet its commitments.

Watch for more on PSP in the coming years. It may revolutionize the process view of software development!

4.5 Metrics

How do you know what's happening? What sort of data gathering systems need to be established for the object-oriented development? What do we need to measure?

We are back to timesheets! If your finance department really needs them, then fill them in but establish your own set of metrics to improve your object-oriented development. You need to measure what is important, one of the major reasons for removing the focus on financial matters. If you continually focus on these financial issues, low-quality products will be shipped to satisfy some financial concerns. You may make budget, but the cost of cleaning up the mess, never mind the loss of customer confidence in the products, far outweighs any hoped-for savings.

This is a statement of a fundamental law: What gets measured gets done.

If your interest is in reducing the number of defects per class, then by recording them not only will you see the scale of the problem but you can begin to tackle the source of the defects and provide feedback to the developers. If your developers see that reducing defects is really important and you are taking the time to analyze them, improvements will begin immediately. But if next week you start to measure lines of code, not only will the developers be confused about your priorities, but you will start to get big programs!

Many books on object technology management give long lists of items that should be measured. Here are some examples:

- *Number of classes in the system.* Indicating "size" of application
- *Ratio of classes reused versus new classes.* Indicating return on investment
- *Number of methods per system.* Indicating functionality
- *Average number of methods per class.* Indicating level of partitioning
- *Number of messages.* Indicating degree of complexity

These are interesting metrics, but they focus on the technical content of the product. What do you do about the number of classes? Or the number of methods? The number of classes and the number of methods may help signify the

FIGURE 4.9. Key Quality Metrics

complexity of what has been built and may aid estimation in the future, but are they important in the long term?

What's important in the long term is continual improvement in the development processes. So you need to measure processes indicators that really make a difference (see Figure 4.9). These are metrics such as the following:

- *Product quality.* Number of defects, number of changes per class after release
- *Flexibility.* Number of enhancements per class, number of systems reused
- *Time to build.* Number of days to a useful set of scenarios
- *Increase of skills.* New business areas entered, increased skill profile per employee
- *Responsiveness.* Number of hours to enhance present system
- *Customer satisfaction.* Number of complaints, number of positive comments

These are critical issues for your development team—they are their measures of success. These are things that really count; not the number of lines of code generated each year, or the number of messages sent. The measures are simple. You can see this is not a "bean counting" method beloved by many process efficiency groups.

Good process measures have the following properties:

- *Quantitative.* Real figures are produced and can be tracked.
- *Responsive.* Figures respond quickly to changes (e.g., number of faults reported per day).

- *Relevant.* Measurement of the key indicators.

- *Significant.* Shows a difference is being made (e.g., process improvements).

- *Understandable.* Lines of code is not understandable to nondevelopers except as an indicator of cost.

- *Easily obtained.* If it costs more to collect than is useful, don't collect it.

In choosing your own set of metrics be sure to involve everyone in the discussions and be sure to make the results visible—graphics and colors are great for this—so that a sense of urgency is transmitted through the measurement and the setting of improvement targets. Ensure that the cost of collecting the information does not exceed the value that may result; having a sophisticated database and analysis program is no help if it simply spits out the answer 42!

When do you start this measurement process? Now! Yes, start now or tomorrow at the latest. Get everyone together, and say that you want to improve such and such, how could this be measured, agree the metrics, sketch out any reporting forms such as for customer faults, photocopy, and start the monitoring. At the end of the week, plot the results and stick them up everywhere. Repeat every week and you will see dramatic changes. Try it—it really works!

4.6 Quality Systems

Zen and the Art of Motorcycle Maintenance by Robert Pirsig is one of the most-referenced books in software (Pirsig, 1974). Why? Because it's a book about *quality.* Its premise is that quality cannot be defined, or as Richard Gabrial calls it, "quality without a name" (Gabrial, 1993). If quality is part of the product—the object—then instruments are capable of being designed to measure quality. If quality is subjective (i.e., an attribute of the customer, the subject) it will vary with each individual customer. What is right for you may not be right for me.

Yet we all know what quality is—or more accurately, we know when it is missing. We might not be able to say what a good report looks like, but we all know a bad one!

Pirsig suggests that quality is separate from object (matter) and subject (mind) and is itself the creator of mind and matter. That when building an object we use quality values to determine the final product; the main problem is that they are often our quality values rather than those defined by others. I don't want to move into the metaphysical, but simply, want to emphasize that defining quality is a difficult undertaking. This is why reaching an agreement on quality values really does matter.

So how do we define quality?

Quality can be defined as degree of excellence, and to measure quality, we identify the attributes in which excellence is required. The combination of these different attributes gives us an overall measure of quality. This measurement is fine, but the comparison must be made between the same things (i.e., compare apples with apples). Using someone else's values can be dangerous as what is found to be useful in one industry sector may not be useful in another (e.g., embedded system products against accounting systems). The same is true of the productivity gains claimed by some suppliers of tools; these claims usually apply to a small sector of the industry and are not applicable to all.

4.6.1 Start with Quality

The use of object-oriented design doesn't give the license to abandon established practices of quality assurance. Quality criteria need to be defined at the start of the project. The basic set of metrics to measure the quality of the design are associated with the classes:

- *Reusability*. Can it be used in more than one application?
- *Complexity*. How difficult is it to implement?
- *Cohesion and coupling*. The dependence of an item upon the implementation details of another; loose coupling is desired
- *Sufficiency*. Enough characteristics to allow meaningful and efficient interaction (e.g., if "remove an item" is necessary, is there also "add an item"?)
- *Completeness*. General interface to be commonly useful no matter the client
- *Primitiveness*. Gives access to the underlying principle of the abstraction

Reusability is the major criterion for all object-oriented systems. It is reusability that gives the leverage to all the benefits from object technology.

Reusability means that the new class is designed to be useful in other contexts. Its methods and interface are such that can provide useful operations to many client classes. And it is the reuse of the classes in other contexts that indicate a well-defined class.

One of the many problems is the increasing complexity of the developing system. Initially the design, even for complex systems is straightforward, with well-defined classes and objects. As the solution domain is explored, more and more complexity is added. For example, the handling of errors always causes any well-structured design to become complicated. While the overall system may be complex, individual classes that make up the system should be as straightforward and understandable as possible. One major technique in establishing the level of complexity is to have the class reviewed by peers from other teams. If they can't understand the class description or its code, you have a complexity problem.

Systems should have loose coupling between classes and high cohesion within the classes. The aim is to avoid any changes to a single class causing a ripple effect among other classes. Cohesion (borrowed from structured design) measures the degree of connectivity between elements of a single class or object, whereas coupling is the degree of interaction between the classes. However, there is a tension between coupling and the concept of inheritance. On one hand, it is desirable to build classes that are weakly coupled; on the other hand, inheritance, which tightly couples base classes to their derived classes, helps greatly to exploit the commonality of abstractions. As a rule of thumb, tight coupling is permitted between base classes and their derivatives but discouraged between other classes. Class designers are faced constantly with such dilemmas associated with the aspects of coupling and cohesion.

For example, when a new operation is to be designed as a new class or a new method within an existing class, there are no hard and fast rules, but if the following set of questions are considered and the answers are mainly positive, a new class is required; otherwise, the operations can be included as a new method.

- Is the operation a meaningful abstraction?
- Is the operation likely to be shared by several classes?
- Is the operation complex?
- Does the operation make little use of the representation of the operands?
- Will relatively few users of the class want to use the operation?

A common early mistake is to include within a class only the operations or properties required by the solution domain and not consider the other operations. To do so is to render the class useless. For example, if designing a `Set` class, it is futile to include only an add set item operation without including a remove set item operation. These errors are usually detected early on in the design when other client classes find the missing operations.

Completeness is similar to sufficiency, but where sufficiency means a minimal interface, completeness means one that covers all aspects of the abstraction (i.e., one that is general enough to be usable, no matter the client class). Unfortunately, completeness can be overdone (e.g., a date class with 55 ways of printing today's date). In an attempt to provide a reusable class, all potentially meaningful operations are included. This not only overwhelms the developer/user, but is generally unnecessary since many high-level operations are composed of low-level ones. This is the aspect of primitiveness. Primitive operations are those that can be efficiently implemented only if given access to the underlying representation of the abstraction. Adding an item to a `Set` is the only way unless the underlying abstraction is made visible to them. However, adding four items to the set is not primitive as it can obviously can be implemented without having access to the underlying representation. However, if an operation requires a lot of computational resources in using an existing primitive class, then this operation is a candidate for inclusion as a primitive class.

4.6.2 Check Quality Frequently

To ensure the quality of the component, we need to frequently check the outcomes from the development stages. With object systems, there is a tendency to rush into coding without carefully considering the design of the solution and system domains. Walkthroughs and inspections are still needed; in fact, I believe they are needed more with object systems. The architecture of the system—the class hierarchy—is crucial to the final system, so it is unwise to ignore it in the early stages.

Design and code reviews need to be established early on in the project lifecycle for these benefits:

- To create a strong foundation

- To enforce consistency throughout the problem, solution, and system domain models
- To encourage reuse and awareness of available classes

The key elements of a successful review strategy are the following:

- Do not review several things simultaneously (e.g., high- and low-level design).
- Follow a disciplined review process with entry/exit criteria, review structure, guidelines, checklist, and standards; the ETVX paradigm is most often used (Figure 4.10).
- Identify the relevant quality criteria; see above.
- Track customer/user requirements; use "tags."
- Record review findings, and track action item to closure.
- Measure and track review process (e.g., size of what reviewed, time, defects found, defect not found).

It has been proven so many times that early detection is cheaper than later detection, hence reviews and inspections take less time than testing and the savings made in detecting faults early significantly outweigh the cost of the reviews. Don't throw this baby out with the bath water in moving to object technology.

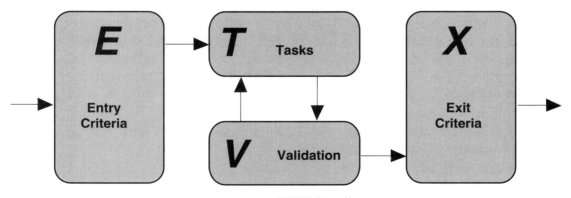

FIGURE 4.10. ETVX Paradigm

4.7 Using and Choosing Tools

One common approach to implementing a particular development method is to provide tools that only support the chosen method (i.e., CASE tools), but they are only part of the list. Equally important are tools to aid testing, and group working, and sophisticated browsers for the libraries of classes.

4.7.1 CASE

First, what does CASE mean to you? Computer-aided software engineering, computer-assisted systems environment, computer-accelerated system engineering? You can take various combinations from assisted, accelerated, system, software, strategy, environment, or engineering; the only common word is *computer.*

I'll use the term *computer-aided software engineering.* What can it do? Is it a language generator from pictures, a 4GL with diagrams? Does it produce test harness and test data? Can it aid and document the capture of the requirements. If it can capture the requirements, document the object model, generate the code, and produce the test cases, then great. That's a CASE tool.

CASE tools are becoming more sophisticated at handling the complete development cycle, and that is the key requirement: do they match your development processes? Do they automate much of the routine work at all levels of the development, or do they simply provide a documentation aid?

They do add much to the development process when used appropriately, but they have another side. CASE tools enforce a way of working. If you want to use the Wirfs-Brock responsibility-driven approach for analysis and Booch for design, as this reflects your business and the skills of your staff, then you can't do it. It's one or none. Some tools do support many methods, but there are few, if any, that allow you to use a different approach for each development stages.

In choosing a CASE tool, you need to be clear on what you want from it. Here are some suggestions, which you might like to add to your own list:

- *Easy diagramming techniques.* Some tools don't yet support drag and drop.

- *Centralized repository.* Common information source allowing different views (e.g., object and entity relationships).

- *Validation and verification.* Some even use AI techniques to ensure the model is consistent.

- *Database design.* You may still be dealing with legacy databases; do you want to have to use another tool to do these designs?

- *Code documentation.* You will have to go back to the code.

- *Code generation.* Does it support more that one language? How "neat" is the generated code? Does the generated code give an acceptable performance?

- *Code reengineering.* Can it build a model from code? This is especially useful for tools that allow you to change the generated code.

- *Class capture.* Can it collect clusters of classes for possible reuse?

- *Class navigation.* Has it got a good browser?

- *Generate documentation.* In textual and pictorial format for differing views: developers, sales, service.

- *Version control.* Will it manage the iterative nature of the code and documentation development?

CASE tools not only ensure some rigor in the development process, but have the added advantage of documenting the evolving system—that is it does if you have got the right tool. CASE tools come in different varieties. Some support the analysis and design function producing repositories that let you do the coding, and some allow you to express the code as pictures. These are often called front-end and back-end tools, respectively.

One of the problems with front-end tools is that they can cause a separation between the design and the code. Should the code change, it must also be reflected in the design model on the CASE tool. If this is too difficult, or tedious, then expect the design model to quickly become out of date. Your hopes for a documented design are dashed.

Similarly, back-end tools mean that the coding may be well-documented, but transforming the analysis and design to the pictures can be unproductive. Some tools create a barrier to the coding process, so that code can be generated only through the tool. This does ensure a rigorous coding model, but can cause significant delays in turning around changes, especially minor changes.

All of these features help you, but will they also help your users? Will the CASE tool provide the system on-time and under budget? Or will the use of the tool slow down the development cycle? In other words, do you really need a CASE tool or could you achieve the same benefits from another technique?

If your development maturity is at the chaotic level (level 1 of the SEI model), using a tool might simply create an automated chaos! With careful introduction, the CASE tool supporting a methodology may provide the catalyst for moving up the maturity levels.

4.7.2 Testing Tools

One of the most frequent questions asked is What tools are available for testing object-oriented systems? Unfortunately, the most common response to What tools do you use now? is Oh! we don't use tools to test the software, we know the developers will thoroughly test the system.

Testing is desirable thing—like going to the dentist. But unless we want our teeth to fall out, we need to undergo the examination. We need the *testware*.

Testware is an asset that is built, used, and maintained. In using testware, you need to be clear of your own objectives. Are they for the purpose of

- improving the quality of the software?
- improving the quality of testing?
- better meeting the release deadlines?
- improving productivity, capacity planning, or performance assessment?

Unfortunately, it is said that most people building software have no understanding of testing. It is seen as a chore, and in some ways it does not guarantee success. If we find lots of errors, we can be confident that we have poor quality software, but if we don't find any errors we cannot conclude that we have high-quality software.

Well, now we have CAST tools: computer-aided software testing. However, sales of CAST tools represent less than one tenth of the $675 million spent annually in the UK on all development tools. Until the whole organization can adopt the idea of automated support to testing, testing will remain repetitive, boring, require such excessive attention to detail that as a result it is often abandoned at the first opportunity—"I know it will work." With object systems, the result will be positively dangerous.

Testing involves a number of different techniques for object systems. Obviously there are the functional tests of the various methods within classes so that they then can be treated as "black boxes." But testing also involves the dynamic nature of the object systems. It means thorough execution of all the pathways, testing and exercising the system architecture, testing any special interfaces to legacy systems, and then testing any special conversions necessary to link with other systems or information sources.

Your own test strategy involves work at three different levels:

1. Testing an individual object
2. Testing a cluster of objects
3. Testing an object system

When testing an individual object, insist on a test method in *every* object that cycles the internal states and validates the attributes. When developers have to provide test scripts for their code, the quality of the production code is usually increased. Alternatively, build another "ghost" object that contains the test methods and exercises the production object. The latter approach avoids the overhead of the test code in the final delivered system (some, including myself, argue that it's better to keep that test code in the production system for tracing the inevitable failures) in that it allows the "ghost" objects to be removed prior to delivery. In effect, a "ghost" object model is developed in parallel to the production object model.

For testing clusters of objects, ensure that every use case scenario has a trigger event object that invokes the messages that exercise all the objects involved in the scenario. A set of these trigger objects is equivalent to a set of user acceptance test scripts.

For testing object systems, especially those that a client-server architecture, special tools need to be used to capture and record the message traffic. If the system has an object request broker (ORB), the test process is straightforward, as they all usually provide message logging facilities; otherwise, access needs to be made to the message handler of the operating system layer.

Tests should be selectable from a menu; they will invoke the necessary files, run one or more series of tests and report the results. By all means remove these features in a final version, although they can prove very useful in providing information to support staff dealing with some form of system failure. It is also noted that if developers have to design tests, they make their software testable and that can't help but lead to higher quality components. At a conference in 1993, Standard Chartered Bank reported that using this approach, testing was now 2.3% of development effort compared with 30% previously.*

Whatever your chosen method, good tests are

- *Effective.* Find errors
- *Exemplary.* Represent types of errors
- *Economical.* To build and use
- *Evolvable.* Maintainable with evolution of the systems

Tools are used to aid this process. Most tools provide all or most of these features:

- *Key capture and playback.* Useful even to capture user interaction
- *Comparison of expected and actual data.*
- *Automatic regression testing.* You don't want the software to regress!
- *Static analysis.*
- *Performance analysis.*
- *Animators.* Particular to certain languages

As a manager, you will have to manage the tests. There might be a small team of testers (no more than five), who are closely involved in the development. They insert special "ghost" classes and methods to determine the quality of the software. This team is separate from the traditional QA department, which inspected the final product.

4.7.3 Configuration Management

A key element of managing the tests is to establish early on in the object-oriented project, proper configuration control. It has been reported that half of all companies have no idea which version of their software users are running! Do you?

---

* Quoted by John Abbott of Standard Chartered Bank at "Managing Software Quality in the 90s" organized by Unicorm Seminars at the US Embassy in London Autumn 1993.

Configuration management is applied to controlling the versions of the individual classes for each "build." Because the build sequence is normally associated with scenarios or use cases, all the methods for a class will not be implemented at the same time. The interface may well be established—the "contract" as it is sometimes called—but there are only "stubs" for the methods. Version control then identifies each unique version of a particular class or cluster of classes (Figure 4.11).

4.7.4 Groupware

Object-oriented development is best done in teams; teams need to communicate, they need to share their work with each other, and they need that sharing of work to be controlled. Many, but not all, CASE tools permit some form of group working. If it is a workstation or PC product for a single developer, then it may appear to be inexpensive when it does in fact cost more money. Why? Because of the expensive development time spent in sharing information, transferring files, coping with the inevitable mix-ups and all occurrences of Murphy's Law.

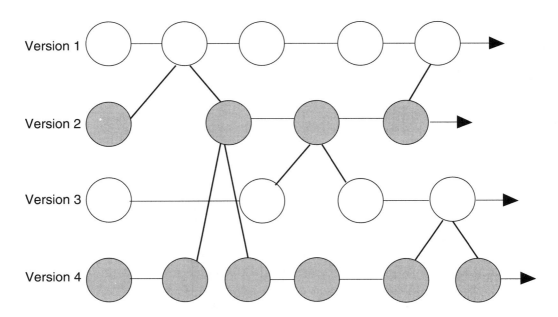

FIGURE 4.11. Involvement of Classes in Configuration Control

Groupware is made up of a number of components:

- Electronic mail
- Calendaring
- Conferencing
- Document data management
- Workflow
- Class management

Email is not groupware, it's a mechanism for communication, which is a useful aid to group working. There is rarely a need to send mail to a close colleague as it's easier to shout across the room. It's when the team is dispersed or using outside services or contractors that email can make a difference. We have all experienced the irritating game of "chase the caller"; they call us, we call back and leave a message, they call back and leave another message, and on and on. Email, and even the much-maligned postal service, does ensure delivery whether or not the contact is there. If nothing else, it makes a physical record of the message.

But email can also be a curse. If your organization uses email extensively, you will relate to that sinking feeling when the mailer tells you that you have 203 messages after you have spent a few days away. The pile of paper on the desk did not look so intimidating as the count of 203 items! You have to read them all before throwing them in the bin; it seemed easier with paper.

Calendaring—I hate the word—is more than your own personal scheduler. It's the team diary showing various milestones, individual commitments, schedules, availability, and any arranged meetings. Using the calendar in a responsible and controlled way ensures that the team resources are allocated effectively.

There are now inexpensive conferencing products ranging from the closed electronic bulletin boards on your email server to video phones to full room teleconferencing. Remember, your team needs to meet regularly, maybe every day for crucial parts of the development, and if the team is dispersed over a wide area you need some form of this support. Companies seem reluctant to use public service conferencing facilities such as CompuServe or CIX. Why? They can be a cheaper alternative to setting up your own Internet server for all the staff in the various locations; especially when you need to pay for the telephone calls!

Document and data management identification is the key to groupware. Sharing information is only good if you can find it, so some form of structuring is needed. It's simply not good enough to provide the groupware and not set up the information infrastructure. Information that is held can be called the *Project Log;* it contains the following:

- Documents—memos, specifications, minutes of meetings, letters, etc.
- Designs—object models in the various stages of development
- Change requests
- Fault log
- Schedules, budgets, costings
- Released source code

Such information is crucial to the ongoing viability of the project. If you lose it, you may lose all! There is a cost to maintaining this information, perhaps to hire a librarian who looks after the structure, files the material, and ensures it is secure both from unauthorized access and from loss or damage. When "all your eggs are in one basket," it pays to check the basket regularly.

Workflow management is a form of groupware, but it has much wider implications. *Workflow* means the automatic flow of documents from one location to another and keeping track of revisions and authorizations. It is usual for workflow to move across team boundaries, and this can be especially useful if certain support services (e.g., the test group or QA specialists) are not located as part of the team.

Workflow is a hot topic at the present time: the paperless office is the dream of many organizations—I don't know why they just don't get rid of the bureaucratic procedures that generate the paper in the first place; it's called business process reengineering. But without spending a lot of money, you can achieve a sort of workflow through shared documents and automatic memos and reminders from the scheduler.

4.7.5 Shareware

Shareware is not groupware. Shareware is software in the public domain which can be used with or without a small license fee. Shareware is mentioned here because there will be an increasing availability of class libraries as object technology matures. Some organizations may be tempted to use such products and must evaluate the quality and the risks associated with "free" software.

Shareware is useful when it provides lots of source code to examine. Much can be learned from reading another programmer's code: good coding as well as bad coding practices, algorithms, partitioning, class design, use of messages, types of objects, etc.

4.7.6 Browsers

Browsers for class libraries can be quite rudimentary in operation. They may provide some sort of navigational picture usually based on the class hierarchy but try and find your way through the morass of detail common in most libraries. It is very difficult to make semantic-style queries or to create filters on this volume of information (e.g., bars, buttons, and scrolling). Like most large volumes of information you need to know your way around before you can find anything, and sitting for hours looking at a screen of class definitions is not my idea of fun. If you think this is exaggerated, look at the two volumes of the Microsoft Foundation Classes. They are at least four inches thick with only two pictures in all the pages!

Furthermore, most browsers do not permit clusters of classes to be assembled for experimentation. If this was allowed, you could determine whether the behavior and performance of a possible candidate cluster of classes meets your requirements—real prototyping!

4.7.7 Choosing a Tool

You have probably noticed that I have avoided recommending any particular tool. This is deliberate. Firstly, there are such a wide range of tools available in the present marketplace, it would be a major research project to identify them. In fact, companies undertake this for you and sell you the results of their work in various reports. Secondly, tools do vary from country to country. There is a marked preference in the US to use American tools because of the support, pricing, etc. In Europe, there is a huge choice between American products and those developed within Europe. American toolsets have been well accepted into Europe up to now, but there is an increasing trend to seek out tools that provide the language of the user (e.g., French, German, etc.). With the increase in multilanguage products, the choice will be even greater.

In choosing a tool, you need to identify your goals, objectives, functions, and attributes. For example,

- user interface style and help facilities,
- networking facilities,
- hardware platforms,
- output devices supported,
- organizational tools,
- customization tools,
- modeling facilities,
- hardware configurations, machine, printers/plotters, use of color,
- security access issues,
- supplier reliability, support, etc.

In undertaking any evaluation of tools, make sure the evaluation is auditable (i.e., you need to be able to contrast and compare the reasons for the selection). To achieve this, the evaluation needs to be treated as a project in its own right; don't leave it to someone to do in their spare time. Toolsets are too important to be a side issue and should involve you as well as the technical staff. Group brainstorming sessions are an effective means to solicit ideas.

Once you have defined your goals, functions, and attributes and have cross-referenced the requirements to business activities, you can use prioritization and weightings to reflect importance of the various criteria. Another major consideration is the various costs: package costs, new hardware support costs, training and operating costs. One of the difficult things is to find the correct level of detail on these specifications. Once you know what you are looking for, it's time to draw up short-lists and send out questionnaires to possible suppliers. You will often get better service from the supplier by being proactive rather than simply accepting all the standard literature. Also, once you have made the contact, keep the supplier informed of progress and your final decision, even if it's a rejection.

It is worth spending time over this process as it can eliminate many possibilities and will make any trialing effective and even unnecessary. While this is expensive in time and resources, it's a lot less expensive than choosing the wrong tool. The suggested project model process (Figure 4.12) follows.

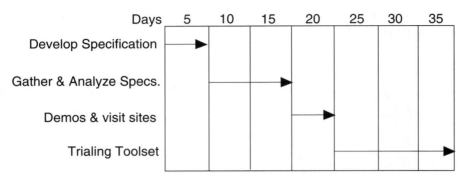

FIGURE 4.12. Project Plan for Choosing a Tool

- Five days developing the requirements
- Ten days gathering tool specifications, summarizing the data and analyzing the results
- Five days looking at pre-trial demonstrations and visiting reference sites
- Fifteen days trialing the chosen toolsets

These estimates represent a worst-case scenario, but by having up-front analysis, you can reduce the traditional costly and lengthy trialing periods.

4.7.8 Some Final Words on Tools

Having tools is not sufficient. The tools need to be used. This may seem obvious, but many organizations buy expensive toolsets for their developers and do not enforce their use. Obviously, the tool should be useful, but it is surprising the number of tools bought by senior executives—usually at a trade show and the result of some special offer—which at best are used casually, but more often than not, end up being shelfware. If the tool ain't useful, it won't be used.

Before closing on the use of tools remember that a fool with a tool is still a fool—if the painter in our analogy does not know how to clean the brushes, then the work of art will always be murky brown.

4.8 Summary

I've had to cover a lot of detail in this chapter. It showed that given the inter-relatedness of the procedures and techniques—the systems—it becomes very important that all the systems reflect the goals of the organization. Be it customer care or time-to-market, the working processes, the object development methods employed, and tools used must all be chosen with care. Systems have levels of maturity, which were first focused on organizations. Now the new ideas applied to teams and to individuals have been covered.

The section on metrics showed how you could know what had been happening in the object-oriented project. It also covered what sort of data gathering systems were needed for the object-oriented development. It was followed by the types of quality systems that are needed, including what to look for in class design and to consider in the development processes.

The final section covered using and choosing tools to support all object-oriented development work. Although it did not give product recommendations, it outlined the criteria for choosing CASE toolsets, configuration management software, testing strategies, and tools to aid verification and validation. It also covered the typical support tools that will be needed for group working (i.e., groupware).

References

Carmichael, A. (ed.). (1994). *Object Development Methods*. New York: SIGS Books.

Booch, G. (1986). Object-oriented development, *IEEE Transactions on Software Engineering*, SE-12 (2).

Jacobson, I. (1992). *Object-Oriented Software Engineering—A Use Case Approach*. New York: ACM Press/Addison-Wesley.

Coleman, D., et al. (1989). *Object-Oriented Development: The Fusion Method*. Englewood Cliffs, NJ: Prentice Hall.

Humphreys, W. (1989). *Managing the Software Process*. Reading, MA: Addison-Wesley.

Pirsig, R.M. (1974). *Zen and the Art of Motorcycle Maintenance*. New York: Bantam.

Gabrial, R. (1993). The quality without a name, *Journal of Object-Oriented Programming*, 6 (5).

CHAPTER 5

STAFF

THREE COMPONENTS ARE NECESSARY FOR SUCCESSFUL OBJECT-ORIENTED systems development: people, people, and people. So says Peter Coad, one of the leaders of object technology and co-author of the Coad/Yourdon object development methodology (Coad, 1991; Coad & Yourdon, 1991a, 1991b). I agree with Peter; in the end no amount of technology will make up for poor staffing, inadequate skills of the development staff, and lack of leadership by the managers.

Organizations thrive and prosper through the contributions made by the people that they employ. Successful products or excellent service come not from an abstract company but from the groups of people that design, develop, build, and support your products or services.

People are the essence of every success: People grouped into teams working to fulfill tasks and activities; committed to achievement, committed to quality and working harmoniously. One of the most significant realizations in organizational development was that groups of people could be deliberately and methodically developed into effective working teams. Once developed, the team is a potent and resourceful unit that can play a vital part in creatively coping with innovation and change, a requirement necessary for any successful organization.

This chapter, then, focuses on people, the staff attribute of the McKinsey Seven Ss.

- How do we find the right staff?
- What qualities do they need to possess?
- What roles and responsibilities are to be filled?
- How are contractors chosen and managed?

Whether inside or outside your organization, hiring new staff is an activity that causes as much stress as house moving or close family crises. First there is advertising the post both in-house or through the trade papers; what words will catch the eye of the right person? Is the salary attractive? Should you use an agency to avoid those hundreds of CVs that will come through the mail? Do you want the world to know of your future directions in IT? When can the interviews be arranged? Who will chase down references? And on, and on, and on.

I don't know about you, but I feel stressed just thinking about it! Let's try and structure this crucial activity to give us some peace of mind.

5.1 Why Recruit?

This may appear to be a silly question, but you need to be clear as a manager if you are recruiting for strategic or tactical reasons.

Strategic recruitment reflects the organization's plans for growth and entering new business domains—diversification. In this situation, you have more of a blank piece of paper so you are able to fully specify the skill set needed and the likely career paths. If the business area is really new to you, you may need to get outside help to identify the skill set you will require for the domain. Obviously, recruiting into a new business area may mean some very senior positions need to be filled. In these cases experience in the new area is more preferred than generalized skills. For more junior positions, then, strategic recruitment is almost continuous. This reflects the attitude that despite the current workloads, such staff will be useful in a very short time. All of this presupposes that you have a clear knowledge of the long-term direction for the business.

Tactical recruitment is usually to fill vacancies. However, if you wait until the vacancy exists—a common situation in the harsher economic climate when recruitment is curtailed—it may, of course, be some time before the post can be filled. Tactical recruitment needs then to be practiced in anticipation of possible vacancies, especially those of a critical nature. Rigid headcounts lead to tremendous frustrations in filling critical posts. While you may need to accept such a situation, be aware of the impact on the schedules caused by the loss of resources and spend real effort in reducing your staff turnover.

5.2 Sources of Staff

Potential staff can arrive from a number of sources.

The first route is when potential staff seek you out (i.e., self-select). This route has the lowest cost as you are only left with the problem of selection. For organizations that have a high profile in the business, this route is very common—Xerox, IBM, and Microsoft must get many hundreds of hopeful letters every week. The problem in this situation that you have a skill need, which may not be matched by any of the hopefuls.

The next route is the traditional advertising for staff. The best source of staff are those who already belong to the organization (i.e., internal recruits). Such staff have not only an understanding of the business, but they may also bring a wider vision of the organization to the team (e.g., sales activities, financial procedures). For vacancies that need external candidates, this may be done through an recruitment agency, which performs the initial screening, or through your own human resource group. This at least notifies the potential staff of the skills and experience you are seeking, but dealing with the volume of replies can be a huge headache.

The final and most expensive way is the use of headhunters (i.e., specialist recruitment agencies). These are traditionally used only for very senior posts, but they are becoming increasingly popular for filling object technology posts. Why? Because when skills are scarce, there is money to be made in finding suitable candidates, and headhunters are motivated by money. They often charge up to 35% of the first year's salary of the hired candidate.

5.3 Qualities to Look for

What are the qualities that you are seeking in the new member of the object-oriented development team? It is easy to list the technical skills you need:

- Object-oriented analysis and design skills in your preferred method
- Proficiency in your chosen programming language (e.g., C++, Smalltalk, etc.)
- Knowledge of the particular operating system environment
- Knowledge of the relevant class libraries
- Exposure to your chosen toolset
- Graphical user interface design skills
- Possible knowledge of database design and access mechanisms (e.g., SQL)

And of course, experience—they must be experienced; you don't want to teach them how to do it. At a recent conference, Bjarne Stroustrup, father of C++, is stated to have said that it takes over two years to be fully proficient in the language. As the "average" C++ programmer in Britain has seven months of experience, this implies that there are no experienced programmers in the UK! How about other countries?

This set of technical skill requirements gives a baseline. Most managers stop there, but unfortunately it is not enough.

As important as technical skill is the new recruits' business awareness. Object technology is most powerful when it is used to model the business world, so the staff need to have a strong focus on your business area. If you are in the oil business or airline services, a thorough understanding of this business is needed. Your business will be special, even unique, but the terminology and jargon, the *semantics* of the business, play a crucial part in building your business models. One question to ask new hopefuls is what business they are in? If they say "DP" or "IT," you should say "Next!" This shows they are unaware that they are part of a business enterprise that needs their support. Don't be misled by hotshot skills in the latest graphical user interface library if the basic understanding of the work processes of your line of business are missing. These hotshot skills might be important for a short time on the project, but in the long term, objects designed to fit your business will make the difference.

Now you may understand why many organizations always use in-house staff for the new projects and retrain as appropriate: object-oriented skills to current development staff, the usual option, or more radically, IT skills to end-users. This builds on the present knowledge already acquired of the business. Technical skills can be learned.

As an example, one of the best teams I have ever worked with in object-oriented analysis was a group of technical writers. They could define the problem scenarios, organize the classes, put them into relationships, and outline the object dynamics in such a clear manner that, to be frank, shook my preconceived notions on the necessity of technical competence for analysts. They would have had a problem in designing the system architecture and detailing the classes, as real technical skills are required, but the point was made evident.

Despite this shake-up, the qualities that we seek are those of a software engineer, a professional who is interested in the technology as well as its application to the business. One who will seek excellence in every endeavor and who will be dissatisfied with poor quality work. One who will think before acting. One who believes that although software is intangible it needs the same rigor and discipline as constructing a bridge or a building. Object-oriented software may be an artifact of the mind realized in a machine, but it requires engineering nonetheless.

Another key element to consider is the question of the position of your organization on the learning curve of object technology. In early days, you will need experienced people who are keen to experiment and to put in the effort required to build a framework for the future—both the future systems and the working practices of the new teams. If you are well established with object technology, you need pragmatists who will form the backbone of the development group.

Figure 5.1 shows that these different types of personalities to fit your learning curve can be categorized as follows:

- *Experimenters.* Those who love to try something new but get quickly bored when there are no more new toys to play with. They usually like to work by themselves and do not provide feedback to others in the team.

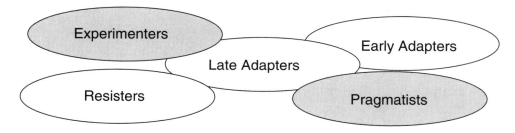

FIGURE 5.1. Different Types of Staff Personalities

- *Early adopters.* Those who try something new, stick with it, and provide a solid skill base to share with others. These form your mentors for the future work.

- *Pragmatists.* Those who are reluctant to try something new but when convinced that objects will be beneficial, will work hard to make it a success.

- *Late adopters.* Those who have to be threatened and coerced into using objects. They can be the most destructive as they will use every excuse to prove objects don't work.

- *Resisters.* Those who are unable to deal with change of any kind. They may quit, be fired, or need to be moved to other areas in your organization.

You will meet every one of these types in your recruitment process. How can you tell their personality? Many organizations use formal psychometric testing to attempt to identify such traits. Some even use handwriting analysis. Such tests have a place if you know how the results will match against your requirements.

One of the worst type of tests, in my opinion, is the so-called IQ test that scores intellectual capacity. For goodness sake, you have selected these candidates on their past academic record, past job experience (if any), professional affiliations, etc.—why waste time in testing intelligence? Use the time for the more important interview activity and skill evaluation.

5.4 The Interviews

Interviewing new recruits is a time-consuming but vital part of the process. Don't let your personnel department do the job for you. They may need to cover the terms and conditions, but the interviewing is up to you and your team. Yes, your team members need to be involved with the interview. After all, they will work with the new staff. They will be busy trying to meet the next deadline, but you could have the whole project go down the tubes if the new team member causes a large disturbance or deep resentment.

The interview is a dialogue during which you learn about the candidate and the candidate learns about your organization and the team. One interview is not sufficient. You are not hiring a fruit packer; you are hiring a person whose intellectual capacity, innovative attitude, and creativity will provide a knowledgeable resource for the future. If you intend to have some ability tests, you should indicate that on the joining instructions, and these tests should be conducted separately from the interview. If it is a senior post—system architect, major designer—you also need to get to know the actual person rather than simply examine the technical ability. This can be done informally over lunch, dinner, or whatever. Too many interviews are done with haste to get back to the mountain of paper and crises that are building on your desk. Those items aren't going anywhere, but the ideal candidate may slip through your hands if you aren't careful.

Have you and your selected team members prepared for the interviews? Are the majority of your team skilled in interview techniques? If not, why not? A short course, or one of the many how-to books will make a tremendous difference. You will all have had experiences of poor interviewing as a young hopeful: when the manager reads your CV for the first time in front of you, when she seemed more interested on what was outside the window, when he kept looking at his watch. You know they weren't interested. What did you do? Did you sit there valiantly answering the questions, or did you get up, say that it appeared that the manager was too busy at the present moment and to avoid wasting each others time would leave, shook hands and walked out. If only! The manager would probably have chased you down the corridor, pleading to be given a second chance.

Not only are the interviewees presenting themselves, you are presenting your organization to the candidate. It is important to give a genuine picture of the organization rather than the more upbeat presentations given to clients. There is little point misleading a potential employee only to have to repeat the process a few months later when that team member leaves after the disillusionment. If your object-oriented project is an experiment to get a grip on the technology and may be abandoned if it does not provide sufficient business benefits, then say so. Most candidates seek some long-term stability, so don't mislead them about the scope of object technology in the organization, when it may be possible that you will revert to COBOL programming.

In presenting the organization, you need to cover not only the salary package, job prospects, and so on, but also the culture, values, and expectations. You need to convey the real truth about the organization.

These new hopefuls are your future; you need to take time to assess their expertise, their credibility, and their communications skills. If they can't communicate at the interview (allowing for nervousness), how will they communicate with the users, never mind the rest of the team. Do they admit they don't know it all; do they know their own limitations? If they don't, they will likely attempt something beyond their expertise and usually wait too long before asking for help. With object technology, the odds of getting into an awful mess are much higher.

What books on object technology have they read? How many do they own? It never ceases to amaze me how few books programmers read other than those directly associated with the task, such as programming manuals. Be impressed if the new hopeful personally owns and has read a number of books on the subject. You might have found one of the 5% who are truly interested in their profession. This is not to imply that reading is a key skill, but a recognition of the individual's interest in the work they have chosen for a career. Remember to test this knowledge, which implies of course, that you have at least read the major works on object technology.

Have the interviewees prepared? Did they bring examples of their work, ones that are not company confidential. If they do bring dubious material, what does that say about their trustworthiness? Would they show your material at their next interview? Has the new hopeful taken time to find out about your enterprise? All of these types of questions will give you insight into the character of the new staff member.

Some organizations now set a small development task for their candidates (e.g., build a small application using only class library components or review class design and coding to identify errors that have been deliberately placed in the work). Often this means the interview period needs to be longer than a single day, which raises the costs not only for the extra resources in preparing the test material and checking the results, but also in possible hotel costs for the candidates. Would you do this for every candidate? Perhaps not, but if you don't, you will need to accept the risk that your choice may be a mistake.

This may seem like a lot of effort, but with modern employment law it can be extremely difficult to rectify such mistakes. Furthermore, you become personally involved with new staff. Before you hired them, they were only new analysts or programmers, but after they are hired, they are John or Mary. It takes a much longer time to admit that it's not going to work out. If John or Mary do not fit in, it's your mistake, not theirs. You have no business blaming that person. You have made a mistake.

Remember that while the time and effort in recruiting may have a significant cost, it's a lot cheaper than a project disaster.

5.5 Using Agencies

Recruitment agencies are loved by some and hated by others. They do provide a first level of selection and ensure some form of anonymity, and they should know the salary market better than you, but do they get results? Often it's a case of "garbage in, garbage out." If you are unable to supply a detailed profile of what you are seeking (i.e., more than a technical profile) you will get a wide variation of candidates. Poor matching is not often the fault of the agency but a result of poor specification by the manager or the manager's personnel department. If you don't get the right caliber of candidates from an agency, look at the quality of your requirement specification before blaming the agency.

Many managers express disappointment with recruiting object technologists through an agency. As yet, there are few specialist agencies for object technology, coupled with a lack of experienced staff on the move. In Britain this excess demand for experienced staff can be seen in the large salaries offered for object technology work on trading systems in London.

Another form of agency, with the same problems as external recruitment business, is your own personnel department, a.k.a., the human resource group. Their name change from "personnel" was meant to imply their full involvement in the resources of the enterprise with the speciality of the people involved. That is fine if that is what they do, but most human resource groups are still fundamentally personnel departments, concerned with terms and conditions, employment contracts, and the like. They are rarely involved in maximizing the human resources with career guidance, training, counseling, etc. As one cynic said, "I was a human resource, but I was wasted."

5.6 Use Your Friends

A more effective method is to use your own network of contacts to find suitable candidates. If you and your team have taken object technology courses, you will have met others in your field. Keep in touch, share progress and information, and build relationships. These relationships will become powerful when you need to recruit or when it's time for you to move on. Networking within your own organization is similar. Current staff may be eager to become involved in this new technology, and the cost of training or retraining is much lower than the cost of seeking new recruits. Look for those who have the qualities of a good software engineer and retrain them in object technology. Once they grasp the concepts, stand back and watch them run with the ball.

5.7 Hiring Contractors

Contractors come in various packages: the "work alongside the team" type, the "give me a chunk to take away" type, and the "we'll do it all for you" type. What type do you want? If you thought hiring a new recruit was tough, try selecting and using contractors. You still need the qualities of the more permanent staff. Not only are experience and technical skills required—but ensuring a transfer of skills to your own team is vital. You don't want the expertise to be lost when the contract is completed. You also don't want to spend a lot of time training them in your business.

It is essential that you follow up references provided by the consulting organization but remember these will be sites that in general will support the consulting organization. Ask instead for a list of past and current clients—encourage boasting—and follow these up as well. You need to hear some bad news as well as the good. Consider only those organizations that have strong recommendations from multiple independent sources. Interview the consultants who will work with the team, not the manager or company chairman. These are the people who will make the difference to your team. You are not just buying the consulting services of the organization, rather you are buying the skills and experience of the individuals assigned to your project. Get the best qualified consultant, not the best qualified consulting organization; reputation and rates are not necessarily a guide to the best value.

Many of you will have already experienced the problem of the senior management being sold services by the top executives of the consulting organization with an impressive list of personnel, most of whom will never work on the project. Insist that the object-oriented consultant is interviewed by you, that they can provide documented success stories, and that the final decision is made by you.

Contractors who work alongside your team must have excellent technical and communication skills. High technical skill is always admired; you might not like the person, but you have to admire their skills. But you must like contractors as well. They must fit in well with the team, use tact and discretion in nontechnical issues and be prepared to do the dull and uninteresting jobs as well as the more glamorous ones. One way guaranteed to demotivate your own team is to give only the interesting jobs to the contractor and neglect the permanent team.

This also applies to contractors who take away bits for development. Avoid giving them all the interesting parts. Using contractors in this manner may have the benefit of saving some costs of providing equipment, desk space, etc., but unless closely managed it may cause problems. Object technologists sell the concepts of components, so there is a belief that it becomes easier to 'farm out' components to some outside organization for production. This is a myth. There may be individual components, but these need to communicate with the other components of the system. That means the designers and the programmers need to communicate constantly to ensure that the final systems work. If the contractor is a part-time member of the team, then that communication channel, unless supported by groupware, will be sporadic and prone to failure. Richard Gabrial recounts how a highly productive and successful object-oriented project team found that changes to the interfaces caused severe ripples through the rest of the system (Gabrial, 1994). The team recognized the problem "and adopted a process of almost-daily meetings to discuss architectural issues, interfaces, algorithms, and data structures. These meetings lasted several hours a day." If your team members are not there, how will they know what affects them?

Contractors are there to provide expertise and extra resources, not to take over the project. If that is what you want, hire an outside contracting agency to do the work for you. If you are going to choose outside contractors to deliver a working system, then a small core team, including yourself, must become fully involved in the project. Too often when work is contracted outside an organization it becomes "out of sight, out of mind." But in these situations much more management is needed. Your own trusted staff needs to work on a daily basis with the outside contractors. Again, how will you know what is going on, and how will your staff hope to gain experience?

This is where enterprises often employ external consultants as mentors to their staff. These consultants help and guide your own staff in the development of the project, but the skills stay with your team. The mentor guides the development process, ensuring that the evolving system in all its stages uses the best practices, is not heading for some tar pit, and continues to meet the requirements. Mentoring has the advantage of using a scarce and expensive resource, the consultant, to maximum benefit for your organization. Finding mentors may be difficult, especially as the requirements will change over the life span of the project, and this is where an independent group of mentors is useful.

5.8 Roles and Responsibilities

Roles and responsibilities depend in many ways upon the services you provide to your enterprise. There are four types of roles for systems departments:

- Technical services cover the provision of data communications, definition of standards and interfaces, provision of technical support, etc.

- Development support is concerned with provision of new systems and maintaining the present systems, especially those at the core of the business activities.

- Business support is the provision of end-user computing, office technology, business product, and business service technology.

- Business service is an emerging role in some organizations and is concerned with integrating business units and systems to provide improved customer services.

You clearly need to understand which of these roles you need to supply to the organization. These roles must be clearly passed on to your staff. If a mission-critical application fails, it is their job to not only recover the situation but to investigate the failure thoroughly to avoid future occurrences.

5.8.1 Object Technology Roles

Job titles such as "programmer," "analyst/programmer," and "business analyst" may satisfy the personnel department, but they do not cover the roles you need to fill for object technology.

First, there are a broad set of roles with titles such as "architect," "engineer," and "apprentice." These reflect the different skill levels of the members of the team. Architects will be highly experienced and have a track record of past achievements in object technology. These are the staff you trust to deliver a successful product. Engineers are the boilermen of the team, providing the technical expertise in a number of specialist areas (e.g., business classes and infrastructure classes such as communication). These are more commonly known as the domain experts. Apprentices are, as the name suggests, learning from the engineers (as the engineers are learning from the architect). They will have language skills, perhaps not fully developed, but sufficient to provide the coding resources under guidance of the engineers.

In object technology development there is less of a distinction between the traditional analyst, designer, builder, and coder seen in most organizations. The close interrelationship of the various domains means that there has to be much more knowledge of all aspects of the development by all members of the team. The distinction between the team members is their knowledge and experience, rather than their title, i.e. every team member needs to be multi-disciplined.

The preceding discussion focuses on the technology team, but a number of support roles also need to be provided. For example, test engineers and their apprentices are needed as are documentation experts and class library specialists. In many cases the number of support staff will equal the number of technologists.

Figure 5.2 illustrates the detailed object technology roles:

- *Class builder.* An experienced developer with skills to abstract and build classes for reuse within present and future projects

- *Reuse engineer.* Has knowledge of major sections (few can know all the library components) of the application library, domain library, enterprise library, and third-party class libraries and coordinates their use in current projects

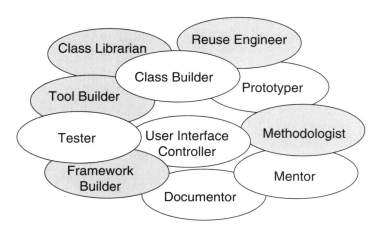

FIGURE 5.2. Roles for Object Technologists

- *Class librarian.* The guardian and protector of the library components
- *Framework builder.* An experienced developer who can provide architectural frameworks for use by future projects
- *Prototyper.* Can elicit information on customer requirements and using powerful tools, provide visual representations to ensure that the requirements are fully understood
- *Mentor.* The guide and counselor in specific areas of the project: analysis, design, programming, language facilities, etc.
- *Methodologist.* Has a deep knowledge of your chosen approach and ensures the appropriate work processes and methods are followed and developed to fit your organization; trains and coaches others in the method
- *Tool builder.* Develops and provides specialized tools for the developers to improve productivity (e.g., debugging aids, data generation)
- *Tester.* Creates the various test harnesses, test classes and methods, test data, etc. for inclusion in the evolving system
- *User interface controller.* Similar to the framework builder in that they ensure a consistent and understandable user interface style with appropriate components
- *Documentor.* May tackle the manuals and training notes, but is now more involved in providing the on-line help facilities associated with modern systems; needs to be involved early in the project life span

One role not mentioned above is that of the maintainer. Most object technology writing focuses on developing new systems and mentions maintenance only as one of the benefits of this new technology, lower maintenance costs. The focus on new systems is understandable as most, if not all, developers want to be involved in new work rather than lost in the maintenance of older, existing systems. But is it really justified?

It's well known that to make a name for yourself and thereby rise within the enterprise, you need to be involved in mission-critical activities. This is why most of the very senior managers come from a sales and marketing background: these are mission-critical activities. All mission-critical systems were developed in the early days of the computerization of the enterprise. They have become the legacy so hated by the IT staff. It's old, boring, difficult to understand, and impossible to change. It rusts; every time you touch it, another thing breaks and needs repair. So out with the old and in with the new!

But these systems are mission critical and need to be kept up-to-date. Legacy systems need to be incorporated into the object world. There needs to be a melding of the new with the old; new graphical user interfaces with standard TCP/IP communications to remote relational databases and batch-like processing. It's not the new-system syndrome promoted by many of the object technologists, but it is the only one that has any future in most enterprises. *Maintenance* was a dirty word, but if you want to advance to the top of your career, get involved with these mission-critical systems.

5.8.2 Team Roles

In addition to the technical roles another set of roles also needs to be allocated. *Team roles* are vital to the success of the task. They ensure that the team achieves its short and long-term goals and that the team remains a cohesive unit.

The first set of team roles are associated with the task function and describe the behavior needed for a team to achieve its goals:

- *Mover.* Initiates, coordinates, and develops procedures by proposing activities, goals, defining problems, suggesting procedures and solutions, and suggesting ways that different issues may be handled; gives direction and purpose, harmonizing and adjusting issues that may cause conflict

- *Collector.* Seeks information and opinions and makes the team aware of the need for information by requesting relevant facts and asking for clarification; asks for opinions to form a team opinion and test for consensus

- *Informer.* Gives information or opinion by offering relevant facts and avoiding reliance on opinion when facts are needed; states information or beliefs and evaluates a suggestion as a basis for team decision

- *Clarifier.* Eliminates confusion and reduces ambiguity by defining terms, interpreting ideas, giving examples, and explaining issues and ideas

- *Philosopher.* Pulls together ideas and related issues, shows contradictions, and defines common models by drawing general statements or models from specific ones and critically examining underlying assumptions and ideas

- *Evaluator.* Measures accomplishment against goals and provides a sense of progress in line with these goals and notes progress and blocks

The second set of team roles is less obvious but needed within every team to maintain team cohesion:

- *Guide.* Helps the team be aware of direction and progress by stating standards to achieve and suggesting activities

- *Communicator.* Provides an interested audience for others, accepts ideas, and goes along with the team; listens, explains, and interprets what others have said

- *Encourager.* Accepts contributions and opinions of other team members, draws out silent members, and gives others recognition

- *Mediator.* Conciliates differences, offers compromises to reduce tension, admits error, and encourages the yielding of status

- *Fixer.* Ensures the physical surroundings and resources are assisting the team

Although two sets of team roles are given and the distinction between task and maintenance functions is useful, it is of course, the case that all functions listed perform both types of role to some extent. Team maintenance is vital to team achievement, and team achievement is important to team maintenance.

An individual team member may have a number of roles: a technical role such as designer and team roles such as philosopher and encourager. A skilled member of the team would ensure that any unfilled roles are assumed as they are needed. Obviously team roles are allocated with some thought to the personality of the team member concerned. Major problems will arise if for example, the most aggressive team member is allocated the role of mediator!

Task and team roles can be allocated, but a further set of roles are also adopted unconsciously by any team.

As more working hours are spent at work than at home, working relationships tend to adopt a family structure: aunts/uncles, brothers/sisters. It is a temporary family usually formed as a patriarchy and undergoing the same con-

FIGURE 5.3. Dealing with New Recruits

flicts as real families; children being rebellious or mischievous to older family members. Family roles are adopted by individuals either as a compensation or projection of other members. So we have the joker, the intellectual, the dunce, and the angry young man. If such roles are unconsciously forced by the team upon an individual, say the role of the dunce, then the role becomes self-fulfilling. This family principle holds true for whole organizations as well as teams.

In summary, it can be seen that roles have important part in team building. Creating teams is a difficult process prone to failure through lack of care in the design and make-up of the team. While technical roles are important, teams can fail if the team roles are not also adopted by the team members. If however, team roles are recognized and consciously encouraged, the team becomes the most powerful force for achievement.

5.9 The First 20 Days

After all the effort, you now have one or more new staff members. What are you going to do with them? Throw them in at the deep end? Let then languish with the set of manuals? Or induct them into the ways of your business as shown in Figure 5.3?

The objective of an induction procedure is to provide new employees and new team members with knowledge of the organizational structure, operating values of the team, the new product, and the background on the main technical components. Its aim is to ensure that new members quickly feel part of the object technology team, that they reach their maximum effectiveness in as short a time as possible, that they adopt the culture of the team and the organization, and that they cause minimum disturbance to the work in hand.

The induction procedure is made up of a series of talks, seminars, discussions, and demonstrations provided by a range of staff. This is not an advocation for a new training department—it's hard enough getting budgets for developers without trying for a training department—but I do suggest that your own team members undertake this process. It's a well-known fact that in trying to teach about your specialist areas gives more understanding to the teacher as well as informing the student. Set some time aside in the schedule to free up staff to develop their knowledge.

It would obviously make sense for these to be organized for a group of new members, but every new member is at least welcomed to the team and given an overview of the information. No new team member should be left more that five days at a loose end. Each new team member will be given an "introductory pack" containing documents such as the object-oriented mission statement, the objectives, project plan, project members names (and photos), their roles, telephone numbers and areas of expertise (with the encouragement to ask for help from these experts), quality plans, etc.

Any induction procedure for all new staff has these major elements:

- Welcome
    - ◆ "Welcome to the object technology team" talk by the project manager

- Organizational structure
    - ◆ Company divisions and groups
    - ◆ Object technology team position in company
    - ◆ Object technology teams and their structure
    - ◆ Object technology team approach

- ◆ Team personalities

- ◆ The new member's position and role in the team

- Operational values and systems

  - ◆ Object technology team mission statement

  - ◆ Object technology team working practices and culture

  - ◆ Document and program structures and access

  - ◆ Time-recording and other administrative reporting

  - ◆ Computing support and location of reference documents

  - ◆ Issue of network passwords

- Product, systems, or services introduction

  - ◆ The customers

  - ◆ The product range

  - ◆ The product design

  - ◆ The product specifications

  - ◆ An overview of your business terminology

- Technical background

  - ◆ The overall system design

  - ◆ Detailed system design (of the area relevant to the new team member)

  - ◆ Class library organization and major branches

- ◆ Techniques used or expected

- ◆ Quality standards

- Training project
    - ◆ A small, well-defined project that requires the use of all the tools and establishes the working practices and operating values such as achieving milestones, reviews, responsibility, and accountability.

The induction procedure, including the training project, should take no longer than one month. At the end of this crucial period, the new member will be fully established on the object technology team and will have overcome the many obstacles in any new project/job.

5.10 The Next 30 Days

If the new staff member has previous object technology experience, they can be assigned tasks in the project team supported by one of the team members, i.e., a personal coach. However, if they need to learn and become proficient in object technology, more training is required. First, they need formal training in the language, the methodology, or both. After this training period, they have some understanding but need to exercise this knowledge to become proficient. A sample application that will take approximately four weeks of effort needs to be developed. If you have a number of new staff members, it is even better if they work together as a small team. This gives you the opportunity to observe their interactions and perceive their characters. It also creates camaraderie; they feel part of something rather than on the fringe. This team, or the new individual, must have a coach assigned to support the activity. It is a proving ground, but your aim should be to help them succeed rather than fail through lack of support.

At the end of this period—50 days—you have integrated the new staff into the organization, developed their skills, monitored their performance, and identified their strengths and weaknesses. They will not be experts, but they will be proficient and an effective member of the team.

Some will say they can't wait for the 50 days, in which case the new staff will be learning on the job and the job may be put in jeopardy as a result. You may not know it at the time—everything appears OK—but when it is delivered or when the volume of information increases, you will find the cracks appearing. With object technology, there is this underlying concern that what appears to work may in fact be seriously flawed under certain conditions.

Be patient, allocate the resources, recruit strategically (ahead of need), and be certain that every new staff recruit will be a valuable and effective member of the organization.

5.11 Summary

Finding the right staff is not simple. It requires strategic planning, a heavy involvement by both managers and senior technical staff, and careful specification of the qualities that are sought in the new recruit. These might include not only object-oriented analysis and design skills in your preferred method, but knowledge of the relevant class libraries or even exposure to your chosen toolset. Furthermore, the personalities of the individuals are of importance depending on the maturity of your own object development. Do you need experimenters who love to try something new but get bored quickly, early adopters who try something new, stick with it, and provide a solid skill base to share with others, or pragmatists who, when convinced that objects will be beneficial, will work hard to make it a success? You might encounter those who find it difficult to adopt the object approach, late adopters, who may use every excuse to prove objects don't work or outright resisters who are unable to deal with change of any kind. Consideration needs to be given to finding staff not only through traditional recruitment procedures but through agencies and friends or contacts, who are often the best source of new staff.

Using contract staff to cover a shortfall in resources can be fraught with problems, but with careful attention to selection, job descriptions, and appropriate management, contractors can prove a useful addition to your project team. All team members need to have clear roles and responsibilities. Roles include those for supporting the object development: class builder, re-use engineer, class librarian, framework builder, prototyper, mentor, methodologist, tool builder, tester, user interface controller and finally the documentor. Roles that enhance the cohesion of the team such as mediator, clarifier, fixer, etc. also need to be determined. If they are not evident, they need to be encouraged in the members or covered by the project manager.

Finally, an induction program for new recruits covering the first 20 days followed by another 30 days under the tutelage of a personal coach have been outlined. This program ensures that your new staff gets the best possible start with object technology.

References

Coad, P. (1991). Why use object-oriented development? *Journal of Object-Oriented Programming*, 4(8).

Coad, P., and E. Yourdon. (1991a). *Object-Oriented Analysis*. Englewood Cliffs, NJ: Prentice Hall.

Coad, P., and E. Yourdon. (1991b). *Object-Oriented Design*. Englewood Cliffs, NJ: Prentice Hall.

Gabrial, R. (1994). Critic-at-large. *Journal of Object-Oriented Programming*, 7(1).

CHAPTER **6**

STYLE

ONE DISCOVERY THAT EVERY NEW MANAGER EXPERIENCES IS THE SUDDEN realization that they are no longer doing proper work. The work is now being done by others. This does not imply that the manager does nothing, although a popular misconception about management being easy arose from the title of Ken Blanchard's book *The One Minute Manager*. The style of working has changed. The manger has become a facilitator, an enabler, a guide, and plays many other different roles required of the situation from moment to moment.

This chapter is about the style of management required to make a success of object-oriented projects. It's a difficult subject. We are all different as individuals—both you the manager and your team members—and as such have different needs and aspirations. How can we use this difference to create the powerful teams to tackle the complex object-oriented projects?

6.1 Recognizing Our Differences

First we need to recognize the differences. For many years I have been skeptical about the general use of psychometric testing in recruiting staff, but recent experiences have made me reconsider my position. At the end of a long weekend on psychological typing based on Jungian philosophy there was a team exercise.* The task is unimportant, but what was for me far more of interest was how we all behaved:

- One member ignored the rest of the team and quietly "did it his way."

- Another did little work but wanted to ensure we were all happy and functioning as a team.

- The third launched into the task with enthusiasm and excitement wanting quick results.

- Another didn't know where to start and wanted continual guidance and constant reassurance.

Our team completed the task successfully, but the interaction was far more instructive. The language and words used indicated the problems we would experience: "quietly," "felt," "togetherness," "quick results," and so on. For the first time I understood why some of my own team members have been easy to work with and why others have been so difficult, why certain teams have been powerful and others cease to function after a few weeks and why others understand the concepts and ideas I write and talk about, while others require more information, more detail, more examples.

The reason? We are all different and need different styles of management to respond to our fundamental natures and characters.

To illustrate this, Table 6.1 outlines some behaviors associated with working (Hirsch & Kummerow, 1989). Examine the two columns and decide which side reflects your own preferences; you will have preferences in both columns, but one will dominate. There is no right way, and neither style is better than the other.

Perhaps you now have some understanding of the reasons why you and your staff may have conflicts. It's only a matter of approach. (As a matter of interest, this test has been conducted with hundreds of managers and developers and the left column behaviors seem to dominate the profession; does that say something about managers or about computing or perhaps about men?)

---

* The course was based on the Myers-Briggs Type Indicator, a registered trademark of Consulting Psychologists' Press, Palo Alto, California.

Table 6.1. Differing Styles of Preferred Behaviors	
Do my best when I plan my work and work my plan	Do my best when I can deal with needs as they arise
Enjoy getting things settled and finished	Enjoy keeping things open for last minute changes
Like checking items off my "to do" list	Ignore my "to do" list even if I make one
Overlook new things that need to be done in order to complete current job	Postpone my current task to meet momentary needs
Narrow down the possibilities and be satisfied once I reach a decision	Resist being tied down to a decision in order to gather more information
Decide quickly and seek closure	Put off decisions to seek options
Seek structure in scheduling myself and others	Resist structure and favor changing circumstances
Prefer to regulate and control my work and that of others	Prefer to free up my work and that of others

A similar consideration also applies to managers; each of you have a distinctive style. This has been categorized as follows (Woods, 1989):

- *The facilitator manager.* Functions through people, has the overview, needs time to think, wants to be involved
- *The resource manager.* Is logical, runs a center of excellence, gets things right, accepts expert views
- *The practical manager.* Solves problems, makes decisions, seeks usability, resents the vague, is the classical manager
- *The action manager.* Uses people, looks for the main chance, inspirational, does things now.

Again, no one style is right; all are valid. They do, however, indicate why problems occur with your peers and with your team individuals.

Do you know the fundamental nature of each individual of your team? You will have some awareness when you have been together a while and you can use knowledge of the differences to make a judgment. But what about a new team or a new recruit? Have you got the time to figure them out? Should you use psychometric testing to understand the individuals and guide your dealings with them? If your company uses such methods, do you have access to the information? If not, why not? Go down to the personnel department and inspect the results of your team members' tests. Use the results to good effect.

Why is this worthy of your efforts?

With object technology more than with other software development approaches, the team is all-important. You can have single developer projects, and these will be successful—but think of the scope and the impact of the business. Will they make a difference? No! The business benefits and the success of the object oriented-approach comes from teams.

6.2 Creating Powerful Teams

The first step with the new team is to change their perspective. Move away from the process view of software development to focus on results. The processes of analysis, design, etc. are still performed but not as large chunks of activities associated with the waterfall model. Others say that object technology can work within that framework, but I am skeptical. If we are honest, did we believe it when the developers said "the analysis is finished"? We only knew if it was finished when the product was finally delivered. Despite all attempts at reviews and walkthroughs, we could have some confidence in the quality of the work, but we still could not be sure that it was complete. Even worse, we planned it to be finished by such and such a date, with all the next phases planned in detail. What is really being said is that "the analysis is to be *stopped* at this date."

In fact there is often an overemphasis on planning both for the project and for the system structure. Architectural planning is very important, but there can be a tendency to over-plan and over-analyze. This is in some ways an effect of the waterfall style of development; reduce the risk at each stage. Against this fixed approach, building smaller things with lots of new starts is more productive. There needs to be the overall scope and architecture hopefully designed to cope with change and expansion, but the power and flexibility of object technology means that the penalty is lower if you change your mind. However, some care does need to be exercised.

When the requirements are unclear, even to the users, rapid prototyping followed by the more formal iterative and incremental (I&I) development will yield useful results. If, however, you launch into I&I development before having a clear understanding of the requirements, you must accept that significant portions of the version will change. This may not be a problem in the long term—the final system meets all the customer/user's requirements—but in the short term, there will be delays, potential cost overruns that can give rise to periods of frustration felt by the developers when they see large sections of their work abandoned. Keeping the motivation high can be difficult in these circumstances.

By getting every developer to focus on results—by *result*, I mean user-discernible deliverables—we use the power of timeboxing to make mini-projects of each set of deliverables. Timeboxing has been found to be an effective method for applying project planning to the object-oriented approach. One of the main excuses not to adopt object technology is the fear that control of projects will be lost. It can happen, let's not be naive, but well-established timeboxes that have been negotiated with the team provide a strong framework for manager's control and monitoring.

Such a timebox would detail the work to be achieved with a cut-off date for completion (e.g., to develop a set of classes to provide a company-style of graphical user interface that accommodates text, graphical, and user information within the Microsoft Windows 3.1 environment by July 1, 1995).

During the period of the "box," checks will be made at regular intervals to ensure progress toward the deadline is being achieved. When the end-time is reached, work stops and the efforts are assessed. If they meet your various evaluation criteria on quality, etc., the work can be accepted; otherwise careful consideration needs to be given to sanctioning further work effort. Any further work will, in effect, be an overrun, but it may be necessary to avoid discarding the delivered components.

Focusing on results means a change in your attitude: don't tell me how hard you work, tell me how much you have delivered. This new perspective forces the developers to work effectively, and to use object technology as it should be used and not simply as another coding technique. They work smarter. And to work smarter, we set SMART goals for each team member.

6.2.1 SMART Goals

SMART goals, developed by Ken Blanchard (Blanchard & Johnson, 1982), set out clearly what you expect of each individual (Figure 6.1). Yes, this is your work: setting goals. It is through agreement on these goals that the culture of consent can be developed. This culture of consent, so ably described by Charles Handy in *Age of Unreason* (1986), is needed by all professional workers. "Kicking" professional workers makes then work harder, but we want them to work smarter; that is, to use their intellect to be inventive, thoughtful, and creative.

SMART goals are

- *Specific*. Is it clearly understandable?
- *Measurable*. What would a good job look like?
- *Attainable*. Is it realistic for this person?
- *Relevant*. Will it make an impact?
- *Trackable*. How will you know?

SMART goals need a sensible time-span for completion. It's too easy to set unrealistic timeframes. For example, if one of the goals is to select and install new CASE technology tools within the next three months, it will fail to meet the deadline. A moment's thought on the work involved—defining the selection criteria, identifying and evaluating the candidates, purchasing and installing the tool, providing training courses, and conducting pilot experimental projects—will easily take longer than three months. So time-span is important. If a new product is planned for next year, what needs to be started now for that product development to begin in the correct fashion?

To set SMART goals there are three stages:

1. Identify the objective/areas of responsibility with a timeline
2. Specify the priority
3. Detail at least three ways in which success can be measured

An example always gives a better idea of the concepts:

1. To develop a set of classes to provide a company style of graphical user

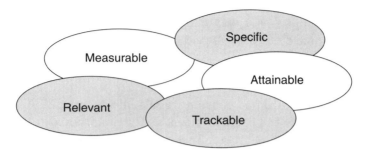

FIGURE 6.1. Key Elements of SMART Goals

interface that accommodates text, graphical, and user information within the Windows 3.1 environment by July 1, 1995

2. Priority: 1

3a. Resultant classes meet needs of current applications

Outstanding: < 5 agreed enhancements after delivery

Acceptable: 10 to 20 agreed enhancements after delivery

3b. Classes reused in future applications development

Outstanding: all classes used in at least four future developments

Acceptable: > 80% classes used in at least two future developments

3c. Classes of high engineering quality

Outstanding: no corrections in first six months

Acceptable: < 5 corrections in first six months

3d. For the classes to be available, initial prototypes completed by 30/5/95

Outstanding: completed by 1/5/95

Acceptable : completed 30/5/95

This example clearly lays out the expectations for a member of the team. It defines the results (1), shows the timebox (1 and 2) and each measurement reflects some of the project goals—fitness for purpose(3a), timeliness (3d), and quality (3c)—as well as attention being paid to important long term factors—genericity (3b). Care needs to be taken over aspects over which there is little control (e.g., reuse of the classes in future developments (3b)). Obviously, the classes need to be useful in order for them to be selected for future developments, but their reuse may not be guaranteed. Try drawing up such goals for the next phase of your current project for each team member.

6.2.2 Means and Ends

In other words, you need to put your *own* goals into *their* SMART goals. Your goals will be aligned with the business need: faster time-to-market, higher quality, more flexibility, extendibility, etc. These goals—the ends—need to be translated into measures—the means—for deployment among your team members (Figure 6.2). This reflects the need for businesses to enhance, change, modify, and respond to new requirements of their customers and your users.

Such performance measures become your checkpoints, and for the team member they become their own control point. Again, more examples show the concept:

- To improve quality you can obviously check the number of defects reported.

- To improve the time-to-market you can set a target of less than 5% schedule misses.

- Increasing flexibility can be measured by the number of user-defined changes accommodated each month, and so on.

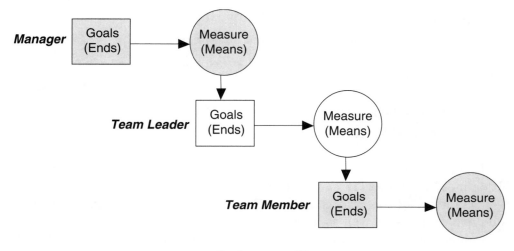

FIGURE 6.2. Deployment of Resources

An example of a typical deployment from manager to team is shown in Table 6.2

There is one more important issue before we leave goal setting: you need to check and monitor progress in meeting these goals. This may seem obvious, but how many times have you experienced the common situation where goals have been set by your senior manager and then ignored? This is nearly as bad as conflicting goals ("I want it fast and I want it right!"). If you take the trouble to set and negotiate goals at the outset, then at least pay attention to them during the life of the project.

6.3 Leadership

This brings us to your own management style. *Leadership* is a much-abused word these days. All organizations call for better leadership—even countries call for better leadership—and then everyone waits for the leader to be appointed. This reflects an old style of thinking that will not fit with the new world of rapid development using object technology.

There was a time when authority came through position or title. This has been called the age of the "heroic manager": the manager who could do it all, know it all, solve every possible problem. Now we are in the age of the "post-heroic manager": the manager who recognizes that authority flows from the one who knows. This manager is willing to accept that what is being attempted by her or his team is complex, intellectually challenging, and that the team

Table 6.2. Example of Deployment of Resources

Function	Goal (End)	Measure (Means)
Manager	Improve customer/user satisfaction	Reduce number of defects after installation
Team Leader	Reduce number of defects after installation	Establish test plan
Team Member	Establish test plan	Define test case scenarios for those components within their responsibility

members have the knowledge. They are in the position to choose the leader for the next particular task in hand. In the early stages, the analysts will lead the group, then designers will take over, and finally the system specialists will guide the implementation. Leadership changes once again during the next turn of the wheel.

What is the manager doing all this time? Providing direction, ensuring team cohesion and functioning, doing the administration, setting goals, and setting an example.

Your style of management is to be a coach, part of the team yet with the ability to withdraw and encourage self-management by the team members. Remember, you can't do it all; you might not even know how to do it, but if you do you should still let the others get on with it. There is a very large product development company with hundreds of developers, where the technical director continuously gets involved in debugging the system. This might make him feel good, but it certainly demotivates the staff, especially when he finds faults and then severely criticizes the hapless developer.

It's amazing how ineffective leaders are at tapping individual talents within their organizations. Many team members complain bitterly not only about how their organizations have misused their professional skills, but about managers who do almost everything to make sure that they do not perform to the fullest of their talents. It's almost as if the leaders are afraid to allow their teams a chance to perform. Delegation is not valued highly by many leaders, which may indirectly affect their own chances of promotion—they are bypassed because nobody is ready to step into their jobs.

Motivation, incentives, and small wins are important aspects of your style in the fast development cycle associated with object technology. Monitoring progress, reporting both up and down the organization, and checking against the metrics and the goals become the natural activities of your day. This has been called "walking your talk." It ensures that there are no communication failures within your team. Often the message "always meet requirements" becomes "meet requirements if practical." "Quality has top priority" is usually "quality if we have time." You can all think of similar crossed wires. But you are responsible for the communication. If you want faster time to market through object technology then effort must be given to create reusable components. If it is an extendible system, inheritance hierarchies need to be flattened; if it is higher quality, then automated test tools may need to be employed.

To test for consistent messages, ask some or all of the following:

- How do people get raises or promoted?
- How do teams get rewarded?
- How are suppliers chosen?
- Who are the heroes/heroines and why?
- What is important in the reviews?
- What makes the boss mad?

Tom Peters says that all there is attention—attention to the large vision and to the small details. Attention is a two-way thing. Are you paying attention now as you read this or are you thinking about the signals that you have been sending to the teams? If you want higher quality, does every meeting and most memos concentrate on this issue? If it's reusability, is this a constant question in all your dealings with the teams? It may seem obvious, but the manager is the only one who must pay constant attention to the critical attributes of object-oriented development; no one else will (Figure 6.3).

So far, we have focused on the style of the manager in performing her or his activities, but what of the style of the organization? How does the organization behave in achieving the business goals?

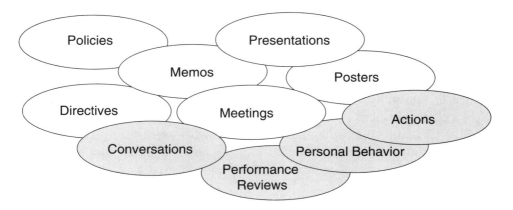

FIGURE 6.3. Vehicles for Improved Communications

6.4 Maturity of Style

Organization style is defined as the characterization of how key managers achieve business goals as well as the cultural style of the organization.

In the initial stages of adopting object technology the atmosphere is chaotic. There is a heavy use of outside consultants, who generally do the work and often do not pass on the skills to the in-house team. This is because the focus is solely on the technical issues with the pressure of work engendering an attitude of "don't bother me, I'm too busy." This in turn leads to a lack of awareness of other issues such as commercial and business, and there's no concern at this lack of awareness. The job gets done somehow, everyone heaves a sigh of relief, vows never to do it that way again, then promptly does it again. Do you work in such an environment? Of course not! *Your* environment is controlled.

A controlled development environment indicates the next stage of maturity. Users are responsible for the requirements, and the IT development group provides the solutions. Delegation is common but with mixed results. IT is upset by the constantly changing requirements of the users, who are now the owners of the system. They also dislike outside interference with their solutions, and all failures are seen as customer/user problems. Yet object technology is meant to overcome these issues. Unfortunately, it doesn't. The rapid development cycle can be seen by the users to be a carte blanche to remain vague and uncertain of requirements. Systems solutions are delivered more quickly but seem constantly to be entering another stage of major enhancement or change. At this point there is an increasing backlog of needed systems. Senior management becomes concerned at this backlog and the lack of coordination between the IT and business groups.

The next stage of maturity is cooperation and collaboration. The focus has returned to IT issues with user groups cooperating with the developers to ensure delivered systems meet the business needs of the whole organization (e.g., a customer class contains sufficient behavior and information to be useful throughout many applications). Logical arguments are used by both the IT and the user groups to set the agenda. This approach ensures that risk-taking is avoided and well-known approaches and technology are used for most of the new applications.

Organizations at this stage find it difficult to adopt object technology throughout the development environment. Critics can always argue well-prepared cases for maintaining the current situation:

- *It's unworkable.* It only works on PCs, not my mainframe.

- *It's too expensive.* New tools and training everyone will cost an arm and a leg.

- *It's high risk.* It is too great a change, little steps are needed.

- *It's not proven.* We only hear about small projects; what about big systems?

- *It's disruptive.* All existing procedures and the quality manuals will need to be changed.

If there is any grain of truth in these arguments, resistance will grow and harden. To change the situation, a product champion is needed.

When product champions appear, this indicates a move to the next stage where there is an integrated environment of developers and users. The focus moves to strategic issues and innovation where the drive is to pursue opportunities. Object technologies' flexibility and extendibility make this a most powerful technology for supporting this stage of maturity. Managers now need to be entrepreneurial in outlook and seek advantages to be exploited and supported within the organization and the business environment.

When the final stage of maturity of organizational style is achieved then IT is used for the competitive advantage sought by many companies. At this stage, all top managers realize the importance of IT, including appointing an IT manager to the board. IT is seen as supporting the business units in real and effective ways. Object technology frameworks provided by the developers give power-users the ability to construct new and innovative systems. In one London dealing house, the developers have provided such powerful business components that the dealers themselves can construct a completely new application within 24 hours.* Now, that's powerful.

Achieving these levels of maturity can only come from your determination to improve the development processes. If we continue to develop in the same old ways, we will get the same results that have led us to this software crisis—"if you always do what you always do, you'll always get what you'll always get!"

---

* Personal communication with team members. Also, Distributed Systems Consultants of London won an award in 1993 for a product that allows investment analysts to do some of their own programming (*Infomatics*, 1993).

Object technology, by itself, will not solve the problem. Object orientation is powerful, but like many powerful technologies, it can cause more chaos than benefit. Your style in managing these projects is crucial.

6.5 Managing with Style

If you adopt the hard-nosed approach to object-oriented project management, where you totally focus on achieving the project goals, squeeze the resources to get the best possible yield, and treat your team members as interchangeable parts of a machine, you may be successful. This approach works in some organizations— usually traditional production-line businesses with larger number of semiskilled workers—but it usually causes tremendous friction. That style of management is guaranteed to fail with knowledge workers, who provide intellectual skills to solve complex problems. Books contain information, but knowledge resides in individuals. A softer approach—a people-oriented approach—is required.

The people-oriented approach recognizes that knowledge workers cannot be commanded, that "kicking" them may make them active but not creative, inventive, and thoughtful—remember we hire them to be inventive, creative and thoughtful! The people-oriented manager allows a quota of mistakes; this is not to condone stupidity nor sloppy work, which should always be condemned, but recognizes that we truly learn from our experiences. When someone tells you "I've had thousands of experiences," there is the ancient reply, "have you had a thousand experiences or the same experience a thousand times?" Who do you think would be the more knowledgeable person?

To release this knowledge the team member needs to be motivated. Technologists are strongly motivated by the technical challenge and the latest innovations as well as the normal items of status and money. In the Shamrock organizations (Chapter 3), the core teams are expected to work long and hard with individual members providing a large number of different roles: multidimensional workers. They are less of an "analyst" or a "designer" or "programmer"; they are, instead, John Brown or June Kwolski. They are known and they expect a career with the organization. In difficult times, it is imprudent to guarantee a future for every individual, but there is a high expectation for advancement and a long-term career based on the delivery of results. Recognition is given to these effective workers in the form of rewards and promotion.

Rewards will be in the form of bonus payments for successful projects and the contribution to the business and promotion to more senior positions. The form of the monetary reward may be based on overall contribution of the delivered product or service to the business—more applicable to senior members of the team—or may be payments for components added to the class library. Individual contributions need to be rewarded, but you send more powerful signals if you reward the team as a whole. This reinforces the team as a working group and encourages self-sufficiency and team discipline. Again, the rewards need to be linked into the project goals:

- If timeliness is crucial, link bonus payments to meeting delivery dates.
- For quality, reward a low number of fault reports.
- If budget is critical, pay increasing bonuses for greater savings.
- For flexibility, set out payment schedules according to the time taken to apply a change or enhancement.

Promotions have to be carefully considered, especially those to a position of manager; a good technician may not make a good manager—you lose the technical skills and gain a poorly managed project. Rewards can simply be public recognition of an individual's contribution to a recent piece of work; for example, the "class builder of the week" award. I can almost hear you all cringe! Just because fast food joints and hotel chains have a smiling picture of the employee of the week in the foyer doesn't mean you cannot mention an outstanding contribution in the monthly in-house magazine or in a report to senior management. Public recognition shows that you value and respect each developer; this is a powerful signal to the rest of the team.

Another powerful form of motivation is the small win. Continual successful completion—a section of the design model, a working scenario based on existing classes, etc.—builds a culture of success within the team. By setting such short-term goals, which is straightforward given the structure of object systems, the team becomes highly motivated and much more able to withstand any setbacks.

So far, we have concentrated on managing the core team. What about the services and the contractors?

One important change in this new model of the organization, is the fact that you are less able to manage the time of the other leaves. These services and contractors effectively manage their own time and often the method of working. When this style of management is required, we move from time-based wage to a fee rate for results. Yes, we are back to specifying the results expected from the other team contributors. These are paid on the results of their efforts—for in-house services it becomes budget transfers between groups rather than actual payments. In some ways, it is a form of piecework: produce a certain result, and you will be paid. When wages form the only reward and a job becomes boring—all jobs have a boring element—then numerous ways are found for avoiding the work.

Some object-oriented project managers adopt the role of college professors. This works well in organizations with a flatter hierarchy and a high percentage of professionally qualified staff. Not only are there fewer layers in the hierarchy but any commands from "above" will be frowned upon. Management is by consent rather than command; you may request action, you need to seek consensus, but try and enforce your notions and there will be the first murmuring of mutiny. Here the relationships are founded on respect. This contrasts with the dictator who overrides most other aspects of the project's or individual's well-being to meet the project goals. These type of managers want rapid response and fast action and typically have a plaque on their wall that says: "don't just sit there – do something!" Unfortunately, something, anything is done. In these situations the plaque should say "don't just do something, sit there!" The aware manager will recognize that when critical decisions need to be made, more time must be given for thinking, for due consideration of the options. The flexibility and adaptability of object technology can be very alluring, but it comes with a price. Undue haste in solving problems will surely lead to total loss of control both of the project and of the system components. The object system becomes like Humpty Dumpty: once broken, it is very hard to put together again.

A further aspect of this new management style to match the teams of object technologists is the concept of trust. I have already written that while a manager needs to have sufficient grounding in the technology, that manager must trust the team to provide the results. This involves monitoring progress—now visible with the increasing use of incremental versions—checking the key metrics (quality, reuse, etc.), and watching for shortfalls in the skill levels.

This trust can also be shown in the allocation of team budgets. Take a deep breath at this point as the next topic will shock many of you.

Teams can be trusted to spend their allocated budgets wisely. Instead of acting as the guardian of the money box, set aside a major portion of the budget and allocate this money to the team to spend as they see fit. You will need receipts to account for the spending, but leave it up to the team to decide on how the money will be spent, whether on a new tool, a set of books, or even a beer bust to celebrate a recent successful delivery. This is not a team budget of

$50 but a budget of $2,500 or more; money which you may even not be allowed to spend yourself without authorization. Experiments have shown that when all spending needs to be authorized by the manager, the team will make numerous requests on this budget (Kanter, 1989). The limit (usually unknown to the team) will be quickly reached, and the developers become disgruntled at the increasing number of refusals. However, when the same sum of money is known to the developers and given to them on trust to spend as they see fit, money is usually returned at the end of the project. Why? Not only do they consider each expenditure with care, they also treat it as *their* money to be managed wisely and conserved in case it may be needed for some unforeseen emergency. Prudence is applied when trust is shown and missing when the same staff are treated as spendthrifts and embezzlers. Banks are the worst form of institutions for this type of behavior: cashiers cannot be trusted as they handle money—there are numerous cross-checks and shortfalls come from their own pocket—therefore, all staff cannot be trusted.

6.6 Managing R&D

A great many explorations of object technology take place in research and development groups. These groups are looking to the long-term application of technology to the business environment (i.e., more than three years ahead). Some will say that three years is too long, there will be too much change in that time. That's true, but many organizations will take that long to evaluate a new technology and implement it into the development teams. There are development organizations who have yet to grasp the nettle of structured design never mind these new-fangled things called objects!

R&D is concerned with ideas and transferring some of these ideas into products. This has been called "kissing technology frogs" (Matthews, 1989). This phrase creates a terrific image and implies that you have to kiss a lot of frogs before you find a prince. That's often the problem with R&D: it expects every project to become the next greatest product for the company, but this is rarely the case. There have to be many failures before the successes are realized. Figures show that less than 5% of R&D projects produce successful products or services (Matthews, 1989).

What does that mean to the explorations into object technology by such research groups? Five key questions need to be answered:

1. Is it possible? Will object technology work for us?

2. Is it attractive? Can it make a difference? What advances will it achieve for us?

3. Is it practical? Assessment, evaluation and selection of technology components

4. Is it desirable? Business case, return on investment, risks

5. How do we do it? Building the initial object systems

Managers often fail to make a clear distinction between "is it attractive?" and "is it desirable?" Simply asking whether it is practical means that a research manager may not have sufficient information about commercial aspects or that a more entrepreneurial manager must accept that there is a high risk and the frog may not turn out to be a prince.

6.7 Do It with Style!

Management style applies to individuals and to teams. Individuals are each different in their own way and you need to first recognize this fact, and then accept that dealing with some individuals will be easier than others. By setting SMART goals the individual will know what you expect of them and how they may be rewarded for their results and efforts. Object technology means innovation, creativity, rapid development and this needs to be encouraged in the individual and in the team.

Creating powerful teams is one of the most significant contributions managers can make toward the success of object technology. This means focusing on results—long hours don't mean much; results count—rather than processes. Your high-level goals, such as improved customer satisfaction, need to be translated into statements relevant to the team leaders and the team members. How can your means become their ends?

Leadership in an object development team is more dynamic in that it moves within the team to those most skilled and knowledgeable about the next phase of the method or technique. Leadership means delegation of responsibility and authority to the members of the team and the adoption of an "open kimono" for the manager. Such trust can be difficult to obtain but has so strong a message it can be made to move mountains.

As the manager of the object-oriented project you have to develop the skills of coach, administrator, communicator, and motivator. This is a shift from task-focused management to people-focused management.

It may appear that you are being asked to be some form of social worker as far as your team is concerned. This is not my intention. But you need to become aware: aware of the different needs of the task, aware of the needs of the team; aware of the needs of the individual including yourself. It is a sad fact that today's managers, including software development managers, are swamped with a tremendous workload. This high pressure leads to a concentration on the issues that are perceived to be important. But how can we trust our judgment under such pressure? Do we tend to look for problems we can understand and cope with? Is it easier to arrange to fix the disk drive than seek the time to understand why Mary and John are not talking to each other? The disk may get mended, but the team and, ultimately, the project will fail if the conflicts within the team are not resolved. We may wish it were otherwise, but we are dealing with people. And the style of dealings with your coworkers and the relationships formed are as critical as the product code. This is your style, and it will be unique to you. Do it with style!

References

Blanchard, K., and S. Johnson. (1983). *The One Minute Manager.* New York: Willow Books.

Handy, C. (1991). *Age of Unreason.* London: Random Century.

Hirsh, S.K., and Kummerow, J.M. (1989). *LIFETypes.* New York: Warner Books.

Kanter, R.M. (1989). *When Giants Learn to Dance.* New York: Simon & Schuster.

Matthews, W. (1990). Kissing technological frogs: managing technology as a strategic resource. *Perspectives for Managers,* 5.

Mitchell, G.R., and W.F. Hamilton. (1988). Managing R&D as a strategic option. *Research and Technology Management,* 31 (3).

Woods, M. (1989). *The Aware Manager.* New York: Element Books.

CHAPTER 7

SKILLS

ASKED WHAT PORTION OF THEIR PROFESSIONAL SKILLS IS USED BY THEIR organizations, the average response by most employees from North America and Europe is 45% (Casse, 1989). What a waste. When confronted with this figure many managers either deny it, express a lack of power, or blame employees. Why has this situation come about?

Most managers work on the basic assumption that people are an important asset that the company must use to the fullest. They are resources. Human resource planning is critical. Planning involves defining the timed phases containing tasks that are allocated to analysts, programmers, etc. In many cases allocation is based on job function or title; it is unimportant which analyst or programmer is allocated to the project as the choice is usually governed by availability. What can the manager do to change the situation and avoid this waste? By moving from managing human resources to managing peoples skills. Staff have professional talents. They are not resources. They *have* resources in their knowledge, skills and experience. Releasing an individual's talent is vital to both personal fulfillment and organizational success.

Skill means a practical demonstration of knowledge and understanding of a concept or technique, whereas talent means the capacity for significant aptitude in an activity. So in this chapter the talents and skills needed by the technologists, the users, and the managers involved in object-oriented projects are explored. For the technologists, the basic set of skills and the concept of a technical specialist are discussed. For managers, the devil's square shows how your current quality initiatives might prove fruitless. Traditional project management techniques may also fail, but your skills can be readily adapted to meet object-oriented projects. Skills needed to avoid the dangers when you become a champion of object technology are also covered. Training programs on management, quality, and technical activities for all levels of the organization will ensure that the skills set for your staff and teams is enhanced and developed. This then, can lead to the concept of skill profiling for object-oriented projects.

7.1 The Technologists

Object technologists need to understand the object-oriented development approach as well as the fundamental components of the technology: the language, tools, environments, and frameworks.

7.1.1 Object-Oriented Development Approach

As discussed in Chapter 4, choosing the most appropriate object-oriented development method is a matter of business environment and developer's preference. However, the skills set for a development team is now focused on analysis and design activities rather than programming. This is not to say that programming is no longer important—many a well-designed system has failed owing to poor implementation—but that the emphasis is now in getting the problem and solution domain model defined. The point must be made again, that *if a change is made to any of the domain model classes it affects each of the other domain models.* A change to the problem domain model must be transformed through the solution and system classes or a change to a system class has an impact on the behavior of the problem domain model. Therefore, much more attention has to be made in the analysis—defining the problem domain model, and in the detailed design—defining the solution domain model. Many developers tell of spending some six weeks defining the problem and solution domain models and then implementing the system in a matter of days.

During the analysis phase the user requirements are captured and defined. This may not be straightforward process, therefore skills in eliciting information must be developed. Then the problem domain models need to be developed.

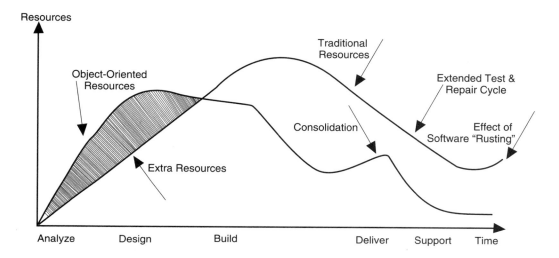

FIGURE 7.1. Different Resource Loading for Projects

Each methodology has a different name for these important diagrams, but they are most often termed the *object model* and show the behavior, attributes, and relationships between the problem domain classes. While skill in the chosen methodology is important, the ability to abstract and partition is crucial—poor partitioning and abstractions cause the failures of many object oriented projects. During the design phase, the skills in detailing the solution domain models, exploiting the class library, identifying the physical architecture, interfacing with legacy systems, and designing intuitive and comprehensible user interfaces are necessary. The project team must be able to cover all these skills (see the section on profiling later in this chapter).

This shift of emphasis affects the resource loading for an object-oriented project (Figure 7.1). Such projects tend to be shorter and have a well-defined end point—further developments are considered new projects—but have more resources in the earlier stages. There is also some extra effort toward the end of the project when the classes may be reworked after consolidation through generalizations and specializations. This contrasts with shape of the resources used on a traditional project when more implementation effort is required, an extended test and repair cycle is needed and after time more development efforts are needed to maintain the system through the effect of software rusting (i.e., the more the code is "touched," the possibility of introducing errors is significantly increased).

7.1.2 Language Skills

Obviously every programmer must know an appropriate object language, whether C++, Smalltalk, Eiffel, or other. But many need to know more than one language. When adopting the iterative and incremental delivery development approach to projects, it is usually assumed that the same language is used throughout the lifespan of the development (i.e., the target language of the final system is the same as the first prototype: an evolutionary prototype). This is not always the case. Whenever the requirement definitions are poor, rapid prototyping is used to reveal the customer/user needs. This often means writing in a 4GL or highly interactive language such as Visual Basic (VB). When the requirements are determined, the prototype is discarded and the actual design and programming take place based on the standard development language. Obviously this means considerable reworking to develop the object model when a 4GL or VB is used.

However, one of the great strengths of object languages—some are better than others in this respect—is the ability to have evolutionary prototypes with the same language throughout. There are the dangers in such prototypes, of cumbersome class trees and inappropriate designs, but with regular reviews and reworking these dangers can be minimized. A further danger is the assumption that the prototype fully defines the requirements. This is rarely the case as complex calculations are simulated in the prototype and never written as a specification.

7.1.3 Skill with Tools

Knowing a language is not enough. The tools that support the language also need to be known. Gone are the days of simple editors and compilation runs. They still exist but are now surrounded by a host of supporting technologies ranging from software engineering (CASE) to computer-assisted system testing (CAST). CASE tools require knowledge of the concepts, the notation and the operation. Unfortunately, as these tools are complicated—any tool that is supporting the concept of development in such a comprehensive way is bound to be complicated—they can be very difficult to operate. Comprehending the tool and levels of sophisticated operation is not to be underestimated. Training courses by the suppliers and a few acknowledged local experts are necessary to gain the benefits from using these tools. The good news is that often only a subset of the complete functionality needs to be learned. Many tool suppliers spend vast development effort adding new functionality only to find that 95% of their users use a fraction of the full functionality; the other 5% who do use the full power are employees of the tool developer! Tool developers take note.

7.1.4 Environment and Frameworks

In addition to the language and its supporting toolset, the target environment needs to be understood. This means knowing in detail the operating system facilities of your chosen supplier whether Microsoft, Sun/NextStep, Solaris, AIX, UNIX, HP, Apple, or Taligent. To understand and effectively use the foundation classes of any operating system is a highly sought-after skill. This is one area where specialization will need to happen. There will be experts in the use of the appropriate application programming interface (API) classes as there will be experts in the business objects that support the enterprise. If you think that this is straightforward, look at the volumes on the Microsoft Foundation Classes (MFC) to overwhelm yourself in detail.

One way of overcoming the raw detail of the foundation classes is to use a framework such as Visual C++, MacAPP, Visual Basic, XVT, Smalltalk Parts, etc. While these do hide the raw API, they in fact add another layer to the knowledge requirements. The level of abstraction may be higher, but there are still an awful lot of classes to understand.

We would expect browsers to help with this respect, but most are mere navigation aids to the on-line help manuals and as such are at a very primitive level. Try browsing more than one library at a time.

Skills are also needed in interfacing to the existing environments of the legacy databases (e.g., Oracle, Sybase, etc). And now with the Common Object Request Broker Architecture (CORBA), Object Linking and Embedding (OLE), and OpenDoc, programmers need to know how objects use the right facilities to be sure of using and exploiting communications for a client/server environment. For many others, the move to a graphical user interface from the existing character-based screen needs thorough training and support in user interface design concepts to avoid visual disasters. One such new system I saw recently had so many windows opened at a time that even the experienced operator had no idea of what was happening and at what part of the business process was the current display. The poor user was lost in a sea of windows (what's the collective noun for windows: pane, shatter of windows, reflection of windows?).

7.1.5 Approach to Training

To minimize the risk of the new techniques for object-oriented project, training, and support (Figures 7.2 and 7.3) in the following areas need to be provided:

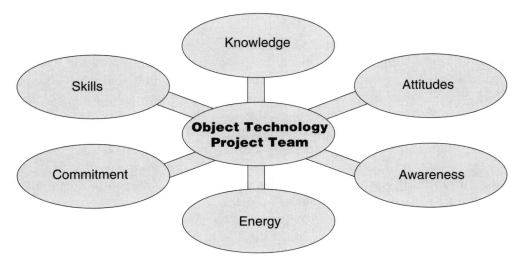

FIGURE 7.2. Training Needs for the Object Technology Team

- *Management.* Self, team, project
- *Technical.* Methodologies, algorithms, languages
- *Quality.* Reviews, walkthroughs, inspection techniques

Team members not only need to understand object technology and develop proficiency, they need to be involved with the management of the project. Evolutionary development, rapid prototyping, joint developments (JADs), libraries of components, etc. are all relatively new concepts to most technologists and the impact on their approach to working must be fully explained. If this is the manager's first object-oriented project, then she or he will also be learning and will make mistakes. Tolerance is needed on both sides.

Learning the concepts of object technology through courses, conferences, and books is the obvious first step, but it is not enough. Real learning takes place on the job, which means developing a significant but noncritical application for the organization. It can also mean joining an existing object-oriented project as an apprentice to become proficient. There is no substitute for attempting to apply the object principles in your own projects; courses may have workshops and hands-on sessions, but they are teaching examples selected to be simply understood and to reinforce a particular topic. By the way, don't choose a course that does not have working sessions; all evidence shows that attendees remember

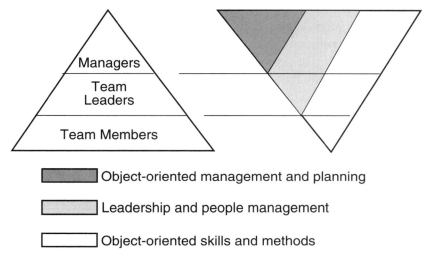

Object-oriented management and planning

Leadership and people management

Object-oriented skills and methods

FIGURE 7.3. Training Needs Throughout the Organization

only 10% of chalk and talk courses, whereas courses that have workshops and hands-on sessions push understanding to over 50%, which with coaching and further support will quickly lead to proficiency.

Generally, most organizations choose the language courses for their chosen development language: C++, Objective-C, Turbo PASCAL, Smalltalk, CLOS, Lisp, etc. Again, such courses lay out the principle concepts, semantics, and syntax of the language, which usually can be learned in a few days as many are extensions to existing languages—Smalltalk is an obvious exception. Becoming proficient in these languages, especially more complex languages such as C++ and Lisp, can take some considerable time.

Object-oriented development is much more than the syntax of the language. It involves design heuristics, performance trade-offs, library extensions, etc., all of which can take considerable time to grasp. For example, you can learn Smalltalk in roughly three days, but it may take up to six months to fully comprehend the extensive library of classes. Learning the library of classes, in all languages and from all suppliers is slow. I really want to emphasize this point: *learning the library takes time.* There is no way you can speed up that process. Sitting and reading the documentation (for the Microsoft Foundation Classes there is four inches of paper contained in two books) or even using the present browsers does not lead to knowledge; it leads only to class blindness. One practical approach to this problem is to allocate sections (branches) of the class library to individual team members to explore, experiment and comprehend. Then to hold regular—even daily—project design reviews to ensure that classes are not being reinvented. Over time the object technology team will have a broad understanding of the complete and expanding library.

One of the most common questions asked is: "which object-oriented language do you recommend?" The problem is that the reply often offends so many programmers. Let's begin by saying that a language is only a language, a method of communicating instructions to a machine. Computer languages are designed for particular reasons: LOGO is for young programmers, BASIC was originally for hobbyist, ADA for real-time safety-critical systems, PASCAL for teaching, C for systems programming, COBOL for business applications, LISP for expert systems, and so on. We all have those that we favor and those that we loath; personal opinions color our judgment.

If you are developing infrastructure-type systems (i.e., operating systems, toolsets, graphical applications, communications products), C++ is an obvious choice. There can be problems however, for the C programmer who has recently learned the object-oriented concepts will often fall back to writing traditional C code at the first opportunity. But why are developers of business applications using a systems programming language? Why is the next accounting and personnel record system being developed in C++? To use the class libraries? Because C++ is object orientation? Because everyone else is using it?

Programmers used to COBOL and other business languages such as 4GLs have an awful time trying to come to grips with the complexities of C++. It used to be said of C that it gave enough rope for programmers to hang themselves; now many are saying that C++ is a short length of cheesewire! C and C++ are *system* programming languages. They are really not appropriate for most business applications; C++ is not an application-development language. I can hear the howls from the technologists. C++ can be used in any domain, but whether your staff can come to grips with its complexity is another matter. Languages such as Object COBOL are available and a number of middleware products provide the object architecture combined with an object request broker (ORB) but allow the objects to be written in COBOL, REXX, etc. as well as C and , C++.*

Managers of business application development must consider carefully the choice of object-oriented programming language. Choosing a language is not to

---

* An example of such a product is "New World Infrastructure—Newi," from Integrated Object Systems, Albion House, Oxford Street , Newbury RG13 IJE, England; telephone +44 1635 522 600.

be taken lightly and is difficult to change once a number of significant applications have been developed.

One recommendation is that managers and programmers exploring object technology learn Smalltalk. This is not to suggest that Smalltalk is better than C++ or any other languages, but it is a true object-oriented language and as such moves programmers out of their comfort zone as they are unable to write in their more normal style.

One final point about language training. We all grasp concepts and new techniques at different rates, so some form of support, say, a telephone hotline or a local technical expert, must be provided. Without this support, much of the early object system will need to be reworked or even scrapped. There is a school of thought that believes that making these mistakes is crucial to the learning process. This is a fundamental truth, so don't find it out on an important new object-oriented system. Find it out through noncritical applications or through reviews and walkthroughs with experienced coaches in object technology.

The final element of training is in reviewing techniques for the major deliverables of the evolving system: object models, class code, test plans, etc. Much has been written about reviews, walkthroughs, and inspections, and it is beyond the scope of this book to cover such material, except to say that all the techniques and process that you have in place for your traditional development approach can be adapted to fit the object-oriented development method (e.g., see Freedman & Weinberg, 1982). The differing models: problem domain, solution domain, and system domain models (e.g., coding) have documentation and deliverables that can be reviewed in a formal documented, comprehensive, and systematic examination. This will

- identify errors and problems,

- suggest better methods and possible solutions,

- ensure that standards and practices are followed,

- provide impersonal constructive criticism of the material under review,

- ensure that knowledge and experience is shared.

Reviews, walkthroughs, and inspections are expensive in time and resources, but without them you cannot be confident of the quality of the delivered system.

7.1.6 Choosing Training Courses

Training courses generally fall into three categories:

- *General technical.* Involves the teaching of skills in the technology and/or the business domain (e.g., accountancy, insurance, utility operations, etc.); usually this is through commercially available courses or organized by the company itself.*

- *Company-specific.* Covers such things as company information procedures, chosen methodologies, language style, documentation formats, etc. These courses will always be done by in-house experts—managers, skilled experienced personnel, training specialists—and their importance has more to do with creating a sense of identity and commitment to professional values and quality standards.

- *Individual-specific programs.* Cover courses such as presentation skills, part-time professional qualifications, personal development programs, and team building. These may be provided by the organization, but are often organized through outside agencies.

When selecting a commercially available course from a brochure, ask the following questions:

What are the objectives of the course?	What will the students be able to *do* when they have completed the training?
Is the course at the right level?	Do you need an overview, introduction, complete course or all three?
What prior knowledge does the course assume?	Teaching C++ to a COBOL programmer may not yield the desired result.
What is the quality of the instruction?	Is the trainer a full-time teacher or an experienced practitioner as an associate teacher?
What are the practical facilities?	Does everyone get their own terminal?

---

* Lists of commercially available training course appear regularly in the *Journal of Object Oriented Programming* (JOOP), SIGS Publications.

Is it possible to see the training material?	Is the material up-to-date and is it comprehensive enough to act as resource after the course?
What after-training support is there?	Can clarification and help be sought?
How long does the course last?	Typically an overview is one day, introduction is two days and a complete course is four or five days.
How much will it cost?	Not only for the course, but the accommodation, transport, subsistence, and the lost resource.
How large are the classes?	Too large a group will reduce the effectiveness of the workshops; seek 10 to 15 as a maximum.

7.1.7 Creating Technical Specialists

It's well known that understanding comes from a cycle of show, try, and teach. You are shown how to do an activity, you try it out, and then you attempt to teach others from your newly acquired knowledge. It is in this latter step—teach—that you formalize and develop your own comprehension of a subject.

Therefore, a further form of training is the identification of technical specialists. These specialists—ask for volunteers—will be responsible for examining all the available literature (>500 pages) of a particular subject of current or future interest to the development organization. Areas where technical specialists would be valuable are method improvements, commercial class libraries, communications protocols, standards, inspection techniques, algorithms, tool development, programming language extensions, etc. Following this research, the technical specialist provides a short training course to the team or group within one month of the assignment start. From then on the specialist monitors developments in his or her particular area and provides expert advice to teams and involvement in reviews and walk-throughs.

Every team member should be a nominated specialist in at least one technical area.

7.1.8 More than Technical Skills Needed

So much for the basic technical skills. What about the human and conceptual skills that are becoming recognized as more important than technical competence? Japanese companies, for example, stress the importance of the human and conceptual skills of their workers and have adopted a culture to encourage their development. Some of the skills can be taught in a classroom, but the emphasis is on practice with regular reviews and comments from peers and co-workers.

High on the conceptual skills list is the ability to abstract useful components for use now and in the future. Abstraction involves the process of generalization and specialization on a set of classes under design or more often those classes created from recent work on an application. This latter process is often called *scavenging*, a bad name, really, as it implies searching among discarded items for something useful. Hopefully, the classes are not discarded and what is found proves to be exceptionally useful for the future. Most developers can abstract to some degree, but with object technology this skill is very important (Figure 7.4).

The most important human skill is the ability to communicate; examine every job advertisement and you will find "ability to communicate," "excellent communication skills required," "verbal and written command of the [English] language," etc.

Have you and your staff gone on a presentation skills course? There are many such inexpensive courses available today, ranging from the chalk-and-talk

Traditional Thinking
mathematical
algorithmic
functional
logical

Object-Oriented Thinking
simulation
objects
messages
environment

FIGURE 7.4. It Depends on How You Think!

style with a notebook to full interactive video coaching. Such skills in presenting are needed by everyone involved in development.

Communication is required with the other team members—remember, if they don't know what's happening, they could really mess up each others' work—and these discussions can lead to exchanges of ideas, classes, and skills (Table 7.1). Communication is also required with the users. Object technology has this close link with the users as it models their world of business objects, so user representatives need to be part of the development team. Communication between developers and users has always been a difficult area. Many developers, especially programmers, are happier talking to machines rather than people. And users are difficult to deal with: they can't decide what is wanted, they change their minds, they expect everything yesterday, they [insert your favorite phrase here].

One of the lessons with object technology is never to ignore the users. They are still the customers of the development process. In these days of customer care, the thinly disguised contempt shown by certain developers toward the users cannot be tolerated.

7.2 The Users

Users themselves are not blameless. They need also to be skilled in communication, they need to be able to conceptualize, they need to understand their own business area and the knowledge it contains. All too often the user representative on the development team is someone who is the least busy or who can be most easily seconded onto the team. This may be because they are inept, about

Table 7.1. Communication for Cross Fertilization	
Objectives	**Approaches**
Exchange ideas and techniques	Informal visits Supplier councils
Provide mutual encouragement	Customer/user groups Professional groups
Inspire high achievement	Peer audits

to move to another area, or, worse, have recently joined the organization. Yet it is the harassed individual who is often the only one who understands the full business process, who knows where it is failing, and who will accept help from any source—they want to make it better. It is such user representatives who can really turn a basic solution into one that has a major impact on the business as a whole.

A powerful new method of communication is the advent of Joint Application Development (JAD) technique, where developers sit down with the users and, using whiteboards, flipcharts, and a computer with appropriate software, develop requirements and early prototypes together. Can you see the rush of developers for the back room in your organization? For others, of course, JAD is long overdue.

Most of you will have experienced "over the wall" communications: users write specifications, throw them over the wall to the analysts, who throw the requirement analysis models over the wall to the designers, who throw. . . . Communication is by missive, understanding is low. JAD breaks down these boundaries. Using users as domain experts, the needs and desires are captured as requirements, analyzed and logical designs produced for the various object models. Various techniques usually associated with the chosen methodology are used to elicit the requirements from the customer/user experts. Traditional requirements suffer from ambiguity, vagueness, conflicting requirements, solution specifications, and numerous other forms of inaccuracy.

Object technology breaks the cycle with the iterative and incremental development approach. The movement is from the known to the unknown parts of the requirements. Object technology supports modeling the real world, but modern businesses want to create a new world, so users are unaware of the possibilities of the new approach. These possibilities can be explored by building rapid prototypes with the users in JAD sessions.

Initially the focus is on developing concrete scenarios of the business models using large whiteboards (more than one helps) and tools such as CRC cards to capture behavior for the classes (Beck & Cunningham, 1989). In my experience, users easily relate to CRC cards and become eager to complete initial specifications (Figure 7.5). It does not matter initially that the model lacks abstractions: generalizations and specialization, these come later in more formal design stages.

The computer may be used for rapid prototyping with the users, but more often it is used only by a junior member of the team acting as a scribe to the JAD team. This scribe captures the decisions and the diagrams from the whiteboard using simple technology such as diagramming tools and word processors; a word processor with outline mode is ideal.

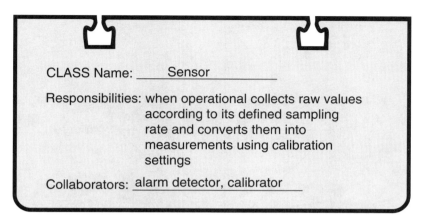

FIGURE 7.5. Example of a CRC Card

JAD workshops bring the users into the development cycle early in the process.

7.3 The Manager

So far, the focus has been on the developers and the users. What about the skills of the managers, your skills? All managers need to be able to deal with the "devils' square" (Figure 7.6), which encompasses the small set of crucial factors that affect every project:

- *Scope.* What will be delivered?
- *Schedule.* When it will be delivered?
- *Cost.* How much it will cost to be delivered?
- *Quality.* How good it will be on delivery?
- *Productivity.* How effective will the resources be during development?
- *Risk.* How likely these targets will not be met?

As risk affects all the factors, and productivity is the ratio of quality and scope to schedule and cost, there are only really four critical factors: scope, schedule, cost, and quality. These form the Devil's Square (Muxworthy, 1990).

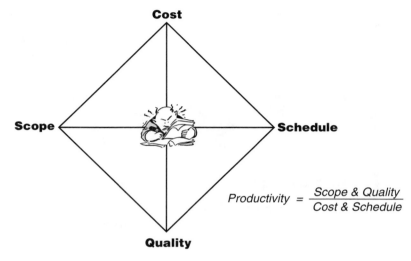

$$Productivity = \frac{Scope \ \& \ Quality}{Cost \ \& \ Schedule}$$

FIGURE 7.6. The Devil's Square

Each corner of the square is one of the critical factors. At the outset of the project all the planning effort goes into getting these into balance. Imagine this square on a pointed fulcrum in the center; each of the four key factors need then to be balanced to achieve a successful project (Figure 7.7) Given what has to be built, sufficient resources and time need to be provided by the organization. Your job as manager is to gather the information, make value judgments, and adjust the factors to satisfy all the constraints. One major constraint is the expectation about the quality of the delivered object system.

Quality is normally fixed and is always assumed to be the least flexible of the critical factors; the customer demands high quality, managers expect it, developers want to provide it. Yet quality is the constant topic on most manager's lips: "we must improve quality," "the quality is not good enough," "make sure the quality is high." Quality improvement is the most common reason for the adoption of any new technology. Why is your organization using or evaluating object technology? I bet that quality improvements is in the list.

Why this problem with quality? The answer lies in the other three corners of the Devil's Square.

When more functionality is required, either the schedule must be adjusted or more resources (cost) provided. If these corners remain the same, the square is out of balance and the only compensation to reassert the equilibrium can be from the quality corner. Quality is always driven down when any of the other corners are altered without matching adjustment of the others. A shorter

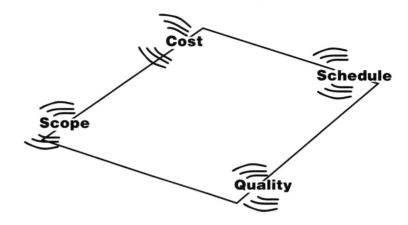

FIGURE 7.7. Balancing the Devil's Square

schedule means less scope can be provided. Shortage of resources through unavailability means either a longer timeframe or a reduced scope. "Creeping elegance" means more resources or a longer time. Any and all of the adjustments makes the assumption that quality is fixed and inflexible. Yet if these compensatory adjustments are not made, the quality will suffer.

It is a fundamental rule: if any change is made to the scope, schedule, or cost without adjustment to the other two factors, quality will be affected.

It's self-evident. Change any factor without adjustment of the others, and quality will fall. This raises a serious question over many so-called quality initiatives. If the manager actually managed the scope, schedule, and cost effectively, most of the quality problems would disappear!

Why is it called the devil's square? It's the devil's own job to keep it in balance!

7.3.1 Fundamental Skills

All management involves these key activities and the skills necessary to support them:

- *Plan*. Define schedule, costs, quality, and resources
- *Monitor*. Progress, detect deviations, execute corrective actions
- *Report*. Progress, problems
- *Manage change*. Specifications, schedules, resource costs, staff

Unfortunately, individual managers tend to favor the planning activities. They seem to feel that the more planning involved, the more certainty that "all will be well." The iterative and incremental delivery approach throws this detailed planning into question. There needs to be a schedule, there needs to be a resource allocation—preferably on a skill profile—there needs to be a quality plan. But there is a distinct tendency with object systems to over-plan at the component level. Can you really be sure in 16 weeks time that Joe Brown will be working on such-and-such component and it will be completed at 12.30 PM on Thursday? Of course not! Yet look at your own plans—are they fantasies? Are they subject to change tomorrow or next week? Are all the components identified? A poor plan is better than no plan, but detailed planning is not relevant to iterative and incremental delivery development.

The manager's focus needs to be on the user deliverables and the execution of delivery. This means hands-on management, not "get on with it and report to me next week." The faster development cycle of object systems may mean that next week is too late for responding to problems with the delivery. You must know what is happening—managing by wandering around (MBWA) is the obvious method (Peters & Austin, 1985). When you find something happening that could be a potential problem, executing corrective action is a priority. Too many organizations report on the slippages in projects and then take no further action. First and foremost action must be considered and then executed, otherwise the situation with this faster development cycle will turn a minor delay into a major delivery crisis.

Further basic skills for managers include developing an awareness of the changes in the business environment—skills in diagnosing new situations, devising solutions for the new situations, applying these solutions, and adapting them according to feedback then drawing upon the experiences for the future. This role is that of analyst and researcher of the organizational environment. Assessment of the technical capabilities, the organizational support and the areas of conflict is necessary before embarking on new development processes. The dynamics of the work processes within development and the relations with the other sections of the organization need to be fully evaluated to determine the impact of the proposed changes. Have you got such skills?

As the project manager you will need skills in specifying the project and team member goals, developing the schedule, achieving commitments, identifying the controls, monitoring, and reporting on these controls.

SMART goals from Ken Blanchard of *One Minute Manager* fame have already been discussed for goal setting for project teams in Chapter 6. It is a fundamental part of the process in setting up the team and the major tool in achieving commitment from the team members. Sets of goals are only meaningful if the tracking mechanisms are in place and feedback is given to the team members, otherwise it becomes another good idea lost in the pressures of delivery schedules.

Delivery scheduling means well-developed estimating skills. Although timesheets are often useless, you will need to track the amount of time spent on each stage and task of the development process. Tom DeMarco and Tim Lister on a recent UK course spent much time decrying the estimating skills of the whole IT profession. They said " you will never be a better estimator than you are a tracker of where you spend your time." If the tracking methods are primitive, your estimating skills will also be primitive. Start improving of your estimating skills and those of each team member by setting up proper tracking mechanisms today.

Managers get swamped daily with the hundreds of priorities that need attention and consideration, from authorizing an expenditure claim to outlining next year's development strategy. Much of what has been written here will seem far removed from the chaos of the development activities and so suggest an ideal world. This is the intention. The intention is to alert you to the dangers that will require all your skills to deal with the uncertainty, the perceived messiness, and the speed of object-oriented development. If you continue along traditional project management lines, object technology will fail completely in your organization.

7.4 Skills for Champions

The first thing to say about becoming a champion of object technology—in fact, any new technology—is that it's politically dangerous. Unless you have a high performance track record with some recent successes, or you have been especially hired to "insert" object technology, you may find it very difficult to persuade senior managers to invest in a number of pilot projects as an evaluation and proving ground. You need to gain their trust.

If your organization is new to object technology, selling is an important skill. Object technology needs a champion at all levels: strategic, tactical, and operational. This means a thorough evaluation of the risks, sensible cost benefit analysis of the move to object technology and a commitment to see it through despite the inevitable setbacks. There will be resistance. Change is seen as a threat in many organizations, and there will be a long queue of skeptics, who will remind you that the same arguments were used about structured methods, about using CASE tools, about downsizing, etc. Never underestimate this resistance. The power of veto can stop most projects or if they let you go ahead, the project will be under such scrutiny that anything less than total success will be used as an excuse to abandon object technology.

You may be tempted to raise expectations in the selling process, to exaggerate a little here and there and to avoid mentioning some of the risks, but the skeptics will be out to get you. They will have noted every comment—in writing if possible—and will use it to form the lynch party should you fail to meet expectations.

Many hopeful managers, excited by this new technology fail to get it adopted by the rest of the group for a number of reasons. Firstly, you must understand the technology. Reading is helpful, but short courses, preferably with course work, will significantly increase your knowledge. Concentrate on the analysis and design issues rather than programming, as crucial decisions are made in this area. Secondly, the customer/users must have a significant role in the pilot projects. Their involvement creates a ground-swell of opinion that object technology will solve many of the present development problems: late delivery, inflexibility, etc. As it is often difficult to effect change from the bottom of the organization, the final key component is an executive champion.

Enlist a senior manager to your cause to provide sponsorship and funding for the trials. This executive will argue the business case with the senior executive or board based on one or more of the key issues:

- Return on investment, which is hard to justify until significant trials completed
- Being done by the competitors and so your organization will fall behind
- Improve process automation and effectiveness
- Overcome cross-functional barriers
- Set a forward strategy for future developments
- Cope with business process reengineering
- Reduction of long term development costs
- Alignment of IT and corporate goals
- Managing organizational change

All types of champions will need commitment. There will be setbacks, there will be resistance, and there will be interference. With strong commitment you will be able to overcome all these hurdles. It is said that you need to be a fanatic to get changes in the organization. A fanatic is someone with strong passions and deep commitment; Winston Churchill once described a fanatic as "one who can't change their mind and won't change the subject." Are you a fanatic of object technology?

7.5 Skill Profiling

One of the more radical ways of approaching project management is through skill profiling.

Implied in each job title or job function is a set of skills. Yet experience shows that individuals may be weaker in certain skills and stronger in others. The job title may be the result of a so-called career progression, which in reality is a progression based on increased payments made to retain the employee.

Skill profiling begins by drawing up a register of the skills valued by your organization. These skills can be categorized in a number of ways (e.g., technical, project management, interpersonal, people management, and business knowledge). For example, the ability to design object-based user interfaces, would appear under technical skills, and the ability to work in small teams would appear under interpersonal skills. While the computer industry has a number of generalized skill models, each organization will have its own subset and own specializations.

Based on this skill register each employee draws up his or her own skills profile. Managers do the same for each of their employees. Any discrepancies—there always are differences—can then be discussed and resolved between the two parties. This is a very powerful process not to be taken lightly or skipped to avoid possible confrontation. Not only are managers alerted to the real training needs of employees, employees recognize their own shortcomings and usually embark on their own improvement programs. Career development plans and company assessments naturally result from this assessment process.

In a similar manner, the skills required in each task of a project are defined. These are the task profiles. The project is broken down into tasks and task-related activities; skill profiles for each of these task activities are then defined. Initially this is a considerable amount of work, but once these task profiles are developed they can be used on future projects with minor changes to reflect the new objectives.

The project tasks are normally grouped into the incremental delivery phases within the defined timeframes. This then gives an overall skills profile for the complete project cycle (i.e., what skills are needed and when they are needed.)

By matching the task profile and employee profiles, the most suitable candidates with the relevant skills are found. If the match process is unable to identify suitable candidates then managers are alerted to any forthcoming tasks where internal resources are unable to cope. This skills shortfall can then be tackled through training or the use of external contractors who are chosen for their suitable skills.

Staffing each activity of the project with the person with the most relevant skills, means that the activity is undertaken in the most efficient manner and that the employee is tied up for shorter periods on any one project cycle. Therefore the manager achieves greater flexibility in planning the staffing of the projects and the effort is worthwhile when the schedules and budgets are met through the right skills being employed in a timely manner.

Busy managers need computer-based tools to help with skills management. There are personnel development tools such as Development Needs Analysis (DNA)* and myriad project management tools, but few if any, handle this approach to managing projects. Such tools are urgently needed by managers to improve their own staff management skills.

It has been reported that the staff management skills of 60% of IT managers are poor or worse, while project and systems managers don't pay enough attention to managing their staff. By changing from managing human resources to skills management, managers become engaged in identifying and developing the talents of their staff. They also become keenly aware of the hopes and aspirations of each and every member of their staff. Staff motivation improves as their skills are recognized, as they enjoy using these skills—we all like to do what we do best—and as they learn new skills as part of their career development.

7.6 Summary

Object technologists must know the technology. This may seem obvious, but it means more than knowing the language. It means developing strong analysis

---

* Development Needs Analysis (DNA) from Mast Learning Systems, 26 Warwick Road, London SW5 9UD telephone +44 171 373 949 is a computer-based system to identify training and development needs for relevant industries.

and design skills based on abstraction techniques to produce the object models. The different approach to object modeling and the different skills needed for rapid application development (RAD) need to be available in the object-oriented project team. Knowing a single language is not enough; knowledge of tools, methods, and environment are all required. This may lead to the creation of the role of a technical specialist whose responsibility is to develop expertise in a particular area relevant to the development organization.

Object-oriented project managers need to adapt their skills for planning, goal setting, monitoring, and reporting. New project lifecycles and product deliverables make these changes necessary. Management of the three corners of the devil's square—scope, schedule, and cost—will ensure that the critical corner for quality will not suffer as a result. If you have become the champion of object technology, you will need to develop your skill as a salesperson while at the same time avoiding over-selling the benefits so as not to create expectations that are too high. You will need to seek a sponsor at the highest level to gain their commitment to the process of changing the way you work for object technology. You will also need to involve your users in the new technology so that they can contribute fully to the success of the project. One way the ensure that success is to develop profiles of skills for your team members (including users) and then match the individual to the task.

It's through planned skill development that your object-oriented projects will become successful. The effective manager of object-oriented projects will care about peoples talents and give those people the chance to perform at the highest level.

References

Beck, K., and W. Cunningham. (1989). A laboratory for teaching object-oriented thinking. *SIGPLAN* Notices, 24, 10.

Casse, P. (1989). Managing people's talents: the leadership challenge of the 1990s. *International Institute for Management Development*, 5.

DeMarco, T., and T. Lister. (1994) *Controlling Software Projects: Management, Measurement, and Estimation.* Technology Transfer Institute of London.

Freedman, D., and G. Weinberg. (1982). *Handbook of Walkthroughs, Inspections, and Technical Reviews.* New York: Little, Brown.

Muxworthy, B. (1990). *Project*, Sept.

Peters, T., and N. Austin. (1985). A *Passion for Excellence.* New York: Random House; London: William Collins.

CHAPTER 8

SHARED VALUES

W HEN THE VALUES OF AN ORGANIZATION CONFLICT WITH THE VALUES OF an individual, tremendous turmoil is created, usually within the individual. If the mismatch persists, the increasing dissatisfaction generally leads to disaffection with the organization and subsequent resignation. Value clashes are one of the most common reasons for individuals to leave a company. Many managers will say that the main reason is salary or the compensation package. This may be the declared statement in the resignation letter, but this is confusing cause and effect. The cause is a mismatch in the perceived worth of the individual's contribution by the organization and that perceived by the individual. The worker no longer feels valued within the organization and decides to leave. Other workers with similar compensation packages stay. Why? Obviously there are as many answers as there are workers, but the underlying reason is that they stay because they still feel valued by the organization. And to feel valued, the culture of the organization supports them in their professional aspirations and personal needs.

This chapter begins with an examination of the limitations of corporate goals and objectives as seen by the individual or project team. It then covers the effect of the organizational culture on shared values; such as matching values to strategy and overcoming the three perennial concerns that affect the value systems.

Value systems of an object-oriented organization include a focus on customer service, building on reuse, empowering of teams, embracing change, making a culture of quality, and encouraging innovation; these are all looked at in detail.

8.1 Corporate Goals and Objectives

Most of the time we accept such things as mission statements and objectives as long as they do not interfere with our own objectives or the corporate objectives that we, as managers, have been trying to implement. Someone whose determination to overcome problems was admired when these were in line with the corporate goals, suddenly becomes "misguided" or "obstinate" when they direct that energy into something else. When a change of values happens to an individual— and that change can be dramatic and sudden— the individual appears "not to be themselves." They have changed. Even more worrying, they can as easily change back!

Corporate goals and objectives seem to work only over a short period. For a time everyone has a common purpose and will put aside their own personal goals for some group goal. But this is only temporary. Eventually, and in a surprisingly short timeframe, the personal ego will dominate and reestablish itself within the individual.

There is also a clash in the goals that come from the differing perspectives of the people involved in the project: customers, technologists, and managers. Customers want the product or system to work, to meet their needs, and if possible to get it when promised. Managers want project control and deliveries on time and within budgetary limits. Software developers seek a technical challenge and the latest innovations. Customers are not interested in the technical challenge, the speed of the processor, or how many classes were built, they want it to work and do what they specified at the start. These differing perspectives lie at the root of most conflicts in organizations.

For the developer the newness of object technology is a great motivator, but after more than ten years is it still new? These new techniques and approaches generate enthusiasm and excitement. This vigor will drive the organization forward for a certain length of time. Then the excitement fades, and the commitment falls when a number of problems happen or when the much-sought benefits are less than expected. Disillusionment then sets in and this suppression of the personal for corporate aims passes. This is often true when small groups grow into larger organizations. The commitment gets diluted, the aims become unclear, and people start to work at cross-purposes.

For object technologists, a successful series of pilot projects developed by a committed team of individuals will encourage their spread throughout the organization. But in spreading, the seeds of future disasters may be sown. The determined team, working closely together with a common purpose is very powerful. However, it is temporary and may not be suitable for all organizations.

8.2 Understanding Organizational Culture

The culture of the organization—a nebulous cloud of attitudes, perceptions, styles, and values—has a profound effect on the workers within it. Yet how many managers take time to assess the culture, to actively develop and change it, to recognize when value clashes occur?

Culture is all-pervasive yet difficult to define. But defining culture is one of the first steps in establishing the shared values—what is important—for the workers. This is usually done through articulation, often in the form of a mission statement, and by examples shown by senior and middle managers. In many ways shared values is one of the "bookends" for a mature organization—the other is strategy (Figure 8.1) The shared values reflect many aspects of the

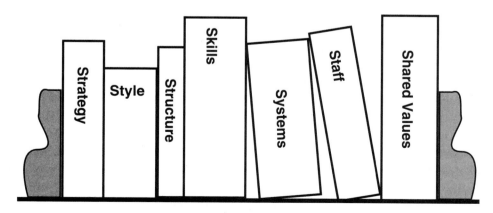

FIGURE 8.1. The Bookends of Strategy and Shared Values

strategy statements. When they don't, the organization is in for a rough time. If one of the strategy statements refers to high quality, the culture of quality must be imbued throughout the organization. Similarly, if the focus is on innovation, then the culture of experimentation, a tolerance for mistakes, etc. are necessary to create a suitable working environment.

Culture encourages the absorption of new concepts and sets expectations, but it is a fragile thing. Some of you will have experienced a take-over of your company by another with different values. In a matter of days, a carefully nurtured and living culture is destroyed. One manager at a large UK bank recently recounted his experience. Their past culture considered that technology was a powerful tool to be used to the benefit of the worker, hence high-specification equipment was provided. This allowed effective operations and provided computing facilities for expansion in the future. Following a take-over by a major competitor, one of the new senior managers had all machines replaced (within 24 hours) with simpler, slower workhorse computers. What do you think was the new value system in operation? Reduce costs of capital equipment and ignore the frustrations and time delays suffered by the staff with the poorer equipment. You can all guess what the resultant atmosphere and the attitude of the workers was like. Many of you will also be able to guess at the subsequent staff turnover.

Robert Townsend in *Up the Organization* stated that the real cost of relocating offices is not in the cost of the move itself, but in the subsequent turnover of staff (Townsend, 1970). If you have a high staff turnover, with allowances for the current economic climate, something is wrong. Look to your company values and to your culture.

Replacing machines is an extreme example of a clash of cultures, but it is more often the case that the culture is too slow to change. This is usually an attribute of large organizations where technology supports the prime business areas (e.g., utilities). Such organizations usually have a long history and move cautiously forward into new areas. There are always examples of brief excursions on ill-advised attempts to diversify. Changing these cultures is particularly difficult. They need to have a receptiveness to new technology itself. In fact, I believe that many of these organizations will fail in using object technology. The whole ethos of evolutionary prototyping is beyond their understanding. It can take such organizations three years to produce a functional specification, so to produce at least 24 deliveries of the product in the same time span is inconceivable. Perhaps if you work for one such organization you should reconsider your future: can you really make it work?

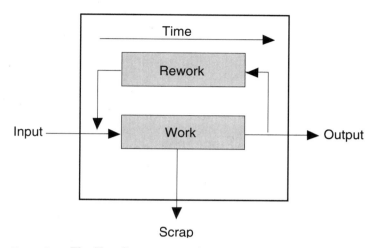

FIGURE 8.2. The Key Components of a Development Process

As I've shown in the devils square (Chapter 7) the four main concerns are scope, schedule, cost, and quality. Scope and schedule tend to lie in the domain of the client or customer. Cost and quality are perennial concerns that have a major effect on the shared values of any organization. Every development process has input (the costs), uses time as a measure of throughput, and evaluates the output for quality (Figure 8.2). These are then translated into various measurements of the performance of the process. For example:

- *Costs.* Labor costs, materials, productivity
- *Throughput.* Process time, number of components delivered, number added to library
- *Quality.* Defects, scrap, rework

"Control costs" (contain, reduce, eliminate), "improve throughput" (shorter delivery times, deliver more), "increase quality" (reduce number of defects, no scrap and little rework) are continual messages from the top team. These can be achieved in software development only by increasing productivity and improving the quality of the delivered components. Back to the concept of the software factory!

How are these perennial messages applied to the shared value system for object technology? The elements of the shared value system are

- focusing on customer service,

- building on reuse,

- empowerment of teams,

- embracing change,

- making a culture of quality,

- encouraging innovation,

Let's look at each in detail.

8.3 Service to Customers

It's no accident that service to customers comes first on the list of shared values. Over the many years of examining software development organizations, one of the most common attitudes encountered is a thinly disguised contempt for the customers. This is outrageous. It shows an arrogance by the technologists as well as a disregard of the fact that their salaries are paid by an eventual customer. They may be developing an accounting system rather than a spreadsheet product, inventory management reporting systems rather than a new computer-controlled machine tool, but the business exists to supply a customer. Even public and not-for-profit organizations have a customer who pays for the product in taxes or insurance premiums. By far the worst examples of thinly disguised contempt is shown by development groups that make internal deliveries to other business functions within their own organization. Software companies, product developers, and system suppliers have a more pragmatic approach as without sufficient levels of sales they will quickly be out of work. Internal IT developers are at last realizing that their work could be outsourced, privatized, or lost in a round of competitive tendering. Their future has become uncertain.

Peter Drucker expressed the concept best when he wrote, "Results depend not on anyone within the business. Results depend on somebody outside—the customer. It is the customer who decides whether the efforts of a business become economic results or whether they become so much waste and scrap" (Drucker, 1989). Have you ever delivered scrap?

Who is your customer? What service do you provide to them? Is customer service critical to the business and therefore to the IT that supports it? Is IT on the critical path holding back further business developments? All are key questions.

The boss of the organization or department who pays for the product or system is not the customer. He or she is the client and while important—anyone who pays the bills is important—the user is the customer. The customer/user of your object-based system is the one to satisfy. Think about it—who does the client ask if the system is satisfactory? Their staff, their team members, their workers—your end-user. Satisfy those customers and you will also find your own staff to be satisfied. Exceed the customer's expectations; object systems break the mold from the current character-based applications that the majority of users see. Give the screen "sizzle," make it easy to use, add extra functionality to the cooperative business objects over and above that in the specification. With the flexible and adaptable nature of objects, this is easy to achieve without spending vast resources.

Modern business practice is moving toward partnerships between suppliers and customers. Can you arrange to be partners with your customers? Can you not only get users onto your development team permanently, but be able to have your own development staff work alongside the users in their place of business? If you can do this, the object-oriented approach to system constructions will yield major intangible benefits:

- Greater customer satisfaction through richly featured systems
- Enhanced corporate or development group image owing to outstanding service
- Greater productivity with use of well-proven components
- Higher morale of your customers by your groups' responsiveness and innovation
- Higher morale of your staff from customer satisfaction.

These benefits become a flywheel to further levels of exceptional customer service.

8.4 Building on Reuse

Two of the most publicized benefits of object technology are improved quality and increased productivity. While it is true that quality improvements can be made through preventing defects by using pretested and proven components, detecting defects is still left to the developers. Object languages and development environments are still primitive in this area; a component may be fully validated and verified, but who can test the "glue" that holds the components together as a system?

However, the focus is on the costs and implications of increasing productivity. Even with object technology, programmers still have to design and write code segments. This we can assume will be done at similar rates as before, therefore, the only way that productivity can be increased is through reuse of existing components. In fact there are increasing reports that in the early days of adopting object technology, productivity drops significantly. Some of this drop is due to the steep learning curve, but much of the lost productivity is due to extra effort required to form the abstractions: generalizations and specializations.

Reuse does not happen automatically, nor is it without a cost.

Reuse has been practiced by some programmers for many years. Code segments, routines, and modules have been part of the toolkit of individuals, and sometimes teams have pooled these components to build libraries for a particular set of applications. There are also many libraries of procedures and functions available for the non-object oriented programmer (e.g., math functions, statistical routines, etc.). The most famous is the NAG library, available in a wide range of languages.

Reuse in object terms can mean a number of things:

- Code reuse by cut and paste will give some leverage but obviously increases the maintenance overhead considerably in tracking the copied code segments.

- Component reuse is what is commonly considered as the principle of object-oriented reuse.

- Design reuse can be very powerful as it builds a common logical model of the business domains.

- Architecture reuse provides patterns of components creating powerful system frameworks.

Another form of reuse is that of the "brain cycles" of the programmer and designer. Hardware costs are reducing considerably whereas staff costs are rising, so any improvement of the brain cycles will result in cost savings. Trading cheap machine cycles for expensive brain cycles means using the computer to mechanize or at least semimechanize the software process. Tools such as syntax-directed editors, which support both the specification and the implementation constructs, can make a significant difference (Bar-David, 1993 and Wills, 1992).

But creating reusable components is difficult.

It's actually easier *not* to develop for reuse! The class under development will satisfy the main application at hand. If it needs to be reused, input from other application teams may need to be sought. This then may cause delays in the present project. Furthermore, who can predict the future requirements for a class? Finally, if many instances of the class are to be used in numerous other applications, the class code needs to be of the very highest quality. To transfer the quality requirements to the provider of the components seems a good move, but this implies that the component supplier can deliver to the expected high quality. Many organizations have had such assumptions dashed in poor quality class components. Counting the cost of poor quality components is not for the faint-hearted.

This leads to the next issue: reuse does not come free.

It takes time. Experience shows that the best classes comes from actual applications development, so you need to wait until classes have been produced before evaluating the candidates and reworking to add to the library. Furthermore, it takes three to seven attempts to reuse a class for it to become sufficiently generic to be useful for all future cases. This means that there has to be a significant number of projects delivered for the class library to be useful and yield the productivity increases expected. This raises a question: if classes require several iterations to get right, how can commercial class libraries exist? Currently most of the commercially available class libraries are focused on software engineering, such as low level components. In the future, it will be a great challenge to provide off-the-shelf class libraries for specific domains that are usable in the first version.

There can be significant costs in developing reusable classes, costs in extra efforts and costs in extended schedules. Project managers can be less than keen to provide reusable classes for others when the extra work delays their own projects. Would you delay your product delivery to provide a more reusable class? Of course not, because when it comes to deliveries, the customer always wins.

In addition to the cost issues, there are other more hidden barriers.

Programmers are at the top of the list. They are notorious for not using other people's software unless in a "packaged" form, such as operating systems, word processors, function libraries, etc. As there are few metrics on quality that can be applied to the new class libraries, programmers generally remain suspicious of one another's code.

The object-oriented language itself may not even support genericity. When reduced to the essential, classes contain data structures that rarely can be expressed other than as a strong type. Strong data typing protects the programmer and the compiler, but gets in the way of some forms of genericity. C++ class designers have to decide which member functions should be polymorphic, whereas in other object-oriented languages, all methods are polymorphic.

Even the available class libraries from suppliers have their problems. There are no standards on aspects such as error reporting, so it can be very difficult to mix classes from libraries from different vendors. Clashes in the namespace (similar class names such as `get_char`) are especially frustrating, although newer products are overcoming this problem. For example, C++ is being extended with the concept of namespaces:

```
Library1:: object object1
Library2:: object object2
```

Many class libraries are huge, and with the current ineffectual browsing tools, it can be very difficult to find suitable classes. Much relies upon the documentation provided as part of the class information. This information needs some form of context or semantic filtering facilities to reduce the scope of interest.

How do managers improve productivity through reuse?

There are four key elements: phased introduction, class library organization, team structures, and the most difficult of all—establishing a new culture where the "library becomes the language."

Reuse needs to be introduced in phases (Figure 8.3). The first phase is reuse by an individual. This is often based on commercial or public domain libraries. These are in effect extensions to the individual's toolkit for object-oriented programming. The danger is that an individual's new classes are simply added into the library for the group without any quality or genericity checks. This situation manifests itself in class libraries that have thousands of components from many contributors, few of which are used more than once. The situation becomes more chaotic as more and more classes are added to the library; it becomes increasingly difficult to find suitable classes, so another is developed, added to the library, and the cycle is repeated until few classes are used more than once.

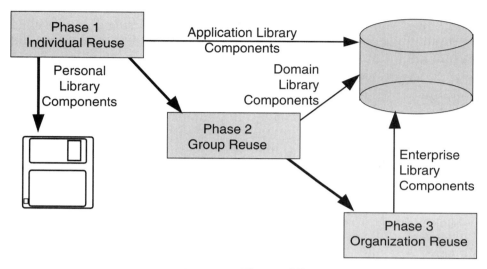

FIGURE 8.3. Phases of Reuse

The next step is reuse at the group level.

The term *group* is used to indicate a business or infrastructure domain. Business groups imply functions such as accounts, engineering, manufacturing, etc. These groups will have libraries that contain classes that reflect their business operations: account number, drawing number, and job number will all be different. Infrastructure groups develop special classes that support the computing environment of an organization, such as real-time, networking, etc. These sets of components are grouped into domain libraries. For effective use of the shared libraries, there needs to be some form of group working software—groupware—to make managing reusable components easy and straightforward.

When mass reuse is introduced throughout the organization or enterprise, the enterprise library will be quite small. If one thinks of the classes that are company-wide, such as customer, employee, product, etc., it will be realized that there are not that many. But those classes that are in this class library really need to be of the highest quality and have the most genericity.

Figure 8.4 shows a profile of the distribution of classes in the various libraries highlighting an emphasis on the domain libraries: GUIs, communications, sales, ledgers, etc., rather than a general class library. The enterprise library provides the foundation business classes (e.g., employee, customer, calendar) used by many of the domains, some of which are used in numerous applications. A

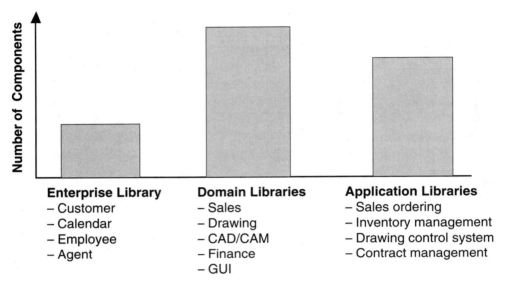

FIGURE 8.4. Distribution of Classes in Libraries

change to an enterprise library item may have a profound impact on many of the domains and applications. For new applications only components in relevant domains need to be examined.

Quality components are crucial to success of the enterprise and domain libraries. If poor quality components are ever delivered, the library will be condemned forever. A host of cynics are ready to show that such an approach does not work, so don't release these components too early.

Library components must also have high performance—efficient use of memory, speed of execution—as these things are still important. Many a novice developer is horrified when in loading a new class they find large amounts of memory lost through the deep hierarchy required to support the one class. Add to performance, robustness, reliability, maintainability, portability, and flexibility, and you gain some idea why building "good" classes is expensive.

There must be more to the library than simply a "good thing," so a crucial element to successful reuse of components is the development culture. This culture has to be one where reuse, rather than creation, is the normal method of development. Such a culture takes time to be adopted, so it must be a constant focus for managers. Exhortations work after a fashion, but positive incentives have more effect. Such incentives can take a number of forms:

- Class authors—teams or individuals—would receive extra payments for new and accepted high-quality classes and royalties for their reuse by others (excluding themselves). This bonus payment scheme will not only help identify generic classes from within projects, but will also encourage "skunkworking" for those really smart/neat classes.

- Class users get awards for exploiting the library to its full potential; this can be tied to the ratio of classes reused against those created. Again, this can be in the form of bonus payments.

- Managers get increased budgets with responsiveness to customer requirements and improved time to reach major deliveries.

- Third-party arrangements include licensed use, leasing, fee rate per use, or percentage of sales.

Do not simply pay for individual classes. Individual classes are interesting, but useless by themselves. What is needed are clusters of classes that provide distinct behavior or functionality. For example, a window display class is better than a button class, and the scenario of placing a customer order is more useful than individual components that make it up. If the focus is on the individual classes, it is similar to counting sheets of paper. You pay for the report, you pay for the cluster—or society or ensemble, as they may be called—of classes. Classes have too fine a grain; pay for behavior, quality, performance, resources used of the cluster.

These schemes may seem difficult to implement in your organization, but unless positive incentives are given, ineffective reuse will occur (Figure 8.5).

If you think it is hard to justify do some calculations on how much it actually costs to develop a new society of classes (design, build, test, deliver) against the time in identifying and reusing one of your software assets. If you can't think of the savings, calculate the revenue-enhancing potential of adding richer functionality or reducing the time to market for your products.* Do the calculations and you will see reuse is very cost effective.

GTE calls its class library team the Asset Management Group. This gives the right emphasis to the importance of the class library and the culture that it provides. The libraries are an asset, a significant one when you consider the cost to

---

* The Gartner Group publishes figures about Brooklyn Union Gas, which had a ratio of 1:20 new to reused code for their Customer-Related Information System (CRIS II); Gartner Group Presentation, 1994.

create them, and the impact they will have on future developments. To help put this in perspective, think of the cost of recreating the source code should all be lost.

However, you have to use the classes in the library. That may seem self-evident, but the cost to produce and maintain libraries of components may be greater than the resources saved in reusing those components. You need to do the calculations and be very selective about which components go forward to be included in the libraries. Most organizations simply put every developed class into one monolithic class library. Do not do that. Classes will never be reused again. Remember the end of the film *Raiders of the Lost Ark* when the Ark of the Covenant was put in that vast warehouse to be lost forever; so it is with uncontrolled class libraries.

Also, be aware that increased productivity means more delivered systems, which in turn means more systems to maintain. Maintenance may be easier with object technology—another publicized benefit—but don't expect to reduce your overall maintenance costs.

I've already written about the structure changes needed. To recap, teams need to be created to look after these library components. If left to individuals, reuse will occur locally and infrequently. If your organization is small or in the initial phases of object technology, you will need the library team role adopted by members of the project team. There is increasing evidence that one-third of

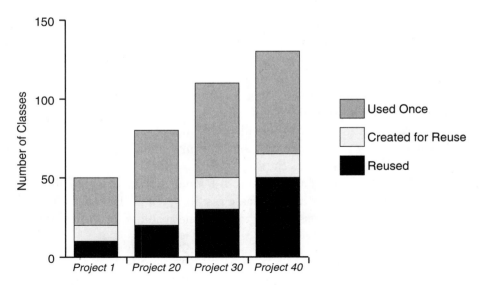

FIGURE 8.5. Ineffective Reuse Through Inadequate Number of Components

your effort needs to be spent on this role; for a six person-month project, two person-months need to be allocated to reviewing, reworking, and reintroducing classes into the projects.

Two more teams or roles are needed: the domain library team and the enterprise library team, whose members have more significant roles than simple librarians. Members of the library teams need to be of the highest technical level. Their skills in modifying submitted classes for generic use and ensuring high-quality improvements are obvious, but these members also need to be good communicators who meet regularly with the development teams to discuss appropriate classes and guide reuse solutions. Large organizations even publish newsletters detailing new classes added to the library and hold class awareness seminars. This awareness of the contents of the class and domain libraries is crucial, for the most common excuse for poor component reuse is, "I didn't know it was there."

There are, however, dangers with separate library teams: specialization and isolation. Members of these teams may will become specialists in ensuring high-quality components and in making classes generic, but often this work takes place in isolation from the project developers, whose new focus is on delivering end-user results. To avoid the charge of the library teams being in an ivory tower, team members need frequent involvement in live application projects. Allocation to the project teams as reuse engineer overcomes this danger.

Will your organization benefit from reuse?

Probably, but do not be unaware of the management issues and the costs. It will take time. One of the major lessons is that the best classes come from previous project developments. It is possible to define and design in a vacuum, but the real advances come from the "foundry" floor of organizations where making it work in a real business environment makes all the difference. You have to do the work. Don't expect significant reuse to occur until many other projects have provided the raw material.

Remember, don't ask what reusing classes can do *for* you, ask what class reuse will do *to* you.

8.5 Empowerment

Empowerment is an overused word. The cynics among us have usually experienced so-called empowerment to find that in reality it means that you have little or no authority but full and complete responsibility. You will get blamed if it goes wrong, but have no power to make it successful! That's not empowerment, that's impotence.

8.5.1 The Project Team

Real empowerment for the development team comes from achieving commitment, setting broad job assignments, decentralizing, and establishing a culture of pride, open information, and embracing change.

In simplest terms, a commitment is an agreement by one person to do something for another. Typically this involves delivery of a specified piece of work by an agreed date for payment or other consideration. In the context of a software project, this means the cooperation between the team members on the distribution of work, allocation of program segments, interfacing between program segments, and adoption of common standards such as naming conventions. As the work progresses, test plans are needed and test data as well as preliminary program versions are required from the other members. To be effective, everyone must know what the other is doing and be able to rely on the work being done as agreed. As the projects become larger and involve greater numbers of staff then this commitment process is crucial to the success of the project. It forms the foundation on which everyone bases their daily work.

The elements of an effective commitment are as follows.

- The person willingly makes the commitment; enforced commitments will fail.
- The commitment is carefully considered and not lightly made.
- Agreement is reached on what is to be done, by whom, and when.
- The commitment is publicly stated.
- The person guarantees their best endeavors to meet the commitment.
- If the commitment cannot be met, advance notice is given and a new commitment reached.

It can be seen that these elements apply to organizations as well as individuals. Organizations, through their managers, make commitments to others, such as customers or internal customer clients. These are the products and services that provide the revenue for the business. This commitment attitude by managers is a clear indication to the professionals of the support that they can rely upon. If a manager ensures that much-needed facilities and services are provided to meet the demands of the project, the manager can rely upon extraordinary effort by the professionals.

Commitment is a way of life. If small commitments are neglected or ignored, it is only a matter of time before much larger commitments are neglected and ignored.

To be effective, the software commitment process must involve all levels of management. Senior management's personal involvement is what motivates the entire process. Professionals know they must justify their recommendations in a visible process that will show up any poor work. This means that

- all commitment for future delivery is personally made by the organization's senior manager,

- these commitments are made only after successful review and agreement,

- the review process is formally conducted to an agreed format, and that format is enforced,

- all material, such as work items, plans, resources, schedules, and costs, is available,

- all parties agree to this plan in writing,

- the risk has been fully evaluated,

- the plans are feasible.

Setting broad job assignments is often expressed by mottoes such as "do the right thing," "solve the problem," "make it happen." These sum up the attitude that encourages workers to seek opportunities, to share in the success and the failures of the work undertaken, and to be involved in the wider issues. If you ever hear, "it's not my job," then consider yourself, or more properly, the organization, a failure in this area.

Decentralization ensures that power is placed closest to the front line of the organization (i.e., the customer or end-user). Decisions can now be made close to the action and trends spotted earlier. If you find that a new business object will speed up the process, then you should be free to allocate resources to get it built. Top management—senior executives and managers—will miss this level of detail and, if involved, are usually slow to respond. In these smaller groupings, it does become possible to create the necessary culture.

One such culture to develop is that of pride. Given that we have the knowledge to do the job, can we really believe that we deliberately set out to do a poor job? No. All of us want to do the best we can and take pride in our achievements. If we as individuals feel that, so do those who work with us. This culture respects people, values them, and recognizes their achievements, which helps to overcome doubts and uncertainties (Figure 8.6). Such constant recognition reinforces the culture and sets up expectations that more is required. When we want these teams to be productive, inventive, and thoughtful—all necessary for object technology—we must nurture this culture of pride.

Tom DeMarco and Time Lister in *Peopleware* write about the "open kimono" for a manager (DeMarco & Lister, 1987). What's under the manager's kimono? Information. No more are power plays relevant; object technology relies on cooperating objects that support the business. They encapsulate information and processes; so should the individual who develops them (i.e., encapsulate such knowledge). Information means an awareness of what's going on, both in the business and the development at hand. Developers must have access to this information or at least know where to go to get it. Many of the past failures in software development were due to poor information exchanges. That's why the requirements and the analysis models were and are still very important. Without them, the information is hidden and will surface late in the day. Open kimono also means sharing the information with others. If you know that there is some risk to the project because of customer difficulties, let the developers know. How many of the developers were unaware of the internal problems that befell TAURUS, London's defunct share processing system?* Its demise came as a shock to most developers, and a group continued to develop the software for three more days as they could not believe or accept the end of their years of work. What a waste of talent. Not at the moment of the cancelation, but later, they felt "scarred" by the experience and wary of committing themselves to future projects.

Open kimono is a shared value; show it by example and expect it from your developers. They should not fear recriminations when they come into your office and say, "We've got a problem. . . ." How many organizations shoot the messenger? This type of barrier inhibits seeking solutions by focusing on the problems.

You, the manager, can often be the cause of much confusion by sending out the wrong messages. Here are some examples of how the communications fail:

---

* TAURUS will become part of the folklore of software disasters in Europe. It was meant to automate company share transactions for the London Stock Exchange and turn it into a paperless operation; in fact it would have generated more paper as every transaction would have generated a statement. It failed in 1993 at a total cost of $600 million.

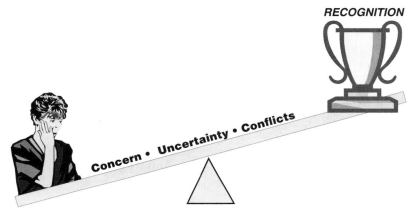

FIGURE 8.6. Recognition Overcomes Impeding Forces

Always meet the deadline	vs.	Accept new work without schedule adjustment
Quality is vital	vs.	Ship it on Friday
Build for the future	vs.	Only meet the stated requirements
Create reusable classes	vs.	Don't waste time reworking for better abstractions

The statements on the left reflect hopes, aspirations, and mission statements, whereas those on the right reflect the daily reality. Which would you believe? Do you act and talk consistently? If you don't, you should not be surprised when your developers focus on problems; after all that is what you do when you go around asking, "Any problems?" How about asking, "Done any good solutions?" or, "Got any good classes built recently?" or, "Did you reuse any of these classes?" All are valid questions, and all establish a mindset to encourage the search for solutions rather than problems.

When the project team is being formed as a mixture of developers, users, marketers, contractors, etc., each will be working toward any of several agenda. An effective way to get the team to focus on the project's aims is to have an "away-break." This is not a suggestion for one of these adventure training courses, although many organizations think them to be a powerful aid to team-building, but a simpler suggestion of getting the team off-site for a couple of days. While they mix informally, some formal team task needs to be undertaken. For example, setting out the project goals as a poster, developing success criteria, identifying threats and risks to the project, brainstorming ideas and directions for investigation, undertaking some general training. One Swedish company maintains its team building activities and rewards their workers by giving them all a training course in some new technology affecting their business. Nothing unusual in that, you think. Except the course takes place every two years on the Mediterranean island of Crete.* Lectures are from 8.30 AM until 1 PM, and the rest of the day is free to be spent with their accompanying partners, whose expenses have been paid for by the company.

8.6 The Top Team's Values

The senior managers and executives of the organization—the top team—are seen as success models by the rest of their workforce. The signals they send out are closely monitored by the rest of the organization, which is looking for clues to the future. If the top team demonstrate cross-functional cooperation, reward innovation and insist on quality so these values will be copied by the staff. If reducing the time to market for new products is important, the top team will be removing every obstacle to achieving this goal (e.g., bureaucratic reporting, purchasing delays, unstable resources, etc.). If, however, the response to ideas is lukewarm, if they are picky about innovation, frosty on skunkworks, and punish well-intentioned initiatives, you can be sure that these new behaviors will die and the organization will revert to its old ways.

Object technology is a challenge to the top team. Their old skills are under threat from the changes in the business environment, and a move to what is still considered by some to be an unproven technology threatens them more. Vast sums of money are spent on IT, so any improvement to costs, whether by cost reduction or enhanced productivity, is gladly welcomed. But if the promised savings are not forthcoming in a short timeframe, they will be looking for another silver bullet.

The top team needs to show a commitment to climbing the learning curve to achieve the high heights of business IT effectiveness in support of the organization.

---

* The enlightened company is Assistor AB of Stockholm, Sweden.

8.7 People-Oriented Values

People deeply resent being treated as resources, equipment, or human capital—all old terms of outworn organizations. This changing view of the workforce has been caused by the following:

- more knowledge-based businesses that emphasize information technology, higher education levels, more team work, and clearly defined individual responsibilities;
- social transformations wrought by an aging population and more women entering the workforce wanting long-term careers;
- economic evolution into global markets requiring recognition of cultural differences.

From these changes there is a new profile of wants and needs being expressed and expected by these workers. Now, they want

- to know more about what's happening in the organization,
- to understand the reasons for decisions and the alternatives that were considered,
- to contribute to the growing future of the organization with ideas as well as individual skills and talents,
- to feel important and have a meaningful role in the organization.

These people-oriented values lie at the heart of all successful organizations. Awareness of these changes and a commitment to the people of the organization have created many of the major success stories of the 90s. If you ignore them, you are in effect saying that you do not wish to be a world-class organization, that you wish to continue struggling with the old ways of working.

By including the people-oriented approach of empowerment, setting believable values, creating a sense of challenge, encouraging ongoing learning, and recognizing individual achievements, you are building on your most powerful asset—your staff.

8.8 Embracing Change

Problems are opportunities. How many times have you heard that? But it really means a willingness to embrace change, and change is something we are guaranteed, along with taxes and death. Opportunities are not threats. Change is to be encouraged; after all, that is why you are using or considering using object technology. It's a change to the development processes.

Change encourages you to determine your important shared values. What phrase best describes your company?

- *Innovative.* Encourage and support experimentation. Use lots of prototypes.
- *Quality.* Thoroughness and attention to detail are important.
- *Commercial.* Productivity and return on investment rule the environment.
- *Service.* Responsiveness and flexibility to customer demands need to be fostered.

If you have all of these in your mission statements, you have a glimpse of the conflicts that will come. Each affects the adoption and development of object-based systems. Fail to recognize and instill the appropriate shared value and you will have disappointments. Again, it's not the technology, it's the culture.

Change must be welcomed, or it will lead to the eventual demise of the organization. Successful companies find it hardest to change. Why? They are unwilling to change what they consider a successful formula, but nemesis will follow, so it is best to consider that the price of survival is eternal vigilance, if not paranoia.

Change must be overcome. Many, many forces that are unique to each organization hold back changes (Figure 8.7). These forces can only be overcome by identifying the discrepancy of where you are and where you want to be. If this awareness is fully developed, the forces against the change will be easily overcome.

Change must be controlled. The flexibility of object systems is both a major benefit and a hidden curse. Unless this flexibility is controlled, nothing will be achieved. Control may be relaxed in the early stages of the project, but when deliveries have been made or major versions developed, formal change control mechanisms should be engaged. Without them you have a foundation of sand.

Change also means that your developers' skills need to be kept refreshed and

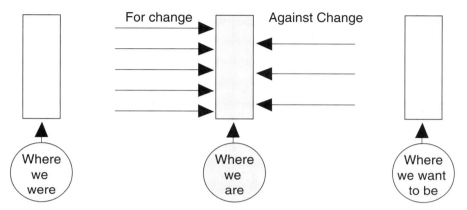

FIGURE 8.7. Create Change by Altering Balance of Forces

current. Skills do atrophy. Skills we use every day are well honed, but past skills, say, in interface building or database management will quickly become out of date if not kept refreshed. Not only do technical skills need further development—new object database techniques, the latest GUI building tool, etc.—but business awareness needs to be awakened. IT and DP staff need to go onto the front line and attempt to use their systems in live situations. Managers at British Airways sit at a booking-in desk once a year. If the process or the systems fail with the passengers for a jumbo jet standing in front of the desk, system reliability will be the hot topic upon that manager's return! Object systems attempt to model the real world so it behooves developers to go into the real world. It also behooves users to come into the development groups. Such cooperation and collaboration shows a sign of a mature development organization.

Prior to collaboration and cooperation, development organizations are often isolationist and viewed from the outside as chaotic and confused. This in turn leads to senior management being concerned over the rising investment in IT and to the continual defense by the DP manager. When cooperation and collaboration are established, shared values, common goals, or sets of related goals have been put in place. This can lead to vigorous pursuit of opportunities by entrepreneurial and intrapreneurial managers. Strategic alliances are formed within and outside the organization (e.g., with suppliers and with customers), to respond to the changing business environment.

Object technology is a framework for establishing these alliances. The object models of the business processes reflect the business operations and using straightforward notations the concepts can be verified by users. Suppliers of object components are able to provide tailored solutions to meet your organization's requirements. Remember, if it doesn't quite fit, you can extend and enhance the functionality.

8.8.1 Changing the Work

It has long been recognized that all improvements must be based on a complete understanding of the work and the work process. Skills can be taught to development staff, but they will only be effective if those skills can be applied to the relevant task or work stage. For example, there is little point providing training on the latest CASE tool if little new program development requiring such a tool is undertaken. This may seem obvious, but consider some of the training courses you have attended in the last two years. Were they appropriate to your work environment?

Many attempts to change the software development activities have focused on improving the skills of the workers. This is correct in that the skills and knowledge are aspects of working, but not of the work process itself. Work is the same whether it requires no skill or high skill, a lot of knowledge or a little. To operate a computer used to require a high level of skill, but now computers are operated successfully by workers (and others) with little or no skill in computers—in some cases they are even unaware that a computer is involved (e.g., in a washing machine).

By recognizing that the skill and knowledge are in the working rather than in the work, we can begin to make work more productive.

It is crucially important to focus on repairing the work process and not on repairing the worker. Part of a manager's skill is in knowing which of these need doing!

Changes start at the top with commitment by the senior management. Changes require leadership based on a conviction that long-term improvements are both possible and essential. Changes to the software process are management's responsibility—it is their commitment, their priorities, goal setting, and allocation of resources that ensure success, and unless everyone is involved, success is limited. Software development is a team business, so all the players need to participate at one level or another. If individuals are not directly involved, they must at least understand what is happening so that they do not inadvertently inhibit the improvements by not following the new experimental procedures.

Once begun, improvements must be continually sought, evaluated, and implemented. It is too easy for the initial momentum to be lost when things take longer or are harder than envisaged. Whenever a crisis occurs, there is a natural inclination to revert to the past methods, but the focus should be on crisis prevention rather than crisis management. Rewards need to be given to the quiet professionals who deliver high-quality systems that meet customer and development goals, rather than the high profile fire-fighters, who are fixing problems that should have been prevented.

All changes require considerable effort on the part of staff and management with regular reinforcement of the benefits that the improvements are making. Athletes require feedback on their performance; software developers require a similar feedback on their own performance. Annual appraisals are a poor method of providing pertinent feedback.

Finally, unless an adequate investment is made in people, resources, tools, and time, the changes will fail. People need to be trained, resources need to be provided—someone needs to do the work!—tools will have to be evaluated, bought, and installed, and that most precious of resources—time—needs to be set aside to nurture the improvements.

8.9 Making a Culture of Quality

The devil's square in Chapter 7 showed that quality is affected more by mismanagement of scope, schedule, and costs than by any other single factor. Most developers do not set out to provide low quality—can you imagine getting up in the morning and thinking, "I'm going to do a bad job today?" They may be inexperienced and need guidance and coaching from more experienced members of the team, but they want to do a good job. This is mainly based in having pride in one's competence, but also stems from the pragmatic view that if there is little maintenance, they can move onto the next project. They get to participate in some new challenge and some new work; otherwise the old history of poor systems becomes like a "sticky toffee paper," which you can't get rid of. Perhaps some staff move to other organizations simply to avoid the continual maintenance of their old systems.

There are of course, exceptions to this view on the professionalism of developers. If you have developers who are undisciplined and deliver poor-quality components, you need to seriously consider their involvement with object technology.

This may seem harsh, but the damage that can be caused by delivering low-quality components cannot be underestimated. To improve this situation, training programs, quality checkpoints, coaching, etc. can be used, but if the inherent desire to provide good work is not present then much of it may be pointless.

It comes down to discipline, self-discipline of the individual developer to ensure that his or her work is of the highest possible quality. Then, like the old Jewish proverb: "if everyone sweeps in front of his own door, the whole street is clean," the quality of the delivered systems will be of the highest standard. Quality lies at the core of everything that is done. It is as much needed by the top team—senior managers—as the most junior developer.

It's not enough to exhort the team to provide better quality. It needs to be encouraged and praised when demonstrated to be present. How? Through measurements of numerous critical quality factors such as downtime caused by the system failures, benchmarks, targets, etc. with the results displayed prominently throughout both the development area and the customer/user area. Charts showing targets and trends of a few critical factors, links to bonuses and rewards all encourage this quality culture.

Choosing which factors to measure is very difficult. The quality improvement world has produced thousands of metrics, yet the challenge is to pick three that are useful. Traditionally this has been defects per line of code or some such measure. This is interesting and may make you feel you have your "finger on the pulse" of quality, but it is not enough. One error—a missing comma—in a program caused the Venus space probe to miss its target and get lost in space. Another US telecommunications company lost its whole telephone network for a day as when it decided not to run its 13-week regression test for a three-line change (Graham, 1993). There are some good defect ratios there!

Quality metrics for your object-oriented systems need to be tied into the business use of the product or service. You must measure the real cost of the missed delivery, the down time, the rework. Again, it comes back to focusing on the outcomes. If you are delivering a product to the marketplace and you miss the launch date, how much revenue has your organization lost? If it's a system for internal use and it fails, how much staff resources become idle, and what's the impact of the lost number of customer contacts, the missed inventory shipping, the delayed bank payments?

Software developers and their managers—yes you—rarely ask how much does a failure costs the customer because they don't want to know the answers!

Every organization will have a different set of customer-based metrics related to the application systems delivered and under development. Be bold, move away from bean counting, set in place critical measurements of your systems, and make them widely available.

8.10 Encouraging Innovation

Innovation, creativity, and thoughtfulness have been constant themes throughout the previous chapters. It is deliberate. Object technology will simply be another programming technique unless its immensely powerful concepts can be used in innovative and creative ways. Imagine breaking down the current barriers between applications when a cooperating business object can be used in a wide range of business processes; e.g., the customer object can not only be used in sales order processing, inventory management and contracts, but can be viewed in a list, a location on a map, and a photograph (Figure 8.8).

Our boxed thinking means that the focus is constantly on solving the everyday problems through automation of the present business processes. Making faster does not mean that it's more effective—it's just faster. Object technology sets the foundation for the future and therefore requires a future-view of the present business processes. It does not even need to be business processes—look at the applications being provided on home computers. Europe is well

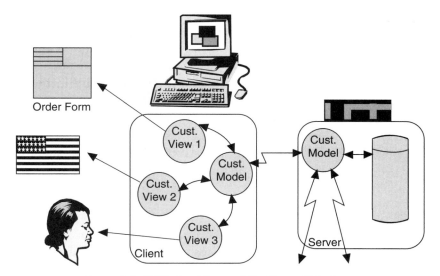

FIGURE 8.8. Differing Views of the Same Object

behind America in the number of computers in the normal household, so there is a huge marketing campaign to get householders to buy these machines. The emphasis is on ease of use, the everyday concepts, and the low learning curve. Instead of having a paper-based personal organizer, you can have one on the computer. They are called Personal Information Managers (PIMs). That's great, but not if they only do the same as the paper-based versions. Why spend some $1,200 on a machine, when I can buy the same functionality for $20 and even carry it around.

The point is this: application of computer technology can only be useful if it does more than can be done manually. If the PIM system can remind me to do my Christmas cards, print them, and do the envelopes, it will be useful. If the object-based accounts system can be enhanced to deal with bank transfers, electronic invoicing, and market analysis by product and by customer, it will be useful. Otherwise, it simply repeats the outworn business processes under such threat from business process reengineering (BPR).

To encourage this innovation you need to use humor, insight, lateral thinking, and imagination to generate ideas. These ideas can then be explored to suggest further concepts, confirm that they are worth building, or rejected as being impractical. Formal mechanisms, such as brainstorming sessions, skunkworks, and suggestion boxes, all need to be used to create this fertile ground for improvements.

One such approach is the formation of creativity circles (Majaro, 1988). Like quality circles, creativity circles are small teams dedicated to generating new concepts, new ideas, new techniques, new approaches, new products, new futures. Such teams need to be used by the organization dedicated to exploit the power of object technology in their products or services. This is more than simply expecting object technology to provide the innovation by itself. Object technology is a technique that will help provide complex systems that are adaptable and maintainable. Real innovation comes from the small starts, the growing enhancements and the rapid construction, reusing components and systems, all of which is supported and encouraged by the technology.

8.11 Summary

Shared values and strategy are the two bookends of a mature organization. Shared values reflect many aspects of the strategy statements. When they don't, your organization is in for a rough time. This can be seen in the clash of values between individuals and the expressed corporate goals and objectives. If managers do not "walk their talk," individuals and teams will become frustrated and demotivated. All of this is reflected in the culture of the organization; if the culture demands high quality, then it must establish the mechanisms and be prepared to take hard decisions such as delaying customer delivery, to ensure that value is maintained.*

For an object-oriented organization, the value system includes

- identifying customers and ensuring that object technology provides the organization with outstanding customer service,
- establishing a culture of quality and measuring key factors in object systems,
- embracing change, innovation, and creativity both in the work processes and in the products delivered by object technology,
- recognizing that reuse does not come automatically, nor does it come free; some form of rewards may be necessary,
- building an infrastructure that ensures reuse of components within and between teams,
- empowering teams through broad job assignments, creating a culture of pride in achievement, and encouraging self-management.

Managers are seen as role models by the team members so be sure you are clear on your own set of values so that your teams may share in them.

References

Bar-David, T. (1993). *Object-Oriented Design for C++*. Englewood Cliffs, NJ: Prentice Hall.
DeMarco, T., and T. Lister. (1987). *Peopleware*. London: Dorset House Publishing Co.

---

* When the cruise liner Queen Elizabeth II sailed at Christmas 1994 with as many plumbers and fitters abroad as passengers it demonstrated a company that put timeliness before quality. It may take years for the owners of the QE II to regain the lost reputation from that debacle.

Drucker, P. (1989). *Managing for Results*. Oxford: Heinemann Professional Publishing.

Graham, D. (1993). Software testing. *Software Management* 42.

Majaro, S. (1988). *The Creative Gap: Managing Ideas for Profit*. London: Longman.

Townsend, R. (1970). *Up the Organization*. New York: Knopf.

Townsend, R. (1984). *Further up the Organization*. New York: Knopf.

Wills, A. (1992). The Fresco System. PhD thesis. Computer Science Department,University of Manchester.

CHAPTER 9

GROWING IN
MATURITY

THROUGHOUT THE CHAPTERS DESCRIBING THE CHANGES THAT ORGANIZA-
TIONS need to make in each of attributes of the McKinsey Seven Ss, there
have been six recurring themes:

- Iterative and incremental development
- Skilled managers
- Product focus
- Productive teams
- Class organization
- Reuse

9.1 Theme 1: Iterative and Incremental Development

The driving force is the iterative and incremental (I&I) delivery cycle, which
has the benefit that both iterations and increments converge toward the final

solution that meets the customer/user's needs. Iterative and incremental development project cycle is based on a product view of the delivery in terms of user features and a process view that identifies the analysis, design, and build tasks required to deliver the next version.

Develop and deliver the increments as complete portions of the final system. Each version is a fully working set of scenarios or use cases within the scope of the new development. When all the scenarios and use cases have been delivered, we have the completed system.

Ensure in this I&I approach delivery of between 5 and 15 scenarios or use cases as using a smaller number increases the risk that when they interact with other scenarios, major changes may be needed to the previous delivered version.

Accept that the I&I delivery cycle means that portions of the system may need to be reworked or modified: the iterations. Take care after every delivery that classes extended and modified to meet the current delivery requirements will not result in a system architecture that may be inappropriate for the next build cycle. Take time after each delivery to review the class hierarchies, reconsider the abstractions, identify more appropriate generalizations and specializations then rework the present version of the system to provide a baseline for the next increment.

Use one or more of the following prototypes to remove risks:

- *Evolutionary prototype.* The language of prototype and the final system are the same, therefore components of the prototype exists in the final system. Beware of inappropriate system architecture and complex class structures in this approach.

- *Revolutionary prototype.* Sometimes called the "rapid prototype," where the prototyping language is different from the final system hence the components are discarded.

- *Revelationary prototype.* Special languages are used for the prototype and then discarded.

Plan the project as deliveries of major user features at sensible intervals and then plan the development activities within those milestones. These milestones, which tie together the technical and managerial aspects of the project, are laid down as time boxes and the development processes and matching resources are planned only for the short term.

Convince customer/users that iterative and incremental delivery will work for them. Demonstrate that the delivered version will be of high quality, that it will be useful, that support will be given, and that it can be changed if it does not meet their requirements. Avoid disrupting the present operation of the customer/users by setting up a beta version group to assess each delivered version.

9.2 Theme 2: Skilled Managers

Develop skills in balancing the devils' square whose corners are the critical factors:

- Scope. What will be delivered?
- Schedule. When it will be delivered?
- Cost. How much will it cost to be delivered?
- Quality. How good it will be on delivery?

Accept that quality is fixed, so any change to scope, schedule, or cost will drive down quality of the final system.

Undertake all of these key activities:

- Plan. Define scope, schedule, cost and quality and allocate resources
- Monitor. Progress, detect deviations, execute corrective actions
- Report. Progress, problems
- Manage change. Specifications, schedules, resource costs, staff

Ensure that proper plans are prepared for the iterative and incremental deliveries, including planning the time-frames, resource allocations, and the quality plan, but avoid over-planning at the component level.

Focus on the user deliverables and the execution of delivery. This means hands-on management as the faster development cycle of object systems may mean that next week is too late for responding to problems with the delivery.

Be aware of the changes in the business environment—diagnosing new situations, devising solutions for the new situations, applying these solutions, adapting them according to feedback, and then drawing upon the experiences for the future.

Specify the project and team member goals and ensure that they are meaningful by putting in place the tracking mechanisms and giving feedback to the team members.

Develop estimating skills with a tracking mechanism on the amount of time spent on each stage and task of the development process. If your tracking methods are primitive, your estimating skills will also be primitive. Start improving your estimating skills and those of each team member by setting up proper tracking mechanisms today.

Become the coach, part of the team yet with the ability to withdraw and encourage self-management by the team members. Motivation, incentives, and small wins become important aspects of your style in the fast development cycle associated with object technology. Monitor progress, report both up and down the organization, check against the metrics and the goals, these are the natural activities of your day. Pay attention to the signals that you send to the teams. If you want higher quality, every meeting and most memos should concentrate on this issue.

Develop the skills of a champion, but unless you have a high performance track record with some recent successes or you have been especially hired to insert object technology, you may find it very difficult to persuade senior managers to invest in a number of pilot projects as an evaluation and proving ground. You need to gain their trust. Sell object technology at all levels: strategic, tactical, and operational with a thorough evaluation of the risks, sensible cost benefit analysis of the move to object technology, and a commitment to see it through despite the inevitable setbacks.

Understand the technology yourself by concentrating on the analysis and design issues rather than the programming.

Allow customer/users to have a significant role in the pilot projects.

Enlist a senior manager as an executive champion to provide sponsorship and funding for the trials.

Profile the talents of your team. Begin by drawing up a register of the skills valued by your organization, categorized in a number of ways: technical, project management, interpersonal, people management and business knowledge. Based on this skill register, get each employee to draw up his or her own skills profile and, as the manager, do the same for each of your employees. Then discuss and resolve any discrepancies. In a similar manner, define the skills required in each task of a project; these are the task profiles. This gives an overall skills profile for the complete project cycle (i.e., what skills are needed and when they are needed).

Match the task profile and employee profiles to find the most suitable candidates with the relevant skills and tackle any shortfall through training or the use of external contractors who are chosen for their suitable skills.

9.3 Theme 3: Product Focus

A product focus—the term *products* is used to indicate business products, product lines, or services—means always having a view of the results of the development activities that are meaningful to the customer/user. Recognize that the customer/user wants the system to work, wants to get it on time, and wants it to meet their work requirements, whereas the developer wants a technical challenge, to use latest innovation, and to work on new system developments. Remember that the customer/user is unconcerned at the various tasks undertaken by the developers, the techniques used or the particular programming language.

Involve the customer/user at all stages of the development. Recognize that as soon as the customer/user is more involved in the project, the risk of change increases as changes in the customer/user environment mean changes to the system. Also, involve customer/users in any evaluation or selection process for third-party products or components that will be used to support their work and with the prioritization of the various projects.

Organize around outcomes not tasks (business process reengineering's first principle). The most important outcome is obviously a valid and verified system, which means the checks and tests to ensure and prove to the customer/user that the present delivered system meets their expectations.

During the movement from conception to completion of the final system, three distinct models are produced: the problem domain, the solution domain, and the system domain models:

- The *problem domain* model focuses solely on the scenarios—sometimes called "use cases"—within the scope of business or problem being considered.

- The *solution domain* model, which encloses the problem domain, is the product of the design phase when various solutions that take account of the numerous constraints.

- Finally the *system domain* model, a product of the build phase, is the realization of the chosen solution.

Classes in the problem domain model will still be discernible in the system domain model similarly solution classes will appear in the system domain model, which will have further classes unique to itself. Document these domain models. Measure what's important:

- *Product quality.* Number of defects, number of changes per class
- *Flexibility.* Number of enhancements per class, number of systems reused
- *Time to build.* Number of days to useful system
- *Increase of skills.* New business areas entered, skill profile per employee
- *Responsiveness.* Number of hours to enhance present system
- *Customer satisfaction.* Number of complaints, number of positive comments

Ensure also that all process measures have the following properties:

- *Quantitative.* Real figures are produced and can be tracked.
- *Responsive.* Figures respond quickly to changes (e.g., number of faults reported per day).
- *Relevant.* Measure of the key indicators.
- *Significant.* Show a difference is being made (e.g., process improvements).
- *Understandable.* Lines of code is not understandable to nondevelopers.
- *Easily obtained.* If it costs more to collect than is useful, don't collect it.

Involve everyone in the discussions if choosing your own set of metrics. Make the results visible so that a sense of urgency is transmitted through the measurement and the setting of improvement targets.

Start the measurement process now!

9.4 Theme 4: Productive Teams

Organize the multidimensional teams, ideally of no more than 7 to 15 members as the leaves of the shamrock. One leaf of the shamrock is the core of professionals who are permanently assigned to the team. These professionals are usually the most skilled and highly trained of the team. They provide the strong architectural framework, they maintain continuity for the duration of the product development, and ensure the quality of the delivered system components. They are highly influential in the design and building of the delivered system. One of the other leaves of the shamrock is the services provided by others within the organization (e.g., publications, contracts, networking services). These professionals are part time members of the team seconded for the necessary periods when their skills and expertise are required; they are the specialists in testing, documentation, infrastructure components, etc. The final leaf is the contractors and other professionals hired to satisfy a shortfall in skill or experience.

Manage appropriately the three different workforces (core, services, and contractors). Each has its own level of commitment and set of priorities.

Improve the skills of the team:

- Every programmer needs to know an appropriate object language and many need to know more than one as the language requirements may change during the life span of the project.

- The tools that support the language also need to be known. The simple editor and compiler is now surrounded be a host of supporting technologies requiring knowledge of the concepts, the notation, and the operation. These tools are complicated, so provide training courses by the suppliers and a few acknowledged local experts to promote, understand, and gain the benefits from using these tools.

- Ensure understanding of the target environment and the details of the operating system facilities of your chosen supplier using the foundation classes of any operating system.

- Skills are also needed in interfacing to the existing environments of the legacy databases and with the Common Object Request Broker Architecture (CORBA) or Object Linking and Embedding (OLE). Programmers need to know how objects use the right facilities to be sure of using and exploiting communications for a client/server environment.

Change the perspective of a new team to a product focus, which means a change in your attitude: "Don't tell me how hard you work, tell me how much you have got done." Force developers to work effectively and to use object technology as it should be used, not simply as another coding technique. Encourage them to work smarter.

Set SMART goals that clearly set out what you expect of each individual. SMART goals are

- specific (clearly understandable),
- measurable (what would a good job look like?),
- attainable (is it realistic for this person?),
- relevant (will it make an impact?),
- trackable (how will you know?).

Use the team performance measures as checkpoints for the team member. For example:

- To improve quality, check the number of defects reported.
- To improve the time to market, set a target of less than 5% schedule misses.
- Increasing flexibility can be measured by the number of user-defined changes accommodated each month.

Encourage the Personal Software Process. PSP is a metric-driven change as well as an empowerment-driven thrust. PSP practitioners establish personal goals for their processes, define the methodology they will use, measure their work, analyze the results, and based on those analyses, adjust their methods to better meet their personal goals. The process is an iterative learning process from their own work and the work of peers. Data is gathered and analyzed so that individual can decide what work best for them and adjust accordingly. The critical sub-processes of PSP are

- the collection of personal measurements—time and defects,

- the planning of the personal activity—size and resource,
- the management of quality—defects,
- the integration of elementary PSP's into a development process.

Empower the project team:

- Set broad job assignments to encourage workers to seek opportunities, share in the success and the failures of the work undertaken, and be involved in the wider issues.
- Decentralize to ensure that power is placed closest to the front line of the organization.
- Establish a culture of pride that respects people, values them, and recognizes their achievements.
- Provide an open information policy that ensures developers have access to all the detail necessary for the objects that encapsulate information and processes
- Encourage change, it must be welcomed, and must be controlled. Change also means that your developers' skills need to be keep refreshed and current.

Provide support for communication; teams need to share their work with each other and sharing that work should be controlled. Provide support in the form of groupware, which has the following elements:

- *Electronic mail.* Internal or remote users
- *Calendaring.* Common diaries
- *Conferencing.* Closed electronic bulletin boards, video phones, or full-room teleconferencing
- *Document data management.* For the vital project log (e.g., memos, specifications, minutes of meetings, designs, change requests, schedules, budgets, released source code)
- *Workflow.* Automatic distribution and scheduling of documents

9.5 Theme 5: Class Organization

Deal with the volume of classes by organizing into different component libraries:

- *Application library* components are associated with a particular project application and are the responsibility of individuals and the applications team.
- *Domain libraries* reflect the business and infrastructure activities of the organization. Business domains contain classes that reflect business operations: account number, drawing number, job number for functions such as accounts, engineering, manufacturing, etc. Infrastructure domains contain special classes that support the computing environment of an organization, such as real-time, networking, etc.
- *Enterprise library* contains classes that are company-wide: calendar, customer, product, employee , etc., which are for mass reuse throughout the organization or enterprise.

Ensure that library components are

- of the highest quality,
- high performance: efficient use of memory, speed of execution,
- robust,
- reliable,
- easy to maintain,
- portable,
- flexible.

Form the class team to look look after the library components. Members are specialists in ensuring high quality components and in making classes generic. To avoid isolation from the project developers whose new focus is on delivering end-user results, class team members are allocated as reuse engineers in live projects. If your organization is not large enough to warrant a separate class team, you need to allocate these roles to members of your core team.

Consider creating the software component factory. Such a software factory produces high-quality components for use by application development teams within the organization. Project teams provide production managers with information on future business directions and current plans for new applications. The factory team review these plans and based on their experience, produce components which can be assembled to provide the relevant solutions. These components are available for other project teams and over time the library components will meet most, if not all of the business requirements. Construction must focus on quality with the all the necessary and costly reviews and inspections. The factory managers need to provide

- component production planning, scheduling, design, and construction,
- sales literature detailing functionality, performance, reliability, size, documentation, and perhaps even price of the components.

And also, develop "classy" skills, such as the following:

- High technical competence: language, tools, environment, etc.
- Ability to abstract useful components for use now and in the future. Abstraction involves the process of generalization and specialization on a set of classes under design or more often those classes created from recent work on an application—often called "scavenging"—to find classes for use in the future
- Ability to communicate effectively with the other team members and with the customer/users

9.6 Theme 6: Reuse

Increase productivity through the reuse of existing components.

Recognize that reuse does not happen automatically, nor is it without a cost. Classes under development will satisfy the main application at hand, but if it needs to be reused extra efforts and increased costs in extended schedules are needed for

- input from other application teams,
- building to the highest quality.

In addition to the cost issues, there are other hidden barriers:

- Programmers are notorious for not using other people's software.
- Object-oriented languages may not even support genericity.
- It can be very difficult to mix classes from libraries from different vendors.
- Many class libraries are huge, and with the current ineffectual browsing tools it can be very difficult to find suitable classes.

Establish a development culture where there is more to the library than simply a "good thing." This culture is one where reuse, rather than creation, is the normal method of development. It must be a constant focus for managers with positive incentives such as the following:

- Class authors receive payments for new and accepted classes and royalties for their reuse by others.
- Class users get rewards, awards, and promotion for exploiting the library to its full potential.
- Managers get increased budgets.

Give it time. The best classes come from previous project developments, so you need to do the projects!

9.7 Growth Towards Maturity

This book is about business process reengineering (BPR) for software development using object technology. BPR has three forms: total transformation, cross-functional redesign, and workplace redesign. Obviously total transformation is the most radical, cross-functional redesign is adopted in order to form the multidisciplined teams and simplify the business processes, and finally, workplace redesign is concerned about the procedures and processes within a specific department. The level of redesign of your organization for object orientation could take any one of these flavors. It depends on the current strength, or maturity, of your organization.

There are five stages of maturity in the exploitation of object technology:

Stage 1. Minimal awareness of object technology or other development methodologies or processes

Stage 2. Awareness of the opportunities and some experimentation with object technology

Stage 3. Knowledge and awareness of object technology, pursuing opportunities in some areas

Stage 4. Skilled staff vigorously using object technology in the majority of developments

Stage 5. Full exploitation of object technology to meet the needs of the organization

If your organization is at the chaotic state, stage 1, of software development where everyone is an expert and there is little planning and control of any development activity, keep well away from object technology. It won't solve your problems; in fact, it will make them worse. You must start to build the foundations.

At stage 2, there is increasing interest in and experimentation with object-oriented techniques. Individual developers read of the methods, managers learn of the benefits of an object-oriented approach, and both groups attend conferences and seminars. Some individual experimentation is attempted and usually a champion emerges. This champion pushes through a pilot project to demonstrate the benefits to senior managers; the pilot is often staffed with other committed enthusiasts. It is usually a success—commitment breeds success—and thereby gains agreement to move to stage 3.

Stage 3 is when some significant pilot projects are attempted with multiple approaches and methods. Members of the group undertake ad hoc training, but experimentation with the techniques applied to the specific business applications is the general way of working. There are attempts to involve customer/users more closely in the development. There is little reuse of any components except within small teams. This is a dangerous period, as a lot of money can be spent on training, consultants, toolsets, etc. with little immediate benefit. The most vocal enthusiasts push forward their ideas (e.g., the choice of language or method) and thereby force upon the organization some long-term commitments. If you choose an inappropriate programming language, it's very hard to change later. As Barry Boehm is quoted as saying, "Choosing a language is like choosing a wife; it's hard to undo after getting involved and not to be taken lightly!"

Stage 4 is the watershed when the object-oriented development becomes well established and stable. The developers are experienced, they have a preferred and chosen method of working, quality assurance is applied at all stages, a training plan is in place for new recruits, and "wrappers" have been developed to encapsulate interfaces to legacy systems. One of the major indicators of this level of maturity is the appearance of the class team. At stage 3, some reuse was achieved, but it was localized and poorly controlled. Now a group of experienced developers create domain classes for use by multiple teams. Another indicator is the customer support team. With the faster delivery of functional versions of the system, an effective and responsive system of customer support needs to be established. It is all very well delivering every six to eight weeks versions of the system but if the mechanism for support is not in place and staffed appropriately, soured customer relations are guaranteed. It is only when stage 4 is achieved that any attempt can be made to have customer/users as part of the development team.

Finally, at stage 5, the "library becomes the language," and developers are wholly committed to supporting the business processes and meeting business requirements is the main objective. Developers may be moved out to be part of the business units with support from a small core development team. These pioneer developers provide a pathway for ideas to flow between the users and the main group. Legacy systems are replaced and from the small object-oriented center, the class team of developers are in regular and formal contact with those placed in the business units. Customer/users now are helped to construct applications from object-oriented components supplied by the developers. This is certainly possible with object-oriented style components; why can't the end-user pull down and use enterprise-wide objects such as customer, telephone, product? Developers now focus on creating frameworks and object-oriented components that support the business applications rather than the infrastructure-type classes such as communications, GUIs, etc.

At stage 5, the organization has embraced fully the object-oriented approach.

9.8 Setting Goals for Introducing Object Technology

It will come as no surprise to find that the goals for improving your organization for object technology need to be smart!

9.8.1 Specific

First, the goal needs to be specific. Introduction of object technology may need to be done in conjunction with improving or changing the development processes. Such improvement goals are chosen from the organization attributes (see method for self-assessment in Appendix A), using the strategy for moving to the next higher process maturity level to guide the choice of which items to improve. If, for example, basic management controls need to be established (moving from level 1 to level 2), this must take priority over installation of tools or defining work procedures even those these may be poor.

9.8.2 Measurable

A measure of success needs to be set for each improvement. This may be associated with reducing the amount of rework, increasing the number of new products supplied, reducing development timescales. Such measures are often supplied as percentages (e.g., reduce the amount of rework by 15%), but it assumes that the current amount of rework is known. If it is not known then such measures need first be collected to establish the baseline.

9.8.3 Attainable

Improvements need to be attainable. If an improvement is announced to the effect that all delivery timescales are to be shortened by 15%, the opposite is sure to happen. Programmers may work harder, but the demotivation in attempting to reach an unattainable goal reduces the overall effectiveness. This is not seen directly until the end of a runaway project when many of the best programmers leave rather than face another punishing year attempting to do the impossible.

9.8.4 Relevant

Improvements must be relevant to the business as a whole. In this case, this is improving the product and the processes that develop the product. It is little use setting goals to improve the manual filing system when the product is of poor quality. The quality charts ensure that the relevant objectives are chosen.

9.8.5 Trackable

The last attribute of the improvements is that they must be trackable. Like any project, a schedule showing work breakdown, resource allocation, deliverables, and deadlines is important. Equally important is the management of the improvement process to ensure that the schedule is being met. Often the use of an outside consultant on a monthly retainer of a couple of days is sufficient to maintain progress on the improvements; they act as the conscience of the management.

Finally, the improvement goals need a time-span for completion. It is too easy to set unrealistic timeframes for the improvements.

A series of small improvements—that can be undertaken at low cost and will improve customer satisfaction through enhanced value, timeliness, and appropriateness should be considered for immediate action. These improvements, although perhaps minor in nature, show the development staff and managers visible progress in the early days of the object technology introduction program.

9.9 Realizing the Vision

We started out with a vision: to deliver quickly, cheaply, and with greater control, the high quality systems of today and tomorrow that meet our customer's expectations and then detailed how you will need to change your software development organization to make a success of object technology.

With the business environment under considerable change both from the demands of the customer and the drive for effective organizations through business process reengineering, you cannot let IT and IT development become a barrier to these forces. Yet too often it is IT that is holding back progress for the business. It takes too long to change a database, too long to incorporate new legislation, too long to respond to moves by competitors, too long by far.

IT is on the critical path. Everything needs to be done to change this situation.

Modern-day change needs creative thinking, and one of the major barriers to this creativity is your and your other managers' mindsets. There is a tendency to be blinkered by our own perceptions and approach problems along the same well-worn pathways. All the brain-storming sessions in the world won't shift someone stuck in this kind of mindset. So be creative and imaginative. Look at the structure of your group and your teams, their skills, the development strategy, the systems of working, your management style, and the values you share with your team members and with the organization. Realize that these have a strong impact on your delivered systems. If you want to exploit fully the benefits of object orientation, you will have to change the organization.

Object technology can help realizing the vision, but only in an organization fit to use such powerful technology. Is your organization fit?

Are you ready to manage your move to object technology?

APPENDIX A

SELF
ASSESSMENT

MANY ORGANIZATIONS HAVE LITTLE IDEA OF THE MATURITY OF THEIR software development processes yet are capable of undertaking an assessment without external help. Much has been written on the subject of software maturity and various techniques have been suggested, some complex, some straightforward. This appendix shows how you may undertake an assessment yourselves for a small to medium sized (20 to 100) development organization. For larger organizations, the assessment would be performed on teams, groups, or whole departments according to the natural divisions within the enterprise.

It outlines the key steps of the assessment process, details the indicators and information that is collected and is then used to determine the score on each of the maturity scales for the organization. From these final scores you will have a baseline from which to plan such changes that are necessary to successfully introduce object technology into your organization.

A.1 Seven Key Steps

The seven key steps in the assessment process are the following:

1. Define scope and agree on objectives
2. Select interviewees and issue list of questions
3. Conduct interviews and collect relevant documentation
4. Analyze all material and draft maturity charts
5. Present maturity charts to managers and selected staff and agree
6. Outline improvement program and detail action plan
7. Present findings, improvement program, and action plan

Step 1

Step 1 is the initial meeting with the site managers to define the scope of the development process that is to be assessed and to agree the objectives. This is a crucial step. There is a real danger that the assessment can stray outside the original scope and become embroiled in company politics or bogged down in areas that are of little or no concern to the assessors. Obviously, a certain number of interviewees will have an axe to grind over perceived shortcomings in the organization and wish to gain an ally in the assessor. Assessors must behave and act neutrally to all factions in an organization. By defining the scope and objectives the assessors are focused on the main task in hand. Also during this step the liaison arrangements between the assessors and the organization are agreed (i.e., nomination of a site representative and a fixer).

Step 2

Step 2 is the selection by the site managers of the staff and personnel to be interviewed. It is useful if the selected staff can be brought together for an initial briefing meeting when the site managers and senior assessors explain the purpose, scope and objectives of the assessment. At this meeting, a questionnaire and guidelines are issued to all the interviewees. Sometimes, it is not possible that this meeting can be called, in which case detailed instructions are sent to each of the interviewees and the site managers encouraged to discuss the assessment informally with their staff. The dates and schedule of interviews is also drawn up in this step.

Step 3

Step 3 is the when the interviews are conducted and relevant documentation collected. This is done on-site. When a team of assessors is involved the interviews are preceded by a short presentation (around 10 minutes) by the interviewee on the specific areas relevant to that member of staff. If a single assessor is used, a one-on-one interview is more productive. Most interviews should be scheduled for one hour, but for senior managers this is often insufficient as wider areas need to be covered; one-and-a-half hours is usually required. Longer interview times yield less results as concentration during the period tends to fall off. Concentration is an important ability for the assessors during the interviews.

Documentation that shows examples of the items under discussion (e.g., sample program listings), are collected, annotated, and filed for later analysis. Documentation that is considered relevant includes the following:

- project proposals and plans,
- feasibility reports,
- requirement specifications,
- design documents,
- company standards and guidelines (procedures, methods, etc.),
- formal review reports,
- change request forms,
- project control documents (timesheets, etc.),
- minutes of meetings.

Step 4

Step 4 is when the assessors analyze all the material—their notes and collected documents—and produce the initial draft of the process architecture and the quality charts. This work is usually done off-site with any clarifications made over the telephone. Some assessment teams prefer to remain on-site so that close liaisons can be made with the staff in the areas under review. This, however, can cause problems, as the possible frequent interruptions will irritate the staff, who are attempting to continue with their normal work. On the whole it is better to be off-site or at least in a separate site location when conducting the analysis.

Step 5

Step 5 is when the results of the analysis—the process architecture and the quality charts—are presented to a group of selected site managers and senior staff for comments and general agreement. This is an important part of the process as it ensures that nothing obvious has been missed, that the emphasis and focus is correct and that the conclusions can be accepted. A major function of the assessment process is communication; so it is crucial that the messages can be understood and accepted. This does not mean the bad news should be avoided, but the style of presentation can help to soften its critical impact.

Step 6

Step 6 is the outlining of the improvement program and detailing the action plan. Improvements are normally grouped into three priorities: high, medium, and low. High priority items need to be tackled as soon as possible as they usually have a significant negative impact on the current work processes (e.g., establishing project plans and schedules or evaluating and selecting a new program development environment).

Also included in this group are smaller improvements that, while not urgent will create a series of successes for the improvement program (e.g., modification of change control forms, alteration of the work spaces). The assessment team must also propose the action plan—tasks and schedules—for the improvement program. Sometimes, the tasks and schedules cannot be produced by the assessment team (e.g., estimates on the establishment of a support team), but it's important that deadlines are indicated on the plan for such action items.

Step 7

Finally, step 7 is when the findings, the improvement program, and the action plan are presented to site managers, selected staff, and the interviewees. A full presentation must be made to all the interviewees and any other staff that will be affected by the improvement program; this is again part of the communication process. Separate presentations are also normally made to senior site managers and possibly to other company managers to involve and commit them to the improvement process.

A.2 Preparing to Assess

In preparing for the assessment a number of tasks need to be undertaken:

- Definition of the scope and objectives (step 1 above)
- Selection of the assessors
- Briefing of the assessment team
- Nomination of site representative, coordinator, and fixer
- Preparation of the questionnaires and briefing notes
- Producing the interview schedule

The definition of the scope and objectives is covered in Step 1. Selection of the assessors can be achieved in a number of ways. If the development group is small (15 to 25 staff), a single experienced assessor is more effective than an assessment team. For larger development groups (more than 25 staff), a team will be more appropriate. This assessment team will be lead by an experienced assessor, but may include other senior staff members from the site. Such staff will require some training in assessment techniques.

Once the team has been selected, they are briefed on the scope, objectives, and schedules of the project. The assessment must be treated as a project. Any attempt to do the assessment in spare time will prove fruitless and counterproductive. Proper resources must be allocated to achieve success. This is often the reason single experienced assessors are used even for larger development groups. Such assessors are often consultants who treat the assessment as a well-defined project, and allocate time and resources to meeting the schedules. They also act as the main agents of change.

A site representative and a coordinator (a "fixer") are nominated by the site management. The site representative is the point of contact between the assessors and the development group. It is the responsibility of the site representative to resolve any problems that may occur during the assessment process (e.g., to resolve schedule conflicts, room allocations, extra expenditure, etc.). Such a representative is usually at a senior level in the organization and has the authority to ensure that the assessment process encounters few difficulties. The coordinator acts as the administration assistant to the assessment team. Their role is to agree interview schedules, reserve rooms for the interviews and presentations, ensure that the facilities are available, and circulate all relevant material. This role is normally undertaken by a personal assistant or secretary to the development group or senior management. Like all things, the more authority such a person can call upon, the easier it is for the tasks to run smoothly.

Questionnaires and briefing notes are prepared for issue to those that will be interviewed. Sufficient time must be given for the interviewees to prepare. A period of two working weeks provides enough time; a shorter time leads to insufficient preparation as most are involved in heavy work schedules, any longer means that any initial preparation is soon forgotten or the preparations are postponed until the last minute.

Finally, the schedule for the interviews is produced. Such a schedule shows the allocation of hourly time-slots to interviewees. They also need to contain

- telephone numbers, which are needed in case the person does not show up or changes need to be made to the schedule;
- free time slots to handle slippages in schedule (some interviews always overrun);
- follow up sessions to allow opportunities for informal discussions of any topics missed or that have arisen since the interviews;
- breaks for the assessors to review their findings and unwind.

A.3 Undertaking the Assessment

There are three major work items for the assessors:

- Interviewing
- Analyzing the findings
- Producing and presenting the results

Facilities required for the interviews must be quiet or at least subject to little disturbance (ask the interviewee to switch off his pager!) and be provided with necessary equipment such as flipcharts, whiteboards, and an overhead projector. The projector is required only if the interviewees are making presentations.

The key skill for the interviews is active listening. This means concentration on what is being said, taking notes, and at frequent intervals reflecting back to the other person a summary of the points made so far. This ensures agreement and avoids misunderstandings. It also encourages the interviewee to be open and forthright with comments and opinions.

A.4 Tools

Tools are needed to serve the assessing work (i.e., interviewing, analyzing the findings, producing, and presenting the results).

Most people have the best tools for the interviewing—two ears and a mind! It is not recommended that the interviews be tape recorded as this starts to move into the gray area of spying, especially as confidentiality is promised. A small dictaphone can however be used after the interview to capture one's immediate thoughts and impressions.

During the interviews, the best tools are many large pads and pencils as note-taking is the main activity.

When the analysis is performed tools can be used to form the results. These include word processors, drafting or drawing packages to produce the diagrams, or even analyst CASE tools if used in drawing mode. However, these tools are really there to produce and present the results, as the main activity uses the analyst power of the mind and not some fancy feature of a tool. If a large amount of documented information is to be reviewed, a simple database containing the title of the document, a summary, and the reviewers comments may be usefully employed. However, like most groupware, a circulating box file can achieve the same effect; it certainly is more than appropriate for the typical assessment material.

By and large, computer-based tools are of little help to the assessment process, but eminently suitable for producing and presenting the results.

A.5 The Results

At the end of the assessment the final report contains the following:

- The process architecture model that matches the organization
- Organization maturity charts
- A set of recommendations on improvements
- An action plan on implementation

By necessity, assessments are critical in nature—it is their prime function—to make a critical judgment on the current situation. This obviously means that the results often appear to be negative in nature. Yet this is never the complete truth. Much is often done well—work is usually to a high standard, products are delivered to customers, and the organization does prosper—but it is done at a cost in terms of resources (money and people), time, and the goodwill and personal well-being of the staff.

Care must then be taken in presenting the results. No one likes to hear bad news. It is important to identify what is also done well in the group and organization. For example, most strong development groups often have

- highly skilled software engineers,
- deep product knowledge,
- strong motivation and commitment,
- self-management skills.

When the bad news has been given and the staff fall on their knees under the weight of criticisms, it is important to give the good news. A better title would be "It isn't all bad. . . ."

A.6 Managing the Assessment Process Itself

The assessment process must be treated as a project. This means that it requires

- planning and scheduling,
- selection of the team,
- breakdown of work tasks,

- allocation of resources for the assessment and producing the results,
- management of team/self,
- reporting procedures,
- keeping of project records (e.g., time sheets, expenses, etc.),
- filing and storage of documents.

Task-based management is the most appropriate style of management of assessment projects. This means that the steps need to be broken down into work items, allocated, and scheduled accordingly. At the end of each step a review should take place to determine the following:

- Is the step complete?
- Is any rework necessary?
- Can we start the next step?

Also part of the assessment manager's role is briefing the assessment team members, ensuring the skill level of the assessors meet the tasks, meeting with the site representative, resolving conflicts and problems, monitoring progress both in terms of the schedule and in terms of the objectives, and ensuring a high level of quality in all areas of the assessment.

During the assessment, a number of problems may be encountered :

- *Missed interviews.* If the interviewee is important (e.g., a senior manager or single representative of a process group), reschedule the interview, otherwise, cancel it.
- *Late to meetings.* This is often unavoidable as arranging to get all staff available over a few days can prove extremely difficult. The danger is that the schedule stretches too long and the momentum is lost.
- *Poor facilities.* Complain to the fixer and if no improvement is made, go up to the site representative.
- *Loss of focus by the assessment team.* Usually caused by too many interviews and being swamped in detail; get them together, review progress so far, and refocus.

- *Large volume of information.* Much of which will found to be copies of existing documents and can be ignored. A few pages of program listings or project plans are normally sufficient despite the attempt by the interviewees to provide complete samples of such information. Cull and discard as required

- *Clash of personalities.* Often occurs when a strong personality at the site attempts to promote their ideas to the assessment team. Careful handling is required to ensure that the strong personality feels that their ideas have been given a fair hearing and due consideration

- *Resentment.* Usually caused by the disturbance to the work schedules. Stressing that the resultant improvements will increase productivity and remove some of the work pressures is often sufficient

- *Resistance to change.* Usually accompanied by "its always been like this, so why change it?" Involvement in the improvement program and good logical reasons to improve the process can alter this resistance

- *Secrecy.* The trouble with secrecy is that you may not know it is happening! It can be discovered only by interviewing more than one person from a process group, but if they all are secretive, there is little one can do

Problems and conflicts always arise during assessments, but these are minor in relation to the problems and conflicts that the assessors find in most development groups and can be easily handled by the assessment manager.

A.7 Seven Key Organizational Attributes

To measure the organization as a complete entity, rather than the individual processes, the McKinsey Seven Ss are used:

Strategy.	Plan or course of action leading to the allocation of a business's scarce resources over time to reach identified goals
Structure.	Character of the organization chart (i.e., functional, decentralized, etc.)

Systems.   Proceduralized reports and routinized processes, such as meeting formats

Staff.   Demographic description of important personnel categories within the development group (i.e., designers, coders, analysts, etc.)

Style.   Characterization of how key managers behave in achieving the business goals; also, the cultural style of the organization

Skills.   Distinctive capabilities of key personnel

Shared values.   The significant meanings or guiding concepts an organization imbues in its members; can also be described as superordinate goals or culture of the organization

Information that is used to measure these attributes is collected during the interviews. It also can be inferred from comments and documents provided by the interviewees. The assessors simply collect as much supporting information as possible with these organizational attributes in mind.

In the following sections each organizational attribute is described in detail with guidelines on the information needed so that each can be measured.

Strategy

The main item is the existence of a strategy document and if such a strategy is widely known by the development group. Published strategy and goals for the product, development, and support activities indicates that strategy issues are well understood and mature within the organization. Table A.1 describes strategy at five levels of organizational maturity.

Structure

This attribute can be derived from the organization charts, but care must be taken with informal groupings that often occur in large organizations. Problems occur when matrix management is practiced by an organization. Table A.2 describes structure at five levels of organizational maturity.

Table A.1 Strategy	
Level	**Description**
1. Ad hoc	Ad hoc acquisition of hardware and software and use of resources
2. Controlled	Attempt to control the use of resources and guide acquisitions
3. Coordinated	Move towards a coordinated strategy
4. Integrated	Active coordination and measuring of attainment of goals
5. Mature	Constant reassessment of strategies and policies to meet future needs

Table A.2 Structure	
Level	**Description**
1. Ad hoc	Software development part of another functional group (e.g., Finance)
2. Controlled	Start of a separate development group
3. Coordinated	A fully centralized managed development group
4. Integrated	Beginning of decentralization with the involvement of end-users
5. Mature	A coordinated but decentralized development group

Systems

Procedure manuals, standards and guidelines relevant to the organization rather than the work processes are used to determine this attribute (e.g., how to purchase supplies, procedures in calling review meetings etc.). Table A.3 describes systems at five levels of organizational maturity.

Table A.3 Systems	
Level	Description
1. Ad hoc	Uncoordinated processes and reports normally of a financial nature
2. Controlled	Beginning of the "computer center" and its attendants
3. Coordinated	Start of the definition of internal processes and procedures
4. Integrated	Formalized internal procedures and start of collection of external data
5. Mature	Fully interorganizational procedures, methods, and systems

Table A.4 Staff	
Level	Description
1. Ad hoc	Small number of programmers
2. Controlled	Software development manager
3. Coordinated	Larger staff including analysts, designers etc.
4. Integrated	Appearance of business analysts and IS planners
5. Mature	Development manager now at director level

Staff

This attribute is indicated by staff titles and roles. Table A.4 describes staff requirements at five levels of organizational maturity.

	Table A.5 Style
Level	**Description**
1. Ad hoc	Focus solely on technical matters and unaware of other issues
2. Controlled	Initial attempts to involve the users with mixed results
3. Coordinated	Democratic cooperation with other departments
4. Integrated	Appearance of the product champion
5. Mature	Developers now part of the business teams

Style

This attribute is determined from the approach by managers to the management and control of both planned and unplanned activities—crises. Team work and cohesion are also important parts of the style attribute. Table A.5 describes style at five levels of organizational maturity.

Skills

This is determined by what skills are needed to do their job, whether technical, managerial or other such as communication (writing and presentation). Also important is the level of knowledge needed by an individual; whether business knowledge or product design and architecture knowledge is needed (i.e., does it require an expert?). Table A.6 describes skills at five levels of organizational maturity.

Shared Values

This attribute comes from the comments and attitudes displayed by the interviewees. Do they have common views? Do they cooperate within and outside their own immediate group? Do they involve themselves in other areas of the

Table A.6 Skills	
Level	**Description**
1. Ad hoc	Technical skills only; generally low level
2. Controlled	More competence in building and delivering complete systems
3. Coordinated	Project management skills to achieve cost and time targets
4. Integrated	Business skills now required and integration within the organization
5. Mature	Board level director skills and very senior management skills

Table A.7 Shared Values	
Level	**Description**
1. Ad hoc	Isolation, secrecy, and confusion with no one knowing what is going on
2. Controlled	Senior management concern about the development group
3. Coordinated	Attempts to gain understanding of other areas and work toward a common good
4. Integrated	Entrepreneurial opportunities identified and followed with vigor
5. Mature	Interactive planning, harmonious relationships, and interdependence

business? Are they encouraged to develop ideas and are they provided with the resources to experiment? Table A.7 describes shared values at five levels of organizational maturity.

Bibliography

Bhabuta, L. (1988). Sustaining productivity and competitiveness by marshalling IT, *Proceedings, Information Technology Management for Productivity and Strategic Advantage*. IFIP, Singapore.

Cash, J.I., and B.R. Konynski. (1985). IS redraws competitive boundaries. *Harvard Business Review*, 63(2).

Earl, M.J. (1988). Information Management: The Strategic Dimension. Oxford: Claridon Press.

Galliers, R.D. (ed.). (1987). *Information Analysis: Selected Readings*. Reading, MA: Addison-Wesley.

Galliers, R.D. (1990). Problems and the answers of the IT skills shortage. *The Computer Bulletin*, 2 (4).

Gibson, C., and R.L. Nolan. (1974). Managing the four stages of EDP growth. *Harvard Business Review*, 52 (1).

Greiner, L.E. (1972). Evolution and revolution as organizations grow. *Harvard Business Review*, 50(4).

Humphreys, W. (1989). Managing the Software Process. Reading, MA:Addison-Wesley.

Pascale, R.T., and A.G. Athos. (1981). *The Art of Japanese Management*. New York: Penguin.

Somogyi, E.K., and R.D. Galliers. (1985). *Towards Strategic Information Systems*. Cambridge, MA: Abacus Press.

Ward, J., P. Griffiths, and P. Whitmore. (1990). *Strategic Planning for Information Systems*. New York: Wiley.

The Concepts of Object Technology

T HE CORE CONCEPT OF OBJECT TECHNOLOGY IS DECENTRALIZED CONTROL. Take for example, a simple program for a desk calculator. It selects the mathematical routine depending on the function key pressed. A central routine accepts input from the keypad and dispatches control to the appropriate routine. This central routine needed to know which routine to activate for each keypress. Conventional operating systems work in a similar manner—the routine to be activated is known to the central controller which has interpreted the command. Think of traditional command-line operating systems such as DOS or Unix, where the command-line string is decoded and the specified routine is activated, unless of course, the command string is unrecognized.

With modern workstations' requirement to support multiple windows, this simple approach is no longer applicable. Here the operations are requested through a mouse click and the action to be taken depends on the position of the displayed cursor. This action is unknown to the operating system and it depends on the type of window in which the cursor happens to be located when the mouse button is pressed. Each window is then carrying its own form of command interpretation. In short, it is regarded as an object with its own behavior. When the mouse is clicked, the dispatcher now searches for the

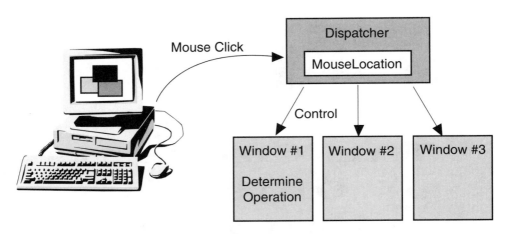

FIGURE B.1. Control Decentralized in the Window "Objects"

window descriptor identified by the current mouse location and transfers control to a routine assigned to that descriptor (see Figure B.1); this routine is often called the handler.

Each type of window will have a different type of handler for the command interpretation. Therefore, instead of control being centralized in a single program, which previously knew the identities of the destination of all commands, it is decentralized in the handlers, whose identity and number are not known in the dispatcher's program text. It comes as no surprise to learn that much of the initial drive toward object technology was by the developers of these modern operating systems.

Objects—in our example, the windows—include information (data) and a set of operations that reflect the object's behavior. The information is encapsulated within the object (i.e., is private), and access to this information can usually be achieved only through defined operations (e.g., GetPosition).* Such operations are called *methods*, and methods are invoked by sending the object a message (see Figure B.2). By convention the name of the message and the name of the method is the same. Figure B.3 shows an example of a window. The window's position (LHCorner), size (Area), and its state (OnTop) are contained within the object and the methods reflect the operations on this information.

---

*Certain languages, such as C++, permit a form of restricted direct access to an object's information (i.e., they break the rules of encapsulation).

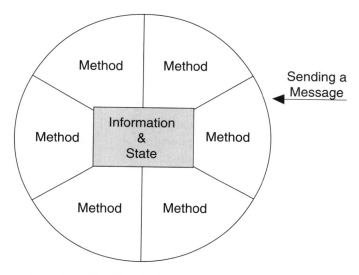

FIGURE B.2. The Terminology of Objects

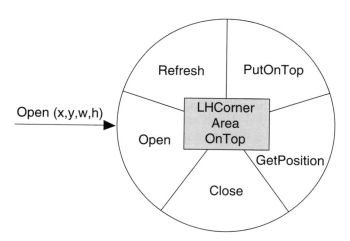

FIGURE B.3. Example of a Window Object

Notice that this set of operations—known as the object's interface—define what can be done but not how it is done.

It could be said at this point that objects simply provide a form of encapsulation and information hiding that is available in many conventional languages (e.g., Modula-2, ADA, etc.). But in these languages, the invocation of a "method" is done by a procedure call determined and fixed at compile time. Objects, however, communicate using messages and while the structure of the message is predetermined, the actual section of code that is activated by the message in the destination object is determined at run time (i.e., when the program code is executed). This is known as *dynamic binding.*

Every message contains the identity of the destination object, the message name, and perhaps some parameters associated with the message; these parameters or arguments may themselves be objects. In our window example in Figure B.3 the Open message has parameters for the position of the top left corner (x,y), the width (w) and height (h). The receiving object (our window) searches its own list of methods for one that matches the message and passes control to the segment of code for that method. When completed, control is returned to the object that sent the message. If a method was not found in the list for an object, then control would still be returned to the sending object usually with some error indicator (i.e., the system would not crash). It should be noted at this point that there is normally a single thread of control (i.e., from sender to receiver and back to sender) and not some form of parallel or concurrent operation.

Because each object can look up its own list of methods for a message and invoke an appropriate code segment, the same message can be sent to different types of objects and thereby invoke different code segments. For example, there may be different types of window objects on the screen, but each type will respond to the Close message and will execute different closedown operations. The sending object does not need to know the type of object that will receive the message, it needs to know only the object's identity (name). This feature of multiple responses to the same message is known as *polymorphism.*

When sets of objects have identical information structures and operations, they are defined as a *class.* A class is then a template for every instance of an object. Our window class is then the specification of the information structure and the operations for our window object, and there can be any number of window objects each with the same interface, the same information structure but each with different information (data) content (e.g., a different position (x,y) of the top left corner). Every object in an object-oriented system is then an instance of a class. To use another example more relevant to application developers, Figure B.4 shows a class definition for an account in a banking scenario. It defines the information structure: Name, PinNumber, Balance, etc., and the account operations: Debit, Credit, CheckPin, etc.—note how the method

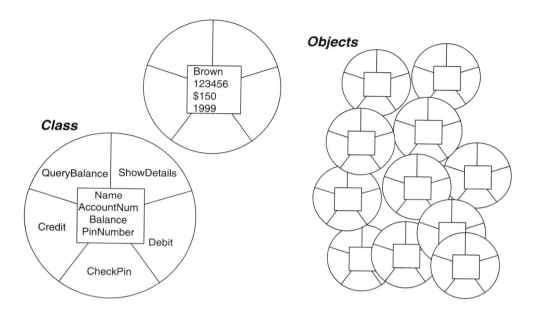

FIGURE B.4. Class Definitions and the Objects

ShowDetails is necessary to display the encapsulated information. There can now be as many instances of the account class as there are customers of the bank; each instance—the objects—will contain different information, but all will respond to the same message interface: Debit, Credit, QueryBalance, etc.

One of the many confusions in the world of objects is the interchangeability of the words *class* and *object*; they tend to be used loosely and imprecisely. It is true to say that an object instance cannot exist without a class definition; hence in this context class and object are synonymous. However in some languages, a class can be defined without there being any object instances of that class—such a class is often called an *abstract class*. It is improper to use the word *object* when *class* is intended.

Why would classes exist without objects? It is desirable to derive a new class from a given class so that the objects of the new class not only share the properties of the given class but also have additional features. Figure B.5 shows how, for example, we can have special classes for handling text, graphics, and pictures from our window class and how from our account class we can derive credit, deposit, business, and mortgage accounts. This is known as *inheritance*.

The properties of the *superclass* are inherited by the *subclass*. New methods may be added (e.g., `CaptureImage` in a picture class), or existing methods modified (e.g., different interest calculations for the different types of accounts). New information structures (data) can only be added (i.e., once defined, they cannot be removed in a subclass).

Inheritance structures define the generalization and specialization of classes within the structure. Figure B.5 indicates that account is a generalization of deposit, credit, business, and mortgage accounts, which are themselves specializations of account. This is similar to the contrast between a top-down (specialization) and a bottom-up (generalization) view.

During analysis, inheritance expresses a semantic relationship between general and specific classes: `DepositAccount`, `CreditAccount`, etc. They are in fact sub-type relationships. However, in design, inheritance expresses a property of

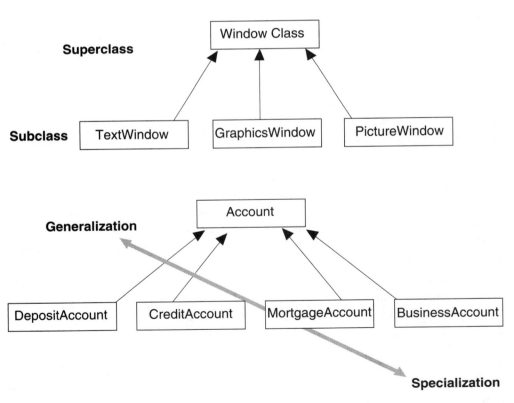

FIGURE B.5. Examples of Class Inheritance

the system not necessarily in the problem domain. It is a mechanism used to encapsulate common structure and functionality. For example, `Viewer` is a class only necessary in the Display context, but it could be a subclass of an existing implementation class `Window`, which contains position, size, status, etc. These differing views of inheritance cause much confusion to novice object-oriented developers.

Some object-oriented languages permit a class to have more than one super-class, which means that the subclass has the combined properties of its super-class; this is known as *multiple inheritance* (see Figure B.6). While multiple inheritance appears attractive and useful in well-defined examples, it can cause grave problems in large inheritance lattices when it becomes difficult if not impossible, to determine the properties inherited by a class. Multiple inheritance is best left to experts.

Inheritance (subclassing) is not the only type of static relationship between the classes. Figure B.7 shows other relationships with special properties:

- *Composition.* A class contains other classes (e.g., the `Vehicle` class is composed of classes `Body` and `DriveTrain`, which themselves contain other classes. A composing class has custody of its components and access to the components can only be made through the composing class. The life span of the objects is then the same as that of the containing

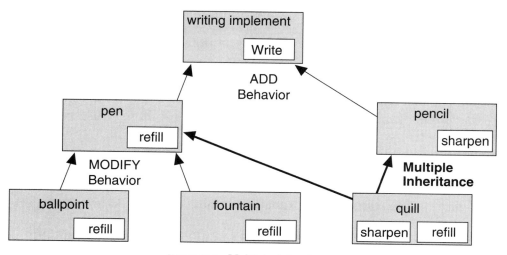

FIGURE B.6. Multiple Inheritance

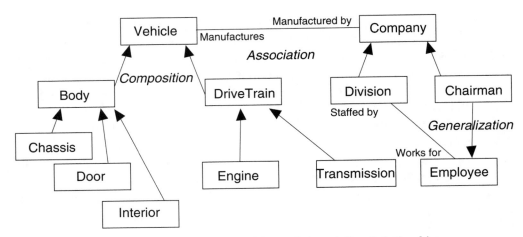

FIGURE B.7. Example of Composition and Association Relationships

object (i.e., when a `Vehicle` object is destroyed, so are the objects for `Body`, `DriveTrain`, `Chassis`, `Door`, `Interior`, `Engine`, and `Transmission`.

- An association. Classes have an association with other classes (e.g., our Vehicle has been manufactured by a Company. This association may be a simple connection between two objects, but if there is any information as part of the association (e.g., date of Vehicle build), it is usual to define classes and thereby objects to support the association. Such objects have an independent life span although the association (simple or otherwise) needs to be managed by other objects within the system.

It is in the area of relationships between classes that demands the most care in designing and building object systems. It is true to say that the structure of the classes defines the structure of the subsystems; get these structures wrong and the eventual system will be flawed.

Yet classes and their relationships give object technology its strength. With the possibility of incrementally enhancing and adapting object descriptions (classes) without touching their inherited code in the process, the concept of reusability and libraries of components becomes a reality. As a rule, object-oriented programming builds on existing applications or parts of applications, known as *class libraries*, that are adapted to specific requirements yet without changing these parts themselves. Thus not only can new classes be derived to support new behavior requirements, but also any later modifications made on these prefabricated application parts will remain completely transparent and be spread to all derived applications without any further overhead (e.g., modified viewing algorithms would enhance all the windows).

To summarize:

- Object orientation is the ability to define pattern templates (of objects) consisting of variables and procedures. Templates are given the name *class*, and instances of class are said to be *objects*. Procedures defined for a class are called *methods*, and invoking a method is called *sending a message*.

- It also possible to derive new classes from existing classes. A derived class is related to the class from which it is derived by the fact that it adopts the latter's variables, adopts or replaces its methods, and may possibly add new methods and variables. This is known as *inheritance*. Inheritance structures show the generalizations and specializations of the classes in the inheritance tree.

- Class can be in different types of relationships with other classes: composition and association. Such relationships imply forms of custody and object life histories.

- When objects can receive the same message or the interface (message contract) is also inherited, they are said to be *polymorphic*.

- Object-oriented programming builds on existing applications or parts of applications—frameworks, class libraries—that are adapted to specific requirements yet without changing the parts themselves.

Object orientation concepts—classes, inheritance, class relationships, and polymorphism—and the introduction of software components as frameworks and class libraries, perhaps provided by other suppliers, will lead to significant improvements in the productivity of software development.

INDEX

A

ADA, 81, 168, 251
Abstractions, 47, 103, 163, 172, 225
Access to information, 28
Adaptor objects, 50
Alliances, 207
Apple, 165
  MAC interface, 2
  MacApp, 165
Applications, 11, 53
  barriers, 11
  explosion in, 11
  teams, 65
Asea Brown Boveri, 60
Assessments, 233–248
  managing, 240
  preparation, 237
  problems encountered, 241
  results of, 239
  steps of, 234

  tools, 239
  undertaking, 238
Audits, 29, 233
Awareness, 8, 66, 178, 205

B

BPR, (*See* Business process
  reengineering)
BS 5750, 85
Banks and banking, 35, 83, 109, 157,
  188, 252
Barriers, 11, 20, 60, 202
  present mindsets, 230
  to reuse, 193, 226
Benefits of object technology, 20
Blanchard, K., 141, 146, 178
Boehm, B., 43, 228
Booch, G., 58, 75, 80, 81, 82, 83, 106
Brainstorming sessions, 212
British Airways, 207

Browsers, 114, 194
Budgets, 156
Business benefits, 38
Business case for objects, 180
Business domain classes, 49, 130, 195
Business environment, 11
Business objects, *See* Cooperative
  business objects
Business process reengineering
  (BPR), 6, 11, 12, 17, 27, 60, 212,
  219, 226
Business strategies, 27

C
C++, 122, 164, 167–169, 170, 194
CASE, *See* Computer-aided
  software engineering
CAST, *See* Computer-aided software
  testing
CIX, 112
COBOL, 32, 125, 168, 170
CORBA, 165, 221
CRC cards, 174
Calendaring, 112
Capability maturity model (CMM),
  17, 19, 96, 97
  self assessments, 228
Challenges, 2
  for managers, 14
Champions, 153
  executive, 180, 218
  skills for, 179, 218
Change, 6, 36, 49, 206–209
  of values, 186
  resistance, 21, 180
  to business, 7, 11, 217
  to products, 7
Class builder, 131

Class definition and specification,
  84
Class librarian, 132
Class libraries, 30, 32, 49–50, 66, 122,
  166, 192, 197, 224, 256
  commercial, 193
  learning, 167
  NAG library, 192
  newsletters, 66, 199
  organization, 49, 194, 224
  teams, 66, 198, 224
Class models, 84
Class team, 66
Classes, 10, 252
  abstract, 253
  clusters, 15–16, 109, 114, 197
  inheritance, 10, 45, 253
  management, 113
  multiple inheritance, 255
  organization, 23, 49
  relationships, 10, 45, 255
Client-server, 7, 12, 13
Coad, P., 119
Coad/Yourdon method, 80, 119
Cohesion and coupling, 102, 103
Coleman, D., 82
Commitment, 2, 25, 65, 119, 181
  effective, 200–201
  of top team, 204, 208
Communication components, 51
Completeness, 102, 104
Complex data structures, 12
Complexity, 102
Components, 33, 67, 90
  farming out, 129
  libraries, 26
  reuse, 49, 52, 66, 150, 192
Compuserve, 112

Computer-aided software
   engineering (CASE), 9, 64, 71,
   76, 111, 146, 164, 180, 208
   choosing tools, 106–108
Computer-aided software testing
   (CAST), 108, 164
Conferencing, 112
Configuration management, 76, 110
   tools, 71
Consulting organizations, 128
Contractors, 64–65, 155
   hiring, 128–129
Conversion strategy, 13
Cooperative business objects, 12,
   173, 202, 211
Cost overruns, 4
Creativity circles, 212
Crisis management, 7, 18
Critical path, 21
Culture, 28
   of consent, 146, 156
   of development, 30–31
   of organizations, 187
   of pride, 28, 201
   of quality, 209–211
   of reuse, 194, 226
   of trust, 156
Customer care, 78
Customer satisfaction, 100, 220
Customer/user, 12, 26, 29–30, 35, 37,
   48, 53, 217–219

D
Data management, 50
DeMarco, T., 5, 70, 179, 202
Decentralization, 28, 52, 57, 201
Delivery cycles, 20
Demand for growth, 7
Department of Trade and Industry

(DTI), 5
Deployment of resources, 149
Design, 89
Development Needs Analysis
   (DNA), 182
Development approach, 20, 162
Development lifecycle, 23
Development lifecycles, 42
   iterative and incremental, 42
   spiral, 43
   waterfall, 42, 87, 144
Development process models, 87–94
Development stages, 77, 87–88
Devil's square, 162, 175–177, 189,
   209, 217
Disasters, 3
Document data management, 113
Documentation, 41
Documentor, 132
Domain models, 53, 169
Downsizing, 12, 59
Drucker, P., 61, 190

E
ETVX paradigm, 105
Eiffel, 164
Electronic mail, 112
Elements for success, 35
Empowerment, 199, 200, 223
Encapsulation, 12, 67, 250
Enterprise classes, 49, 195
Error handling, 103, 194
Estimating skills, 179, 218
European Airbus, 6
Expectations, 12, 37
   conflicting, 20
   customer/user, 12, 34
   exceed, 191
Explosion in applications, 11

Extensibility, 20

F

Flexibility, 20, 34, 100, 145, 148, 220, 222
  controlling, 206
Focus groups, 62
4GL, 44, 106, 164
Framework builder, 132
Frameworks, 26, 50
Free-form organizations, 58
Fusion method, 80, 82

G

GTE, 197
GUI, *See* Graphical user interfaces
Gabrial, R., 101, 129
Gartner Group, 197
Generalization, 47, 163, 216, 254
Geographical information systems (GIS), 30
Goals, 25, 78, 148, 155, 218
  alignment, 27
  corporate, 186
  differing, 186
  introducing object technology, 229
  limitations, 185
  SMART, 146, 178, 222
Goldberg, A., 58, 82
Graham, I., 44, 210
Graphical user interfaces (GUI), 7, 12–13, 20, 38, 50, 122, 133
Groupware, 76, 111–113, 223

H

HP, *See* Hewlett-Packard
Hammer, M., 11, 28, 39, 59, 60
Handy, C., 63, 146

Hardware/software gap, 7
Headhunters, 121
Henderson-Sellers, B., 66
Heterogeneous platforms, 7
Hewlett-Packard, 58, 66, 82, 165
Hierarchical organizations, 58
High-tech solutions, 7
Human resource group, 121, 127
Humphreys, W., 17, 76, 96, 97

I

IBM, 121
IQ tests, 124
ISO 9000, 18, 85
IT strategies, 28
Incremental development, 26, 42, 216
Induction procedures, 135–136
Industrial Systems Development, 96
Infrastructure classes, 50, 130, 195
Innovation, 27, 28, 59, 62, 204, 211–212
Intel Corp., 61
Intelligent machine tools, 35
International Standards Organization (ISO), 17, 96
Interviewing, 124–126
  books read, 126
  development task, 126
  portfolio, 126
  preparation, 125
Iterative and incremental delivery, 42, 45, 88, 95, 145, 178, 215–217
Iterative development, 42, 215

J

Jacobson, I., 40, 80, 82, 96
Job assignments, 27, 201

Joint application developments (JAD), 166, 174

K
KPMG Peat Marwick, 4
Kanter, R.M., 59, 157
Knowledge workers, 15

L
Languages, 167–168
  skills, 164
Leadership, 62, 149
  of teams, 62
Learning curve, 30, 31, 123, 204
  personalities to fit, 123
Legacy systems, 13, 21, 30, 133, 165, 228
Levels of maturity, 18–19
Levels of strategy, 26
  business, 26
  IT, 28
  organizational, 27
Listening teams, 62
Lister, T., 5, 70, 179, 202
Look and feel, 12
Love, T., 69

M
MBWA, *See* Managing by wandering around
Maintainability, 20
Maintainer, 132
Maintenance, 18, 41
  costs, 41
Management By Objectives (MBO), 15
Management problems, 8
Managers, 143
  as coach, 149, 218
  categories of, 143

communication, 151
  heroic, 149
  people-oriented, 154
  post-heroic, 149
  signals, 203, 218
  skills, 159, 177–179, 217
Managing by wandering around (MBWA), 178
Mars Inc., 61
Matthews, W., 157
Maturity charts, 234
McKinsey Seven Ss, 19, 242–247
Means and ends, 148
Mentors, 124, 129, 132
Methodologies, *See* Object-oriented methods
Methodologist, 132
Methods of working, 85
Metrics, 99–100,
Microsoft, 28, 33, 64, 69, 121, 154, 165
  foundation classes, 114, 165, 167
Milestones, 47, 216
Misconceptions, 14
Misconceptions, 14–16
Mission statements, 24, 79, 206
Mission-critical activities, 132
Modern workstations, 9
Modula-2, 251
Multiculturism, 52
Myers-Briggs personality typing, 142

N
National Computing Centre (NCC), 5
New World Infrastructure (Newi), 168
Noise, 70

O
OBA, *See* Object Behavior Analysis

Object Behavior Analysis (OBA), 58, 82
Object Modeling Technique (OMT), 58, 75, 80, 82, 83
Object linking and embedding (OLE), 34, 165, 221
Object messages, 84, 250
  definition and specification, 84
Object models, 40, 84, 163, 207
Object request broker (ORB), 109, 168
Object technology concepts, 249–257
  decentralized control, 249
  dynamic binding, 252
  encapsulation, 250
  messages, 250
  methods, 250
Object-oriented analysis, 83, 122
Object-oriented concept, 9, 10
Object-oriented databases (OODBMS), 50
Object-oriented design, 84, 122
Object-oriented methods, 75, 79, 122
  books on, 80
  camps, 80–82
  maturity of use, 85
  plea for cease-fire, 81
Objectory, 80, 82, 96
Obstacles to object technology, 24, 30
Occam's razor, 33
Office accommodation, 70
Open kimono, 158, 202
OpenDoc, 165
Operating systems, 8, 9, 51, 122, 165, 193, 249
  environments, 165
  handlers, 250

Organizational pyramid, 57, 59
Organizational strategies, 28
Organizational types, 58

P
PIMs, *See* Personal Information Managers
PSP, *See* Personal Software Process
Personal Information Managers (PIMs), 212
Personal Software Process (PSP), 97–99, 222
Personnel department, 124, 127, 144
Peters, T., 24, 59, 60, 151, 178
Pilot projects, 21, 187, 218, 227
Pirsig, R, 101
Planning, 18, 47, 144, 161, 216
  over-planning, 144
Polymorphism, 10, 257
Power-users, 153
Primitiveness, 102
Problem domain model, 13, 40, 162, 219
Process and growth models, 61
Process architecture, 90–93, 235, 236
Process maturity, 96
Process measures, 100, 220
Procurement, 16, 52
Product focus, 23, 35, 144, 219–220
Product lifespan, 94–95
Productivity, 21, 192, 194, 225
Project bidding, 66
Project failure, 5
  business issues, 6
  concept of failing, 21
  people issues, 8
  technical issues, 7
Project log, 113

Project plans, 47, 89, 217
Project sponsor, 65
Project's sociology, 8
Promotions, 155
Prototyper, 132
Prototypes, 20, 44, 164, 216
  dangers with, 164
  evolutionary, 44, 164
  revelationary, 45
  revolutionary, 44
Prototyping, 13, 114, 188
  rapid, 145, 166
Psychometric testing, 124, 141

Q
Quality, 15, 33, 53, 79, 145, 150, 151, 169, 210
  charts, 236
  defining, 102
  devil's square, 162, 175–177
  improving, 191
  key metrics, 100, 210
  measuring, 15
  of components, 196
  systems, 101–105
  "without a name", 101
Quality circles, 62
Queen Elizabeth II (QE II), 213

R
R&D, 157–158
  "kissing frogs", 157
Rapid application development (RAD), 44, 152, 183
Reality test, 25
Recruitment, 120–129
  agencies, 121, 127
  hiring, 120
  new recruits, 86, 135, 228
  of friends, 127
  qualities, 121
  sources, 121
  strategic, 120
  tactical, 120
Relational databases, 30, 31, 50, 133
Requirements, 34, 42
  analysis, 88
  customer/user, 8, 13
  deferring, 49
  definition, 88
  fixing, 16
  poor, 16
  tagging, 42, 105
Resistance, 20
Resource loading, 163
Reusability, 20, 102
Reuse, 191–199, 225–226
  incentives, 196–197
  phases, 194, 228
Reuse engineer, 131
Reviews, 18, 35, 104, 144, 201, 216
  design, 104, 168
  of prototypes, 164
  technique, 169
  strategy, 105
  walkthroughs, 104, 169
Rewards, 197, 209
  to individuals, 154–155
Risks, 16, 43, 204
  devil's square, 175
  reduction, 144
Roles and responsibilities, 130–135
  class library, 199
  system department, 130
  team, 133
  technology, 131

Rumbaugh, J., 58, 75, 80, 82
Runaways, 4

S
SMART goals, 145–146, 148, 222
SPICE, 17, 96
SQL, 50, 122
Safety-critical systems, 5, 79
Scavenging, 172
Scenarios, 40, 46, 82, 84, 109, 197,
    216, 219
Schumacher, E.F., 28
Screen "sizzle", 191
Semantics of the business, 122
Service to customers, 190–191
Services, 64
Sets of objectives, 25
Shamrock organization, 57, 63, 154,
    221
Shared values, 185–214
  culture, 188
  levels of maturity, 247
  McKinsey Seven Ss, 19, 243
  value conflicts, 185
Shareware, 113
Shelfware, 86
Shlaer/Mellor method, 80
Silver bullet, 9, 10, 17, 25, 204
Simms, O., 12
Skill profiling, 181–182, 218
Skillbase, 86
Skills, 161–183, 220, 221
  atrophy, 207
  communication, 173
  human and conceptual, 172
  levels of maturity, 247
  McKinsey Seven Ss, 19, 243
  managers, 175–181, 217
  presentation, 172

technologists, 162, 208, 221
  users, 173–175
  waste of, 161
Skunkworks, 59, 197, 204, 212
Small is beautiful, 28
Smalltalk, 2, 82, 122, 164, 167, 169
  Parts, 165
Software Engineering Institute
    (SEI), 17, 76, 96, 108
Software crisis, 2, 9, 98, 153, 209
Software development process, 17
Software engineering, 15, 63
Software factory, 52, 57, 67, 225
Software management, 15
Software rusting, 163
Solution domain model, 40, 84,
    219
Specialization, 47, 163, 216, 254
Spiral development model, 43
Staff, 119–140
  hiring, 120
  levels of maturity, 245
  McKinsey Seven Ss, 19, 243
  turnover, 188
Stages of maturity, 227–228
Standard Chartered Bank, 109
Standards, 86
Strategy, 23–55
  levels of maturity, 244
  McKinsey Seven Ss, 19, 242
  object oriented, 32
  shared values, 187
Stroustrup, B., 122
Structure, 57–73
  functional-style, 60
  levels of maturity, 61, 244
  McKinsey Seven Ss, 19, 242
Structured techniques, 9, 83
Style, 141–159

levels of maturity, 152, 246
  McKinsey Seven Ss, 19, 243
  preferred behaviors, 142–143
Subclass, 254–255
Success criteria, 204
Sufficiency, 102, 104
Suggestion boxes, 212
Superclass, 254–255
Suppliers, 64, 115, 191, 207
System architecture, 45
System domain model, 40, 84, 220
Systems, 75–117
  layers of, 76
  levels of maturity, 76, 245
  McKinsey Seven Ss, 19, 243
  types of, 75

T
TAURUS, 202
Taligent, 165
Teams, 8, 24, 57, 62, 119, 135, 144,
  221–223
  accommodation, 60
  building, 204
  case teams, 28
  communication, 111, 203
  core team, 64
  motivation, 46, 145, 150, 155
  multidimensional, 53
  multidisciplined, 60, 62
  perspective, 144, 222
  roles, 133, 198
  size of, 62, 221
  structure, 57, 194, 198
Technical skills, 122
Technical specialists, 171
Tester, 49, 132
Testing, 16, 39, 76, 79, 89, 108–110
  good tests, 110

strategy, 109
  tools, 76, 108, 110
Testware, 108
Third-party products, 37
TickIT, 18, 85
Time boxes, 47, 145, 216
  example, 147
Timesheets, 77, 99
Tool builder, 132
Tools, 21, 106
  choosing, 114
  skill with, 164
Top team, 27, 38, 204, 208
Touchstone, 25
Townsend, R., 188
Training, 165–171, 118
  choosing courses, 170
  courses, 166–167
  needs, 166
Training projects, 138, 227

U
Use cases, 40, 46, 109, 216, 219
User discernable deliverables, 35
User interaction model, 84
User interface controller, 132
User representative, 173–174

V
VB, *See* Visual Basic
Value systems, 186
Viewpoints, 36, 89
Visual Basic, 46, 50, 53, 164, 165
Visual C++, 50, 165

W
Walkthroughs, 35, 104, 169
Waterfall development, 42, 87, 144
Weinberg, G., 169

Window handler, 10
Wirfs-Brock, R., 58, 80, 82, 106
Woods, M., 143
Work processes, 42
 change, 208
 formalization, 85
 performance, 189
 procedures, 85
Workers, 8, 185
 wants and needs, 205

Workflow, 113
Wrappers, 30, 228

X
Xerox, 1, 82, 121
 PARC, 82
 STAR user interface, 1

Y
Yourdon, E., 9, 80 373

Add these essential books to your object technology reading list!

Explore the leading methodologies

OBJECT DEVELOPMENT METHODS

(Part of the ADVANCES IN OBJECT TECHNOLOGY series)

edited by Andy Carmichael

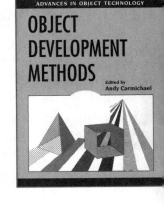

Object Development Methods addresses how object technology can be applied to systems analysis and design. It includes:

- a comprehensive survey and comparison of the leading methodologies including Booch, Texel, Rumbaugh, Shlaer/Mellor, Jacobson, and Coad/Yourdon among others

- an exploration of the common concepts and underlying structure of each methodology.

A must-read for anyone interested in distinguishing and learning how to evaluate, the leading object-oriented methods.

ISBN: 0-9627477-9-3   347 pages $39

A book whose time has come...

Objectifying Real-Time Systems

(Part of the ADVANCES IN OBJECT TECHNOLOGY series)

by John R. Ellis

This essential book presents a methodology for creating a real-time information processing system Requirements Model. The methodology presented is an evolution of popular Real-Time Structured Analysis (RTSA) techniques into object-based Real-Time Object-Oriented Structured Analysis (RTOOSA).

By reading this book, you'll get:

- leading-edge information including more than 100 helpful figures and examples;

- a guided tour through the steps of applying object-oriented techniques to daily projects

- an accompanying diskette which contains the source programs used throughout the book to enable the reader to experiment and verify executions without having to key in code.

ISBN: 0-9627477-8-5   525 pages (including diskette) $44

OVER 100 FIGURES AND EXAMPLES!

SIGS BOOKS ORDER COUPON

YES! Please rush me the following books:

☐ ___copy(ies) of **Inside the Object Model** (ISBN: 1-884842-05-4)
at the low price of $39 per copy.

☐ ___copy(ies) of **Object Lessons** (ISBN: 0-9627477-3-4)
at the low price of $29 per copy.

☐ ___copy(ies) of **Directory of Object Technology** (ISBN: 1-884842-08-9)
at ☐ $69 (Individual Rate) per copy.
☐ $169 (Corporate Library Rate) per copy.

☐ ___copy(ies) of **The Dictionary of Object Technology** (ISBN: 1-884842-09-7)
at the low price of $55 per copy.

☐ ___copy(ies) of **Object Development Methods** (ISBN: 0-9627477-9-3)
at the low price of $39 per copy.

☐ ___copy(ies) of **Objectifying Real-Time Systems** (ISBN: 0-9627477-8-5)
at the low price of $44 per copy (including diskette).

RISK-FREE OFFER! *If you are not completely satisfied with your purchase, simply return the book within 14 days and receive a full refund.*

Total Purchase

Inside the Object Model	$_____
Object Lessons	$_____
Directory of Object Technology	$_____
The Dictionary of Object Technology	$_____
Object Development Methods	$_____
Objectifying Real-Time Systems	$_____
Postage	$_____
NY Resident Sales Tax	$_____
TOTAL	$_____

METHOD OF PAYMENT   ☐ Check enclosed (Payable to SIGS Books)

☐ Charge my: ☐ Visa   ☐ MasterCard   ☐ AmEx

Card#:_____Exp. date: _____

Signature: _____

SEND TO:

Name _____

Company _____

Address _____

City/State _____

Country _____Postal Code_____

Phone _____

Fax _____

Postage and handling per Item: U.S. orders add $5.00; Canada and Mexico add $10.00; Outside North America add $15.00. Note: New York State residents must add applicable sales tax. Please allow 4-6 weeks from publication date for delivery.
Note: *Non-U.S. orders must be prepaid. Checks must be in U.S. dollars and drawn on a U.S. bank.*
PBA1

Distributed by Prentice Hall. Available at selected book stores.

RETURN ORDER TO: SIGS Books, P.O. Box 99425, Collingswood, NJ, 08108-9970, USA.
Fax: 609-488-6188 Phone: 609.488.9602